The

INDUSTRIAL RAILWAYS

of

BOLTON, BURY

and the

MANCHESTER COALFIELD

Part 1

Bolton and Bury

by

C.H.A. Townley
C.A. Appleton
F.D. Smith
J.A. Peden

This book is dedicated to the memory of Frank Smith, who sadly passed away before it was published. Without Frank's indefatigable research in the Record Office archives and in the columns of the local newspapers, there would have been very little to write about.

© **C.H.A. Townley**

C. A. Appleton

F. D. Smith

J. A. Peden

1994

Townley etc
    The Industrial Railways of Bolton, Bury
    and the Manchester Coalfield
    Pt. 1 Bolton and Bury
    1.
    I. Title

ISBN 1–870754–30–1

Typeset and printed by
Stroud Printing Services Ltd.

Runpast Publishing
10 Kingscote Grove
Cheltenham
GL51 6JX

CONTENTS

A scene at Yates Duxbury and Co Ltd's paper mills at Heap Bridge, near Bury. The Barclay locomotive of 1904 climbs the steep gradient from the No 2 Mill to the exchange sidings with the former Lancashire and Yorkshire Railway. The photograph was taken in December 1970, long after most of the steam locomotives had disappeared from the industrial railway systems of South Lancashire.

J A Peden collection.

CHAPTER 1

INTRODUCTION

The present book continues the theme of two earlier volumes [1,2], dealing with the industrial railways of the Wigan Coalfield. We now move on to the districts to the east, starting our explorations in Bolton, Radcliffe and Bury. We then turn south to Kearsley, Clifton, Pendleton and Salford. From here we follow the Liverpool and Manchester line through Eccles and Patricroft to Kenyon Junction, before moving north to deal with Atherton and Tyldesley. Our final chapters cover the Bridgewater collieries, Manchester Collieries Ltd and the National Coal Board. We have chosen our southern boundary deliberately to exclude the Manchester Ship Canal railway system, which has been the subject of a recent comprehensive study [3] by Don Thorpe. We have attempted, as far as possible, to bring our story up to date to the end of 1993, when the text of our book was completed.

Our main purpose is to trace the history and development of the various industrial railway systems and the locomotives which worked on them. However, to understand the subject properly we need to know how the mines and works which they served developed. We hope that what we have written will prove of interest to the industrial archaeologist as well as to the railway historian.

Throughout the whole of the nineteenth century and the first three decades of the twentieth century manufacture and finishing of cotton textiles provided the main source of employment. Coal mining and engineering followed closely behind, along with paper manufacture, concentrated in the valleys of the Irwell, the Croal and the Roch. Neither the textile industry nor the paper industry, important though they were to the local economy, feature prominently in the present work. With very few exceptions, these mills relied entirely on road transport to bring in their raw materials and take away their finished products.

The very many engineering works which were set up early in the nineteenth century to supply equipment to the developing textile and mining industries are also mostly outside the scope of the present book. We have confined our attention to those which engaged, at one time or another, in locomotive construction and those which, exceptionally, had their own private railway systems.

Much of our material concerns the coal industry and its railways. In the northern and central parts of our area, coal had been mined for several centuries, but only in a very limited way to meet a very local demand. The first exploitation on any significant scale took place in the latter part of the eighteenth century, when the Duke of Bridgewater opened up his Worsley mines and built his canal to reach customers in Manchester and further afield.

Coal output increased rapidly in the early part of the nineteenth century to supply the needs of the expanding industries as well for household use by the growing population. Outside the territory worked by the Duke of Bridgewater's Trustees, much of the development was undertaken by members of three families, the Scowcrofts, the Fletchers and the Knowles, already well established as colliery proprietors in the neighbourhood of Bolton. We have had some difficulty in distentangling the various partnerships formed by their descendants, particularly as much of the relevant genealogical information is lacking.

Unlike other parts of South Lancashire, a rail outlet was not always essential. Many of the collieries, particularly those around Bolton, Farnworth and Radcliffe were within a short distance of the mills and factories which they supplied. Coal was often delivered direct from the pit head to the customer by horse and cart. Where access was difficult, a horse worked tramroad was usually built to the nearest suitable road, where a landsale yard was established. Other pits made use of the Manchester, Bolton and Bury Canal and, again, most of the traffic seems to have been over relatively short distances.

Long after the main line railways reached the area, many collieries continued to make use of either canal or road transport. A short length of the Manchester, Bolton and Bury Canal remained in use to convey coal from Ladyshore to cotton mills in Bury until 1949. Coal traffic on the Bridgewater Canal continued until the 1970s.

Other firms took advantage of the greater flexibility offered in the distribution of coal by rail and laid in standard gauge sidings at an early date. Much of the traffic was of a short distance character, to one of the many yards provided by the main line companies in the Bolton and Bury districts or in Manchester and its suburbs, from where coal was distributed to industrial and domestic customers by road. Only a handful of the larger companies, mainly in the southern part of our area, sought markets further afield.

The majority of the private railway systems were relatively small, often confined to a few sidings alongside the main line. However, one, constructed by the Trustees of the Duke of Bridgewater to supplement and later replace the extensive underground canal system at Worsley, eventually had over twelve miles of main routes, served by a fleet of around twenty locomotives. It formed one of the largest private railway networks in the North West and had many interesting feature. A relatively large amount of material relating to its history and to its operation has fortunately survived.

One aspect of coal distribution calls for special mention and that was the widespread use of containerisation to avoid excessive handling between pit head and customer. The use of containers, called boxes locally and generally with a capacity of around 1½ tons, was adopted by many of the collieries served by the Manchester, Bolton and Bury Canal. Where the pits were linked to the canal wharf by a horse worked tramroad, it was the practice to convey the boxes on flat wagons and to use a crane to transfer them to the boats.

As early as 1829 containers were being used on the Bolton and Leigh Railway and were subsequently employed quite widely for rail transport by many of the South Lancashire collieries. Later versions carried 3 or 4 tons and some were still to be seen in traffic after the second world war. More information about them can be found in two recent articles [4,5].

Returning to the present day, the scene which we describe has now all but disappeared. The textile industry went into decline in the late 1920s and many of the spinning and weaving mills, dyeworks and bleachworks closed down. There were further massive closures in the years following the second world war, although many of the mill buildings still remain, adapted to other uses. There was a similar, but less dramatic, decline in the papermaking industry and several substantial works are still in production.

Coal mining around Bolton, Bury and Radcliffe had effectively ceased by the turn of the century, with a few minor exceptions. In the southern part of our area, it continued until well after the second world war. Government legislation between 1926 [6] and 1930 [7] encouraged amalgamation and rationalisation, which resulted in the formation of Manchester Collieries Ltd to acquire the majority of the mines. Nationalisation followed in 1947, when the National Coal Board was set up [8]. In the 1960s there was a rapid run down of the industry in South Lancashire. In the area covered by our book, after the closure of Astley Green in April 1970, only Agecroft Colliery remained and production here ceased in July 1990.

Many of the sites which we describe have been redeveloped. Opencast coal mining, new housing estates and motorway intersections have destroyed the majority of the industrial remains and we only have photographs, maps and the memories of the older generation to remind us what it used to be like.

By way of background, we have provided a chapter summarising the history of the canals and the public railways. Without the improved transport facilities made available at first by the canals and later by the railways, industrial development would undoubtedly have taken a very different course. Our treatment of this topic is necessarily brief, but we have also included some information about projected railways which would have served the area as well as those which were actually constructed.

As in our previous work on the Wigan Coalfield, we have had to rely on a variety of sources, none complete in itself. In the majority of cases, the coal was worked by the colliery proprietor under lease from the landowner. The documents relating to these leases, where they exist in the archives, provide at least partial evidence for the dates of opening of the various collieries and their transfer to new ownership.

Before the days of the Limited Liability Company, most firms operated as legally constituted partnerships and the changes which took place as partners retired or died are recorded in the London Gazette. From the mid 1850s until 1881, details of mine ownership were recorded in the Mineral Statistics published by the Geological Survey. These also provide information on blast furnaces and wrought iron manufacture. From 1883 onwards, lists of coal mines were provided in the Annual Reports of the Inspectors of Mines.

Local papers have proved an invaluable source for information about all aspects of industrial activities - the opening of new mines and new works, bankruptcies, sales of plant, new owners and final closure. Sometimes there are references to industrial railways, perhaps the opening of a new line but more usually to an accident on an existing one.

The gap in large scale Ordnance Survey maps between the late 1840s and the 1890s has again caused difficulty in locating the position of some of the developments which we know about from written records. In some instances we have been able obtain supplementary information from estate plans and from Parliamentary Deposited Plans.

Through the courtesy of the Estates Surveyor, British Rail Property Board, North Western Region, we have inspected the complete set of Line Plans for the area. These were produced by the railway companies and show the track layout, including that at the various private sidings. Details of the agreements relating to the sidings are often included as well as information about land ownership. Some older issues of the Line Plans are available in the Greater Manchester Records Office and we have been able to refer to these.

Further information about private sidings is available from the special diagrams which were prepared by the main line companies. We have been able to examine those for the Lancashire and Yorkshire Railway, dating from the 1900 to 1914 period, again through the courtesy of the Estates Surveyor. Those for the London and North Western Railway have been lent to us by the Librarian of the Manchester Locomotive Society.

For our locomotive information we have relied heavily on data contained in those locomotive manufacturers' records which have survived. We have also referred to lists compiled by organisations such as the Industrial Locomotive Society and the Industrial Railway Society, but we have omitted some information which could not be verified independently. We have made considerable use of the notes which we took at the various collieries and works, from the 1940s onwards, during our conversations with the older generation of employees whose memories often went back to late Victorian times. Finally, much of the later history, from the mid 1930s onwards, comes from personal observations by the authors and their colleagues.

We wish to acknowledge all the help which we have freely received from members of staff at the many libraries and record offices which we visited in our search for material. Without their assistance the book would have much less informative. Our investigations took us to the Local History Departments of Public Libraries at Bolton, Bury, Leigh, Radcliffe, Salford and Wigan, to the Salford Mining Museum, to the University Library at Cambridge, to the Map Department of the British Library and to the Bury, Greater Manchester, Lancashire, Salford and Wigan Record Offices.

We must also express our gratitude to all our friends who have assisted in the preparation of the book. Ken Plant made information available from his extensive collection of locomotive builders archives. Dennis Sweeney unearthed important facts about the history of the railways at Leigh. Harold Bowtell, Philip Hindley, Cyril Golding and John Ryan were able to fill in many gaps in our knowledge of events in the period after the second world war. Finally we wish to acknowledge our special debt to Mike Pain, who has provided a superb set of maps from our very rough drafts.

Those who so generously made available photographs from their collections are acknowledged individually in the captions. Our special thanks go to Bolton Museum and Art Gallery for permission to reproduce the picture of the Hope Foundry in Chapter 3 and to Radcliffe Library in respect of the photograph of Radcliffe Power Station in Chapter 6. Some of the illustrations are copies of rather faded and damaged originals. We trust that readers will appreciate that they have been included for their historical importance rather than their photographic merit.

We are conscious that our research is far from complete and that much more information, at present buried in the archives, still remains to be discovered. We hope that the present work will provide the starting point for others to a undertake more detailed investigation of some of the topics which we have touched on.

Locomotive Summaries

A summary is provided at the end of most of the chapters which gives, in tabular form, details of the locomotives referred to in the text.

The tables are set out in order of name or number; type of locomotive (wheel arrangement, position of tanks, position of cylinders); maker; maker's number (where known); date of construction; cylinder dimensions (bore and stroke); diameter of driving wheels.

The Whyte system of classification has been used to describe the wheel arrangements of the engines, with the addition of 4w and 6w to indicate four or six wheels with gear or chain drive.

The position of the water tanks is denoted by ST for saddle tank, T for side tank and WT for well tank. Tk indicates that we lack information, other than knowing that the locomotive in question was a tank rather than a tender engine.

Cylinder position is denoted by IC for inside the frames and by OC for outside the frames. VC indicates vertical cylinders.

A vertical boiler is denoted by V and a geared drive, on a steam engine, by G.

Diesel locomotives are identified by a D after the wheel arrangement, with M added for mechanical drive, H for hydraulic drive and E for electric drive.

In the case of electric locomotives, OHW denotes current collection from an overhead wire system and Batt that the supply came from storage batteries on the locomotive.

We have used the conventional abbreviations for the locomotive builders, with a few extra which are relevant to our own area. A full list of the abbreviations is given below.

AB	Andrew Barclay, Sons & Co Ltd, Caledonia Works, Kilmarnock
AE	Avonside Engine Co Ltd, Bristol
AtW	Atkinson Walker Wagons Ltd, Frenchwood, Preston

AW	Sir W G Armstrong Whitworth and Co (Engineers) Ltd, Newcastle on Tyne
BH	Black, Hawthorn & Co Ltd, Gateshead
BW	British Westinghouse Electrical and Manufacturing Co Ltd, Manchester
Bs	Barclays and Company, Kilmarnock
CF	Chapman and Furneaux Ltd, Gateshead
Ch	Alexander Chaplin & Co, Cranstonhill, Glasgow
DA	Daniel Adamson, Dukinfield
DC	Drewry Car Co Ltd
DK	Dick, Kerr & Co Ltd, Britannia Works, Kilmarnock
EB	Edward Bury, Clarence Foundry, Liverpool
EBS	E Borrows and Sons Ltd, St Helens
EE	English Electric Co Ltd, Preston
EEV	English Electric Co Ltd, Vulcan Works, Newton le Willows
FH	F C Hibberd & Co Ltd, Park Royal, London
GB	Greenwood and Batley Ltd, Leeds
HC	Hudswell, Clarke & Co Ltd, Railway Foundry, Leeds
HCR	Hudswell, Clarke and Rodgers, Railway Foundry, Leeds
HE	Hunslet Engine Co Ltd, Leeds
HF	Haigh Foundry Company, Wigan
HH	Henry Hughes & Co, Falcon Works, Loughborough
HL	R & W Hawthorn, Leslie & Co Ltd, Newcastle on Tyne
H(L)	Hawthorn and Company, Leith, Scotland
Hor	Lancashire & Yorkshire Railway Co, Horwich Works
JF	John Fowler & Co Ltd, Leeds
K	Kitson & Co, Airedale Foundry, Leeds
KS	Kerr, Stuart & Co Ltd, California Works, Stoke on Trent
LE	Lowca Engineering Co Ltd, Whitehaven
LMM	Logan Mining and Machinery Co Ltd, Dundee
MR	Motor Rail Ltd, Bedford
MV	Metropolitan-Vickers Electrical Co Ltd, Manchester
MW	Manning, Wardle & Co Ltd, Boyne Engine Works, Leeds
NBL	North British Locomotive Co Ltd, Glasgow
NG	Nasmyth, Gaskell & Co, Bridgewater Foundry, Patricroft
NW	Nasmyth, Wilson & Co Ltd, Bridgewater Foundry, Patricroft
P	Peckett & Sons Ltd, Atlas Works, Bristol
P&K	Pearson Knowles Coal and Iron Co Ltd, Dallam Forge, Warrington
RH	Ruston and Hornsby Ltd, Lincoln
RHR	Rothwell, Hick and Rothwell, Bolton
RS	Robert Stephenson & Co Ltd, Newcastle, later Darlington
RSH	Robert Stephenson and Hawthorns Ltd, Newcastle and Darlington
RWH	R & W Hawthorn & Co, Newcastle on Tyne
S	Sentinel Waggon Works Ltd, Shrewsbury, later Sentinel (Shrewsbury) Ltd
Sdn	Swindon Works of British Railways
SS	Sharp, Stewart & Co, Atlas Works, Manchester. Later Atlas Works, Glasgow
VF	Vulcan Foundry Ltd, Newton le Willows
WB	W G Bagnall Ltd, Castle Engine Works, Stafford
WCI	Wigan Coal & Iron Co Ltd, Kirkless Workshops, Wigan
WkB	Walker Brothers & Co, Pagefield Works, Wigan
YE	Yorkshire Engine Co Ltd, Meadow Hall Works, Sheffield

Also mentioned are :

Crook and Dean	Phoenix Foundry, Bolton
Wm Dean	William Dean, Phoenix Foundry, Bolton, successor to Crook and Dean
Gibfield	Gibfield work shops of Fletcher, Burrows and Co Ltd
Hargreaves	John Hargreaves Junior, Bolton
H'worth	Timothy Hackworth, Shildon, Durham
Haydock	Haydock Foundry of Richard Evans and Company
Hick	Hick and Company, later Benjamin Hick and Sons, Soho Ironworks, Bolton
Lewin	Stephen Lewin, Poole
Stothert and Pitt	Stothert and Pitt Ltd, Bath
Stoke	Stoke Works of North Staffordshire Railway
Tayleur	Charles Tayleur & Co, Vulcan Foundry, Newton le Willows, later Vulcan Foundry Co (qv)

References

References to the background literature are given at the end of each chapter. The following abbreviations have been used:-

BMB	- Bolton Metropolitan Borough Local History Library and Archives
BRO	- Bury Metropolitan Borough Record Office
GMRO	- Greater Manchester Records Office
LeiRO	- Leicestershire Record Office, Wigston
LRO	- Lancashire Records Office, Preston
PRO	- Public Records Office, Kew
SAO	- City of Salford Archives Office, Irlam
SMM	- Salford Mining Museum, Buile Hill Park
WRO	- Wigan Metropolitan Borough Record Office, Leigh

BC	- Bolton Chronicle
BEN	- Bolton Evening News
BJ	- Bolton Journal
BLN	- Branch Line News
BT	- Bury Times
Cbn	- *"Carbon"* (House Journal of Fletcher Burrows Ltd and later Manchester Collieries Ltd)
CG	- Colliery Guardian
CJ	- Contract Journal
EA	- Eccles Advertiser
EPJ	- Eccles and Patricroft Journal
FJ	- Farnworth Journal
LC	- Leigh Chronicle
LG	- London Gazette
LJ	- Leigh Journal
MG	- Manchester Guardian
MJ	- Mining Journal
MM	- Machinery Mart
PC	- Preston Chronicle
RT	- Radcliffe Times
WEx	- Wigan Examiner
WO	- Wigan Observer

Maps

The following symbols are used throughout on the maps, with the exception of those in Chapter 2

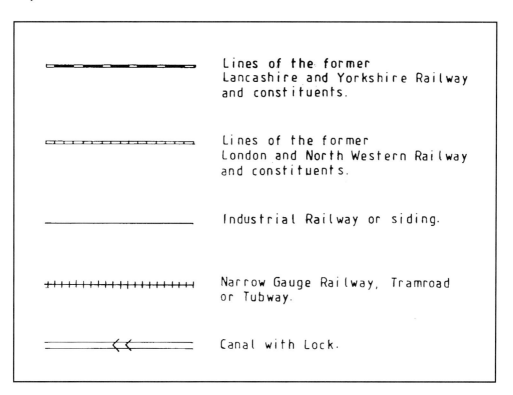

In the text we have used "tramroad" to describe a narrow gauge horse worked line. We have used the term "tubway" to denote a narrow gauge railway on which the tubs from the pit were used to convey coal overground, often over considerable distances and usually employing endless rope or chain haulage.

References to Chapter 1

1 "*The Industrial Railways of the Wigan Coalfield - Part 1*" - Townley, Smith and Peden - Runpast Publishing, Cheltenham, 1991

2 "*The Industrial Railways of the Wigan Coalfield - Part 2*" - Townley, Smith and Peden - Runpast Publishing, Cheltenham, 1992

3 "*The Railways of the Manchester Ship Canal*"Don Thorpe - Oxford Publishing Co, 1984

4 "*The Box Wagons of the South Lancashire Coalfield*" - A J Watts - In "*Platform Nine*" - Jnl of L&Y Soc, Summer, 1982

5 "*The Box Wagons of the South Lancashire Coalfield - Part 2*" - A J Watts - In "*Platform Ten*" - Jnl of L&Y Soc, Autumn, 1982

6 16 & 17 Geo V cap 28; 4th August 1926

7 20 & 21 Geo V cap 34; 1st August 1930

8 9 & 10 Geo VI cap 59; 12th July 1946

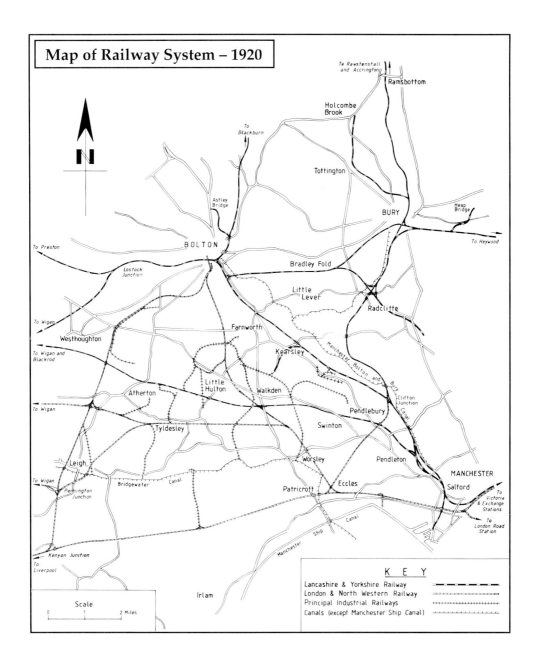

Map of Railway System – 1920

CHAPTER 2

THE CANALS AND PUBLIC RAILWAYS

Before starting our exploration of the private railways and their predecessors, the horse worked tramroads, we need to understand something about the history of the canals and the main line railways. A unique feature of the area was the large underground canal complex, constructed by the Duke of Bridgewater to give access to his coal mines, which eventually extended from Worsley to the outskirts of Bolton. As far as more conventional waterways were concerned, the district was not well served. The first to be constructed was the Duke's own canal from Worsley to Manchester and Runcorn, while at the southern edge of the territory we cover, the rivers Mersey and Irwell had been made navigable in the eighteenth century. To these were added, around 1800, the Manchester, Bolton and Bury Canal and the extension of the Bridgewater Canal from Worsley to Leigh. Here, we can only give a summary of the main developments. Readers who wish to study the history of the canals in more detail should consult Hadfield and Biddle's *"The Canals of North West England"* [1], which we have used extensively as a source document.

The first public railways, the Bolton and Leigh and the Liverpool and Manchester, appeared on the scene towards the end of the 1820s. The Manchester and Bolton, Bolton and Preston and Leigh to Kenyon lines were built soon afterwards. In the rush of speculation following the success of these early railways, many more lines were planned. The majority of the schemes were soon dropped. Several progressed as far as the submission of a Bill to Parliament, although very few were actually authorised. The Deposited Plans show many proposals for branch lines serving collieries and other works and it is interesting to speculate how the course of industrial development might have been altered if the lines had been built. The relevant parts of their routes are shown on the maps which accompany the subsequent chapters.

By the mid 1840s, the railways within the area we cover had passed into the hands of two major companies, the London and North Western and the Lancashire and Yorkshire. The only exceptions were the East Lancashire Railway, from Clifton Junction to Bury and beyond, and the Bolton to Blackburn line. By 1859, both had been absorbed by the Lancashire and Yorkshire Railway.

The monopoly held by the two companies, which tended to work together rather than in competition, was one of the factors which led to the agitation for a ship canal from the Mersey to Manchester. The Manchester Ship Canal, opened in 1894, was the last major transport development in the area before the new road schemes of the 1930s and the 1960s.

Up to the first world war, the railways continued to play a major role in the transport of both goods and passengers. From 1920 onwards, there was increasing competition from buses and from motor lorries. By the 1960s, rail traffic had declined and many of the lines in the area were abandoned. With the demise of coal mining and much of the heavy industry and with the closure of the docks on the Ship Canal, goods traffic has all but ceased and the few lines which remain open are almost exclusively used by passenger trains.

The Mersey and Irwell Navigation

Navigation works on the Mersey and Irwell rivers from Manchester to Warrington were authorised by Act of Parliament as early as 1721 [2] and were completed in 1736 [1]. There were considerable improvements in the 1780s and 1790s, which included straightening the more tortuous sections of the waterway and the provision of extra locks [3]. The Runcorn and Latchford Canal was constructed to avoid difficulties of navigation on the Mersey below Warrington and was opened in July 1804 [1]. The Mersey and Irwell was later absorbed into the Bridgewater undertaking, which in turn was taken over by the Manchester Ship Canal Company.

The Bridgewater Canal

The earliest of the true canals, from Worsley to Knott Mill in Manchester, was constructed under the auspices of the Duke of Bridgewater and opened throughout on 1 Aug 1765 [1]. The original scheme, authorised in 1737 [4] but not pursued, was to make the Worsley Brook navigable to its junction with the River Irwell. In 1759 an Act [5] was obtained for canals from Worsley through Patricroft to Salford and from Worsley to Hollin's Ferry on the Irwell. A further Act [6] in the following year authorised a new line between Patricroft and Manchester, crossing the Irwell by the Barton Aqueduct and passing through Stretford.

The primary purpose of the Duke's canal was to provide a cheap means of transporting coal to Manchester from the mines which were then being developed under the Bridgewater estates. An underground canal was driven from the main waterway at Worsley to serve the working faces and to enable coal to be loaded into boats near the point of production. We shall describe, in Chapter 11, how the underground canal system was extended as mining progressed until early in the nineteenth century it reached the outskirts of Bolton.

Only a short section of the Hollin's Ferry line was actually constructed, primarily for the drainage and reclamation of Worsley Moss. The roads and causeways were built up using colliery waste, brought by boat from the mines. Work to reclaim the Moss started by the Duke in 1769 [7].

With construction of the new line from Worsley to Manchester well under way, the Duke turned his attention to a more ambitious scheme for a canal from Stretford to Runcorn, which would give access to the Mersey Estuary. Authorised in 1772 [8] and opened throughout on 21st March 1776 [1], the new canal extended the market for Worsley coal and at the same time provided a route for goods between Manchester and Liverpool, competing with that of the old-established Mersey and Irwell Navigation Company. After May 1777 [1], when a junction with the Trent and Mersey Canal at Preston Brook was opened, the Bridgewater Canal formed an integral part of the chain of communication between Manchester, the Midlands and the south of England.

Proposals to link the Duke's canal with North Lancashire were put forward by the Lancaster Canal Company in 1793. The intention was to extend the Lancaster's authorised line from Aspull, near Wigan, passing through Leigh to a junction with the completed section of the Duke's Hollin's Ferry line [9]. The Bill, presented to Parliament in 1794, was thrown out [1].

Next year the Duke obtained Parliamentary authority [10] for an extension of his own canal, following a similar route to that proposed by the Lancaster as far as Astley Green and then taking a more southerly course from there to Leigh [11]. The Leigh extension was opened about the end of 1799 [1]. It acquired a considerable coal traffic from the new collieries which were developed in the 1830s and 1840s in the neighbourhood of Atherton and Tyldesley as well from the Bridgewater pits along its route.

It was left to the Leeds and Liverpool Canal Company to provide the final link with the North Lancashire canal system. Plans had been submitted to Parliament in 1800 [12] and again in 1808 [13], but the scheme was not approved until 1819 [14]. The new canal, which was opened at the end of 1821 [1], ran from the Leeds and Liverpool's main line at Wigan to an end-on junction with the Bridgewater at Leigh.

Following the Duke of Bridgewater's death in March 1803, the canal, along with the colliery property, was administered by his Trustees. Income from the Trust went to the Marquis of Stafford and after 1833 to Lord Francis Egerton [15]. It was Lord Egerton who acquired a controlling interest in the Mersey and Irwell Navigation at the end of 1843 and subsequently resold his shares to the Trustees. The Mersey and Irwell came under the control of the Bridgewater Canal as from 17th January 1846 [1], although the Navigation Company continued to exist as a separate entity.

Traffic remained at a high level on both the navigation and the canal, but, with increasing threat of railway competition, the Trustees decided to sell out. In 1857 a plan [16] was produced of the canal from Leigh to Manchester and from Stretford to Runcorn, together with land at various places, which was "proposed to be sold to the North Staffordshire Railway Co". Evidently these negotiations fell through and it was not until 1872 that the Trustees were successful. The Bridgewater Navigation Company was formed by the Sir Edward Watkin, Chairman of the Manchester, Sheffield and Lincolnshire Railway, and Mr Price, Chairman of the Midland Railway, [15] and took control on 1st September. Subsequently a number of improvements were carried out, particularly on the Mersey and Irwell Navigation [1].

The Bridgewater Navigation Company, and its subsidiary the Mersey and Irwell Navigation Company, were bought out by the Manchester Ship Canal Company on 4th July 1887 [1], in accordance with its Act of 1885 [17]. The Ship Canal used the course of the Irwell and Mersey rivers for much of the length from Manchester to Warrington and many of the old navigation works disappeared. The whole of the Bridgewater Canal was retained and a new swing aqueduct was constructed at Barton to replace the original Brindley structure.

Some commercial traffic continued on the Bridgewater Canal until the second world war, after which it gradually faded away. Lighterage between Manchester Docks and Trafford Park finally ceased in the 1970s and, according to Salford Mining Museum notes, the last coal traffic on the Leigh Branch, to Stretford Power Station, finished in 1972. Still owned by the Manchester Ship Canal Company, the canal is now used only by pleasure boats.

The Manchester, Bolton and Bury Canal

The eastern portion of the area covered in the book was served by the Manchester, Bolton and Bury Canal, which was relatively late on the scene. It was authorised in 1791 [18] and opened throughout by the end of 1796, with the exception of the short connection between Oldfield Road and the River Irwell, which was not completed until December 1808 [1]. The canal passed through Pendleton, Agecroft, Clifton and Prestolee, where, at the top of the locks, the lines to Bolton and Bury diverged.

From the beginning the main traffic was coal, much of it destined for wharves in Salford, Bolton and Bury, from where it was distributed by road to industrial and domestic consumers. The increase in demand for coal in the early years of the nineteenth century, coupled with the ease of transport by canal, led to an expansion of the coal mining industry in places such as Little Lever, Darcy Lever and Radcliffe where it had long been established on a small scale. At Clifton, Matthew Fletcher built a short private canal to provide an outlet from his collieries at Wet Earth and Botany Bay. Further south, at Agecroft and Pendleton, where the coal seams were much deeper, new collieries were opened in the 1820s and 1830s.

Various extensions were proposed. One was for a canal from Bury to Sladen, near Littleborough, following the valley of the Roch for most of its route [19]. Another was a continuation of the Bolton branch along the Croal valley to a junction with the authorised line of the Leeds and Liverpool Canal at Red Moss [20,21]. Bills which included both schemes, submitted to Parliament 1793 and again in 1794, were rejected [1].

An independent company was successful in obtaining an Act in 1794 [22] for a canal from Bury through Tottington, Haslingden and Accrington to join the Leeds and Liverpool at Church. The project was fraught with engineering difficulties and no work was ever carried out. The company was wound up a few years later. In 1800 there was a further proposal to extend the Bolton line to join the Leeds and Liverpool Canal [1], but the idea was dropped a few years later when the Leeds and Liverpool decided to join the Lancaster Canal at Johnsons Hillock, near Chorley instead of building its line through Red Moss.

As we shall see later, the Manchester Bolton and Bury Canal Company was authorised in 1831 to convert its canal into a railway. In the event, only the railway from Salford to Bolton was constructed and the whole of the canal was retained. Both later became the property of the Lancashire and Yorkshire Railway Company.

Coal carried on the canal remained at a high level until the early years of the present century, but then declined when many of the collieries which it served went out of production. Traffic on the southern end ceased in 1936.

The sections of the canal from Bolton to Prestolee and from a point 167 yards west of Ladyshore Bridge to the south end of Clifton Aqueduct were abandoned under the London Midland and Scottish Railway Act of 1941 [23]. The Lancashire County Council, Bolton Corporation and the Urban District Councils of Little Lever and Kearsley were authorised to take over the portions within their jurisdiction and to fill them in under the Railway Company's Act of 1947 [24]. The same Act relieved the LMS Railway Company of its obligations, under the Canal Company's Act of 1831, which prevented it from stopping up the canal until certain railways had been completed !

A limited amount of coal traffic continued to be handled between Ladyshore Colliery and Bury, but this ceased when the colliery closed in 1949. A few boats were retained at Bury to move coal, delivered by road, to a mill across the canal. The Ladyshore to Bury and Clifton to Salford portions of the canal were abandoned under the British Transport Commission Act of 1961 [25].

Opposite Page Top
The pair of locks at Ringley on the Manchester, Bolton and Bury Canal, photographed in 1903, with the very large cotton mill at Prestolee in the background. The canal ran on a ledge on the hillside for most of the way between Clifton and Bolton.   John Ryan collection

Opposite Page Lower
A view on the Bury Branch of the canal, near Ladyshore. Note the empty boxes on the two rather spartan boats.   John Ryan collection

The Liverpool and Manchester Railway

The first serious proposals for linking Liverpool and Manchester by rail appeared in 1821, although surveys had been made as early as 1797 and 1798 for two horse worked tramroad schemes [26]. It was not until 1826, after several unsuccessful attempts, that Parliamentary approval was finally obtained [27] for a line from Liverpool to New Bailey Bridge in Salford. Liverpool Road was substituted as the Manchester terminus in 1829 [28].

The railway commenced operations in September 1830 and from the outset there was a considerable trade in general goods, particularly cotton. In the area we cover the railway had little influence on colliery development, the seams being too deep to be mined successfully until many years later. Some coal was conveyed to Manchester, after the opening of the Kenyon and Leigh Junction line, from the Hulton collieries and possibly from Fletcher's collieries at Atherton.

In the mid 1830s consideration was given to connections with other railways which had reached Manchester. Plans were drawn up in November 1836 [29] for a junction with the Manchester, Bolton and Bury. In 1838, a more ambitious scheme was adopted for a station at Hunts Bank to serve the Liverpool and Manchester, the Manchester, Bolton and Bury and the Manchester and Leeds Railways. The new Victoria Station was opened on 1st January 1844 [30] when it was first used by Manchester and Leeds trains.

The connecting line to Victoria Station from the west was constructed by the Liverpool and Manchester Railway under Acts of 1839 [31] and 1842 [32]. It was opened for traffic on 4th May 1844 [30] and left the original L&M line outside Liverpool Road Station. A junction was made with the Manchester, Bolton and Bury immediately to the west of that company's Salford Station.

In August 1845 [33], the Liverpool and Manchester was absorbed by the Grand Junction Railway. A year later, the Grand Junction amalgamated with the London and Birmingham and Manchester and Birmingham Railways to form the London and North Western Railway [34]. However, before leaving the Liverpool and Manchester Railway, we must mention two schemes which were in hand when the 1845 amalgamation took place.

A connection with railways terminating on the south side of the city centre was made when the Manchester South Junction and Altrincham Railway's branch to Ordsall Lane was opened to traffic on 1st August 1849 [30]. The railway had been authorised in 1845 to build a line from London Road to Altrincham with a branch from Castlefield to join the Liverpool and Manchester [35]. The capital was provided by the Manchester and Birmingham and the Sheffield, Ashton under Lyne and Manchester Railways and by Lord Francis Egerton, beneficiary of the Duke of Bridgewater's Trust and soon to become Earl of Ellesmere. In 1847, the Earl of Ellesmere sold his interest in the line, which then became the joint property of the London and North Western and the Manchester Sheffield and Lincolnshire Railways, successors of the other two original subscribers [36].

A further connection with neighbouring railways was provided by the Liverpool and Manchester's branch from Patricroft which joined the Manchester, Bury and Rawtenstall Railway at Molyneux Junction, near Clifton, and thus opened up a route from east Lancashire to Liverpool. The line was authorised in 1845 [37] and was opened on 2nd January 1850 [30] for all classes of traffic. The passenger service was, however, short-lived, being suspended after three months [30].

Branches were proposed to Worsley Basin and to John Lancaster's Patricroft Colliery [38]. They were not specifically mentioned in the Act, but, under Section 58, the railway company was empowered to sell the Worsley Branch to Lord Egerton or to the Bridgewater Trustees. In the event neither branch was built, although some earthworks were completed at Monton where the Worsley line would have diverged from that to Molyneux Junction [39].

The Bolton and Leigh Railway

The Bolton and Leigh Railway, authorised in 1825, was, in contrast to the Liverpool and Manchester, first and foremost a mineral line, promoted to connect the Hulton Collieries and those at Atherton with coal yards in Bolton and with the canal at Leigh. The Act [40] included three branches at Bolton, to Great Moor Street, to Deansgate and to the Manchester, Bolton and Bury Canal. A short branch at Chowbent, shown on the Deposited Plans [41], was omitted from the Act.

The portion of the railway from Pendlebury Fold to Lecturers Closes at Bolton was opened for coal traffic from William Hulton's collieries on 1st August 1828 [42]. The entire line through to Leigh was complete by 30th March 1830, when the locomotive SANS PAREIL hauled a coach conveying the directors on an inspection tour. It was stated that "it is now considered that the road is open for the conveyance of all sorts of goods" [43]. It is possible that some form of passenger service was also provided, perhaps only of a temporary nature. In December 1829 the company was given permission to borrow a carriage from the Liverpool and Manchester Railway to experiment with carrying passengers between Bolton and Leigh [44].

Of the branches at Bolton, that to Great Moor Street must have been completed by autumn 1829 at the latest. A short extension which crossed Weston Street on the level to serve William Hulton's coal yard alongside the George Inn was opened on 5th October of that year [45]. The passenger station at Great Moor Street probably did not come into use until 1831.

The date of opening of the Deansgate Branch does not seem to have been recorded. It was probably in 1829, as an engraving of that date shows railway tracks and wagons in the Union Foundry, adjoining the branch. The warehouse at the Deansgate terminus was stated to be under construction in August 1830 [46]. The branch to the Manchester, Bolton and Bury Canal was never built.

Stationary engines were erected at Chequerbent and Daubhill to work the trains over the inclined planes which were built to carry the line over the high ground south of Bolton. Locomotives were used on the level section between the two inclines and from Atherton to Leigh. Initially horses seem to have hauled the wagons between the foot of the Daubhill Incline and the Bolton terminus. By June 1831 it had become the practice for the locomotives to work right through with their trains, being attached to the rope on the inclines.

An extension over the canal at Leigh to join the Liverpool and Manchester at Kenyon Junction was constructed by the nominally independent Kenyon and Leigh Junction Railway, incorporated in 1829 [47]. The line provided a through route from Bolton to Manchester and Liverpool and later to Warrington and Wigan. It was opened for goods traffic on 3rd January 1831 [48]. The Bolton and Leigh was authorised "to take a farm of the tolls" by its Act of July 1831, in other words to work the line and keep the receipts in return for a lump sum payment [49].

In April 1831, the Bolton and Leigh Railway was leased to John Hargreaves Junior, who was then responsible for working the trains and providing the motive power - an early example of franchising a railway to a private operator. It was under his auspices that a through passenger service was started between Bolton and Liverpool on 11th June 1831. We return to the subject of the locomotives used by Hargreaves in Chapter 3.

In 1835 plans were drawn up for a branch in Bolton from Lecturers Closes to the Manchester, Bolton and Bury Railway at Orlando Street. At the same time a line was proposed from Bag Lane to Hindley, with several short branches to serve individual collieries [50]. The former was authorised in the company's 1836 Act [51], but the latter was not. The 1836 Act also empowered the Bolton and Leigh to lease the Kenyon and Leigh Junction or to purchase it outright.

The branch to the Manchester, Bolton and Bury was never constructed. Instead a lift was installed at Great Moor Street to enable wagons to be moved between the Bolton and Leigh line and the Bolton and Preston line, which passed below in a cutting. The date when the lift was constructed has not been discovered. The layout of the connecting lines on both the high and low levels is shown in some detail on the 1/1056 Town Plan, published in 1849, so the lift must have been in use before then.

In August 1845 the Bolton and Leigh and the Kenyon and Leigh Junction companies were absorbed by the Grand Junction Railway [33], itself a constituent of the London and North Western Railway [34], formed a year later. We shall be following subsequent developments later in the chapter.

The Manchester, Bolton and Bury Railway

A number of proposals for railways between Manchester and Bolton appeared in the 1820s. Several were sufficiently well supported for submissions to be made Parliament

In 1825, Deposited Plans [52] were prepared for a line from the New Bailey in Salford to Park Field in the centre of Bolton, with a branch from Cross Lane to a wharf on the Mersey and Irwell Navigation, opposite Hulme Hall. North of Cross Lane the line would have passed Pendleton Toll Bar and then have kept to the Irwell Valley as far Clifton. Here there was to be an inclined plane to gain the higher ground and the line then would have run to the west of the main road through Kearsley and Farnworth before reaching Bolton.

A second scheme was also put forward in 1825 [53]. This was intended to start from a junction with the Liverpool and Manchester Railway, which at that time was still waiting for Parliamentary approval, about half a mile east of the present Eccles station. The proposed line to Bolton then proceeded on an essentially straight course through Moorside, Wardley and Farnworth to terminate in the Bolton Station of the Bolton and Leigh Railway, then under construction.

In 1830, there were two further proposals which were in direct competition with each other. One was for the construction of a line from Manchester through Bolton and Chorley to Preston [54,55,56], the other for the conversion of the Manchester, Bolton and Bury Canal into a railway.

The main line of the Manchester to Preston Railway was to run from New Bailey Street, in Salford, to a terminus adjacent to the Lancaster Canal basin in Preston. Between Salford and Kearsley the route was a short distance to the west of that eventually adopted by the Manchester, Bolton and Bury Railway.

Numerous branches were proposed to serve the coal mining areas. One of these was to leave the main line near Clifton Hall Farm, passing to the north of Pendlebury, where there was to be a short spur to Mr Knowles' coal pits, and then running through Wardley and Walkden to terminate at the Peel Colliery at Little Hulton. The Halshaw Moor Branch was to leave the Peel Branch near Clifton and to run past Clifton Moss Colliery, then to the south of Kearsley and on to Farnworth.

There were to be branches leaving the main line near Moses Gate to serve the Great Lever Works and collieries in the neighbourhood of Raikes Hall. At Bolton, there was to be a junction with the Bolton and Leigh Railway, as well as a separate terminal station in Bradshawgate. A branch to Bury was proposed from Moses Gate, passing through Farnworth Bridge, Little Lever and Black Lane.

The Manchester and Preston project did not materialise and the way was open for the Manchester, Bolton and Bury Canal Company to proceed with its conversion scheme. The Act which it obtained in 1831 [57] authorised the abandonment of the canal between the Irwell Basin and Prestolee, but this could not be done until the railway had been completed at least as far as Clifton Colliery and Kearsley Colliery.

The portion of the canal between Bolton and Bury had to be kept open. Between the Irwell Basin and Prestolee, the railway was to follow closely the course of the canal and in some places was to be built on its bed. Between Prestolee and Bolton it was to be on a site between the canal and the River Croal.

Two branch railways were also authorised. One was to leave the main line at Giants Seat and, passing through a tunnel under the high ground, was to run through Radcliffe to terminate alongside the canal basin at Bury [58].

The second was the Kearsley Moor Branch which was to leave the main line near the south end of Clifton Aqueduct and run past the Botany Bay and Wet Earth Pits of Fletcher's Clifton Colliery. It was then to follow the course of the Unity Brook as far as the Kearsley Vitriol Works. Beyond there it was to run to the west of Farnworth, through Dixon Green, to terminate at the boundary of Farnworth Township, near Fishpool. A short sub-branch was also authorised, from a point to the west of the Bolton to Manchester road to the Buss Pits, which formed part of Fletcher's Kearsley Colliery, and to the Clifton Moss Colliery of Andrew Knowles [58].

The Deposited Plans show that it was intended to continue the Kearsley Moor Branch to a junction with the Bolton and Leigh at Daubhill [58]. However the portion beyond the Farnworth boundary was dropped from the Act, as was a short branch near Manchester, from Pendleton to Strangeways.

Powers were granted to make use of stationary engines and inclined planes. The Sections accompanying the Deposited Plans suggest that these were only to be employed on the Kearsley Moor Branch, to overcome the steep rise up the valley of the Unity Brook.

The Act contained several sections protecting the interests of Ellis Fletcher. The Company was not to take over or use any railway or canal belonging to him. He was also to have the use of the branch railway to his collieries free of toll.

There followed several changes of plan resulting in a complex series of proposals for the main line and for the branches. The maps in Chapters 3 and 6 will be of assistance to those readers who wish to follow the story in detail. The routes of the very many projected lines across Kearsley Moss are shown on the maps in Chapter 11.

Within a few months of the 1831 Act passing into law, the company made a revised application to Parliament and obtained a new Act in 1832 [59]. This repealed the powers to drain the canal. The company was now obliged to maintain the navigation for ever and the line of the railway was altered accordingly. This involved deviations of the original route between Giants Seat and Clifton Hall and between Agecroft and Oldfield Road. There were also to be deviations between Foggs Brook and Prestolee and on the Bury Branch.

The 1832 Act authorised an extension of the railway to New Bailey Street in Salford and from Church Wharf to Bridge Street in Bolton. Also authorised were branches at Bolton, from Strawberry Hill to Bradshawgate, and at Salford, to serve cotton mills situated between Windsor Bridge and Oldfield Road.

The Kearsley Moor Branch now left the main line by a triangular junction near Clifton House, instead of at Clifton Aqueduct. The Act required the Bradshawgate branch and the Kearsley Moor Branch, at least as far as the vitriol works, to be opened at the same time as the main line.

Several lines shown on the Deposited Plans [60] were dropped from the Act. These included a branch from Prestolee to Ladyshore Colliery and Mount Sion Print Works and two short branches in Darcy Lever, to Fogg's Colliery and to the Plantation Pit.

Although construction of the railway had started in 1833, at the Salford end, there were further changes to the route. In November of that year, a revised plan [61] was put forward for the Bury Branch, which it was now proposed to extend to New Hall Hey, Rawtenstall. The new line which, however, did not receive Parliamentary approval, was intended to avoid the tunnel and other difficult earthworks between Giants Seat and Radcliffe. It was to leave the Bolton line near Farnworth Bridge and then pass through Bradley Fold, Elton and Ramsbottom. There would have been a short branch from Elton to a terminus in Bury near the canal basin.

In November 1834, the company made yet another application to Parliament to revise the portion of its main line between Clifton Hall and Bolton. This was now to follow much the same course as that projected by the Manchester and Preston Railway in 1830, to terminate in Bolton on the west side of Bradshawgate, at Trinity Street. As a consequence, the junction with the Kearsley Moor Branch was altered again and was now situated near where the new line crossed Unity Brook. To provide access to collieries and works on the original route, a branch was proposed to the canal near Damside Aqueduct. This was to leave the main line at Farnworth and run past Hacken Colliery, from where another short branch was to be built to the canal at Strawberry Hill [62].

The new line from Clifton to Bolton through Farnworth was authorised in 1835 [63]. In place of the proposed branches to Damside and Strawberry Hill, the company was required to construct the major part of the line from Clifton to Bolton through Prestolee, authorised in 1832, as well as the branch to Bradshawgate from this line at Strawberry Hill. The 1832 line from Clifton to Bolton, at least as far as Hayes, Hamer and Jackson's works at Haulgh, together with the Bradshawgate branch, had to be opened within two years of the completion of the new line. The Kearsley Moor Branch, at least as far as the vitriol works, had to be opened on the same time scale.

With its route finally settled, construction of the main line from Salford to Bolton proceeded rapidly. Opening for public traffic was on 29th May 1838. Plans were made in 1845 to extend the line to a terminus nearer the centre of Manchester, at Blackfriars Bridge [64]. This idea was dropped and instead, starting in October 1846, some passenger trains ran through to the new Victoria Station [65], over the connecting line built by the Liverpool and Manchester Railway.

An independent access to Victoria Station was not provided until much later, when Salford became a through station and separate tracks were laid down by the Lancashire and Yorkshire Railway. Authorised in 1861 [66], the new lines were opened on 1st August 1865 [65]. The junction between the L&YR and the LNWR, situated to the west of Salford station, was subsequently removed and replaced by one on the approach to Victoria Station [67].

At Salford, land had been acquired under the 1832 Act for a goods yard adjacent to the canal. As the railway was at this point on a viaduct, a hoist was provided to reach ground level. A branch to the yard, which left the main line at Oldfield Road, was opened in April 1867 [65]. In 1871 powers [68] were obtained to purchase the site of the New Bailey prison in order to extend the yard and lay additional tracks across Irwell Street.

We return now to the northern part of the Manchester, Bolton and Bury Railway. Construction of the Kearsley Moor Branch was deferred and an extension of time was granted in June 1838 for the portion from the main line to the vitriol works [69]. The line was completed as far the connections with Fletcher's Manor Pit by April 1840 [65], but the remaining section from there to the vitriol works was never built. As envisaged in the original Act of 1831, a rope worked incline was provided to overcome the 1 in 15 gradient up the valley of the Unity Brook to the Manchester and Bolton Road.

No work ever seems to have been carried out, as required by the 1835 Act, on the Clifton to Bolton line via Prestolee or on the branch from Strawberry Hill to Bradshawgate . The Bury Branch, authorised in 1831 and amended in 1832, was also allowed to fade away. The result was that the mining districts of Darcy Lever and Little Lever were deprived of rail transport and the collieries were obliged to continue to use the canal.

There was one last project in 1839, when plans [70] were submitted to Parliament for a line from Stoneclough to Rawtenstall, passing through Ladyshore, Radcliffe and Bury. However, nothing more is heard of the proposal and Bury had to wait for nearly another decade until the first railway arrived.

The independent life of the Manchester, Bolton and Bury Canal and Railway Company came to an end in 1846, when it was absorbed by the Manchester and Leeds Railway [71]. In the next year [72] the Manchester and Leeds changed its name to the Lancashire and Yorkshire Railway and we shall follow its subsequent history later in the chapter.

The Bolton and Preston Railway

We have already mentioned the scheme of 1830 for a railway from Manchester to Preston through Bolton and Chorley [54, 55, 56]. Beyond Bolton as far as Chorley the main line would have followed closely the route later adopted by the Bolton and Preston Railway.

Numerous short branches were proposed leading to industrial establishments - to Mr Mackenzie's Colliery, near Chauntry Brow at Blackrod, to the Waterhouse Estate and its collieries, to Cross Hall Print Works, near Chorley, to the Duxbury Park collieries and to Burgh Colliery. There would also have been a branch to Horwich, with a spur serving Mr Wright's stone quarry. Of particular interest in the context of the present work was the branch, about a mile in length, which would have left the main line at Lostock and run to Pendlebury Fold to serve William Hulton's collieries.

The 1830 project fell through, but the part north west of Bolton was revived, without the branches, by the Bolton and Preston Railway in 1836 [73]. Parliamentary authority was obtained in 1837 [74] for a line starting at an end on junction with the Manchester, Bolton and Bury at Bolton and terminating near the Lancaster Canal basin at Preston. It had been intended to utilise the trackbed of the canal company's Preston and Walton Summit tramroad to gain access to Preston, but a further Act in 1838 [75] substituted a new route from Chorley to a junction with the North Union Railway's Wigan and Preston line at Euxton.

The line was opened for traffic on 4th February 1841 between Bolton and Rawlinson Bridge, near Chorley, and throughout on 22nd June 1843 [65].

The company was purchased by the North Union Railway in 1844 [76]. Two years later, the North Union itself was vested in the Grand Junction and Manchester and Leeds Railways [77], the lease subsequently passing to the London and North Western and Lancashire and Yorkshire companies.

The North Union Company was dissolved in 1888 [78] and in 1889 [79] its assets were transferred to the two lessees. The portion of the North Union line from Bolton to Euxton, previously worked and maintained by the L&YR, was transferred to that company, while the LNWR acquired the portion from Parkside to Euxton. Euxton to Preston, previously worked and maintained on a joint basis, was vested equally in the two companies.

The Blackburn Railway

The Blackburn, Darwen and Bolton Railway was incorporated in 1845 [80] and was authorised to build a line joining the Manchester, Bolton and Bury at Little Burnden, about half a mile south of that company's terminus. An alternative route south of High House Fold, Entwistle, passing through Astley Bridge to join the Bolton and Preston Railway, which was shown on the Deposited Plans [81], was specifically ruled out.

In November 1845 the company submitted plans [82,83] for a deviation at Bolton, from the authorised line at Craddock Lane to the Manchester, Bolton and Bury station. A branch to Bury was also proposed, starting from a triangular junction with the main line at Turton and running across country through Edgeworth, Quarrelton and Walves to join the Liverpool and Bury Railway at Elton. Only the deviation at Bolton was authorised in the company's Act of 1846 [84].

The name of the company was changed in 1847 [85] to the Bolton, Blackburn, Clitheroe and West Yorkshire Rly. This followed an amalgamation with the Blackburn, Clitheroe and North Western Junction Railway, which had been incorporated in the previous year to build a line northwards from Blackburn to Elslack [86]. The line into Bolton was opened for traffic on 12th June 1848 [65] and in 1851 the shorter title of the Blackburn Railway was adopted [87].

In the 1857 Parliamentary Session, the Blackburn company submitted a Bill for an independent line to Manchester, which, however, was defeated due to the opposition of the Lancashire and Yorkshire [65]. The Deposited Plans [88,89] show that the railway was intended to start at a junction with the Blackburn line near Craddock Lane and pass through Tonge, Bradley Fold, Radcliffe, and Whitefield to terminate at Ducie Street, near Victoria Station.

The Blackburn Railway was vested jointly in the East Lancashire Railway and the Lancashire and Yorkshire Railway in 1858 [90]. It came into the sole ownership of the L&YR on the amalgamation of the ELR with that company in the following year [91].

The East Lancashire Railway

As we have seen, the powers obtained in 1831 [57] by the Manchester, Bolton and Bury Canal and Railway for the construction of a branch to Bury were not implemented. Later proposals by the same company, in 1833 [61] and 1839 [70], for lines to serve Bury and Rawtenstall proved equally abortive.

Then, in 1844 the independent Manchester, Bury and Rawtenstall Railway was incorporated. Its Act [92] authorised a line to join the Manchester, Bolton and Bury at Clifton, with running powers from there to Salford. The name was changed to the East Lancashire Railway in 1845 [93] as the result of amalgamation with the Blackburn, Burnley, Accrington and Colne Extension Railway. Public services between Manchester Victoria and Rawtenstall commenced on 28th September 1846 [65], the trains running over the Liverpool and Manchester Railway's connecting line between Salford and Manchester.

In November 1846, the company submitted proposals [94] for a separate line to Manchester, from Buckley Wells, south of Bury, through Whitefield and Prestwich to a terminus at right angles to Victoria Station. Like the Manchester and Bury Atmospheric Railway scheme a year earlier, which generally followed a similar route [95], the East Lancashire project did not proceed much beyond the preparation of the plans. Although the Blackburn Railway proposed a line serving the same districts in 1856 [88], Whitefield and Prestwich had to wait until 1879 before they were served by rail.

As the result of an increasingly difficult relationship with the Lancashire and Yorkshire regarding the use of the line between Clifton Junction and Salford, the East Lancashire put forward further proposals for an independent access to Manchester in the 1853 Parliamentary Session. The new railway would have started just north of the junction at Clifton and followed a course to the east of the L&YR line to Salford [96]. A compromise was reached with the L&YR and in 1854 [97] the Clifton Junction to Salford line was vested jointly in the two companies. It became the sole property of the L&YR when the two railways amalgamated in 1859 [91]. The amalgamation Act granted running powers to the LNWR, subject to certain restrictions, from Molyneux Junction through Radcliffe to Bury.

The Liverpool and Bury Railway

In the early 1840s, two competing schemes were put forward for lines to Liverpool. The Liverpool and Bolton Direct Railway was intended to run from Bolton to Garston, which was then being developed as a port for the shipment of coal. It would have passed through Lostock, Westhoughton, Bamfurlong, St Helens and Huyton, by-passing Wigan. Plans were submitted to Parliament [98], but the project was dropped.

The Bolton, Wigan and Liverpool Railway followed a similar course as far as Westhoughton and then passed through Pemberton and Rainford to a terminus on the north side of Liverpool, again avoiding Wigan [99]. An extension from Bolton through Bury, to join the Manchester and Leeds Railway at Heywood [100], was subsequently proposed and the name was changed to the Liverpool and Bury Railway.

The Act of Parliament in 1845 [101], incorporating the company, authorised construction of a line from Liverpool to a junction with the Bolton and Preston Railway at Lostock and a line from the Manchester, Bolton and Bury at Burnden as far as Bury, terminating at a point about ten chains east of the bridge over the River Irwell. Between Bury and Heywood, powers were granted to the Manchester and Leeds Railway [102]. The Liverpool and Bury Act also authorised a branch to Great Lever Colliery from the point where the Bury line crossed the Rover Croal.

A second Liverpool and Bury Act in 1846 [103], which authorised an extension at Liverpool to Tithebarn Street, also included a branch from the main line near Lostock Junction. This was to terminate near the White Horse Public House on the Manchester to Preston Road at Westhoughton and was intended to serve William Hulton's collieries.

The Manchester and Leeds Railway took over the Liverpool and Bury in 1846 [104]. Next year, the Manchester and Leeds became the Lancashire and Yorkshire Railway and the Act [72] which authorised the change in title also gave powers for the construction of additional railways at Bury. One was a short extension from the Heywood line to the Parliamentary termination of Liverpool and Bury on the east side of the bridge over the Irwell. The other was a connection between the East Lancashire and Lancashire and Yorkshire stations.

The line from Heywood to Bury opened for traffic on 1st May 1848. The whole of the former Liverpool and Bury Railway's main line and the spur to the East Lancashire Railway at Bury were opened on 20th November of the same year [65]. The colliery branches to Great Lever and to the White Horse at Westhoughton were never built.

Proposed Railways Serving Tyldesley and Little Hulton

By the end of the 1840s there were railways serving all the major manufacturing centres and, with three exceptions, all the areas producing significant amounts of coal. Only the collieries in the Croal and Irwell Valleys north and west of Clifton, the mining complex operated by the Bridgewater Trustees and a number of independent pits in the neighbourhood of Tyldesley and Little Hulton remained unconnected.

We have seen already how it had been the intention of the Manchester, Bolton and Bury company to construct railways which would have passed along the valleys of the Croal and the Irwell. The route finally adopted for the Manchester and Bolton line and the abandonment of proposals for a branch to Bury meant that the collieries here continued to use on the canal for distributing their coal. The Bridgewater Trustees were likewise able to rely on their own canal system and their underground waterways and had no real need of main line rail transport in the first half of the nineteenth century.

The collieries in and around Tyldesley and Little Hulton were less well placed, as they were remote from either railway or canal. Although there had been a number of proposals which would have provided them with a rail connection, many had to make do with horses and carts until the 1860s.

In 1830, there was a rather speculative proposal for a railway from Liverpool to Leeds and the Humber. The Deposited Plans [105,106] show a route through Westleigh, Tyldesley and Swinton, joining the projected Manchester, Bolton and Bury Railway south of Clifton. A second line left that railway's proposed Bury Branch at Radcliffe and then struck off across country to Rochdale. Similar proposals, now confined to the portion from Liverpool to the Manchester, Bolton and Bury, were put forward to Parliament in 1831 [107] and 1832 [108]. A further submission was made in 1834 [109], which took a more southerly course east of Roe Green to join the MB&B near Agecroft.

None of these schemes materialised. Then in 1845, no less than three separate proposals emerged which would have served Tyldesley and the surrounding area.

The Deposited Plans [110] of the so called Parkside Extension of the Liverpool and Leeds Railway were for a line which left the Liverpool and Manchester at Parkside and ran through Leigh, Tyldesley, Little Hulton, Kearsley, Radcliffe and Bury on its way to Rochdale and beyond.

The other two proposals were almost identical to each other. That for a railway from Liverpool to Preston and Manchester and Southport, to quote the title from the Deposited Plans [111], included a line which was intended to run from Burscough through Wigan, Atherton, Tyldesley, Ellenbrook, Roe Green and Irlams o' th' Height to join the Manchester, Bolton and Bury near Agecroft. There were also branches from Atherton to the Bolton and Leigh Railway, from Tyldesley to collieries in the neighbourhood of Little Hulton and from Roe Green to join the Liverpool and Manchester Railway east of Eccles. The Manchester, Wigan and Southport Railway followed the same route, but omitted some of the branches [112].

All three projects failed to obtain Parliamentary approval in 1846, but the Manchester and Southport Railway was more successful in the following year. The Act of 1847 [113], which incorporated the company, authorised a main line from Southport to a junction with the MB&B near Agecroft, 2¼ miles from Salford, on the same route as the second and third of the previous year's proposals [114]. A number of branches were also authorised. Within the area covered by the present book these comprised :

- A branch from Atherton to the Bolton and Leigh at Bag Lane
- A branch from Shakerley to the Liverpool and Manchester 20 chains east of Barton Moss Station, with a spur to the collieries south of Tyldesley

- A branch from Little Common, Tyldesley, to Wharton Colliery at Little Hulton, with a spur to Hulton Park, to serve the Hulton collieries
- A branch near Worsley to the Sandersons Pit tramroad of the Bridgewater Trustees, continuing, after a reversal, to Wardley Colliery.

Shortage of funds prevented any construction east of Hindley and the powers for this portion of the line were allowed to lapse. There was a further, but unsuccessful, submission to Parliament in 1852 [115] for line from Wigan to Clifton following the previously authorised route as far as Tyldesley. From here the new line would have taken a more northerly course through Walkden and then across country to join the Manchester to Bolton line at Clifton Junction. It was proposed to gain access to Wardley Colliery by means of a branch from the main line at Linnyshaw Moss, from where there was also to be another branch serving the Kearsley Vitriol Works.

The Manchester and Southport was closely allied with the Lancashire and Yorkshire, which was empowered by the 1847 Act [113] to purchase the railway when half the capital was subscribed. The two companies merged in April 1855 [65] and the L&YR made one last attempt to secure a line from Wigan to Clifton in the 1861 Parliamentary Session [116]. The branches to the Bolton and Leigh and Liverpool and Manchester lines were dropped, as was the spur to the collieries south of Tyldesley. East of Tyldesley, the route was similar to the 1852 proposal and included branches to the Hulton and Wharton Hall Collieries, to Wardley Colliery and to the Vitriol Works.

On this occasion the Lancashire and Yorkshire was in competition with the London and North Western Railway. The L&YR proposal was thrown out and it fell to the LNWR to provide the railways which eventually served the collieries in Tyldesley and Little Hulton.

The Lancashire and Yorkshire Railway 1847 to 1895

We now return to earlier times and take up the history of the Lancashire and Yorkshire system following its formation in 1847. We shall look first at the lines serving the Kearsley district.

No work had been carried out by the Manchester Bolton and Bury Railway on its Kearsley Moor Branch beyond the connection, near the incline top, giving access to the Manor Pit. The earlier powers had apparently lapsed and in 1847 there was another move to reach the Vitriol Works. The Manchester and Leeds Railway No 3 Act of that year [72], under which the name was changed to the Lancashire and Yorkshire Railway, authorised the Clifton Branch Extension. This started from a junction with the Clifton Branch, as the Kearsley Moor Branch was now known, 15 chains west of the Manchester and Bolton road and ran to a point 19 chains north-west of the vitriol works of Harrison Blair.

In 1849 [117], powers were obtained for two further short railways. One was to leave the original Clifton Branch 21 chains west of the Manchester and Bolton road and join the Clifton Branch Extension near to the Vitriol Works. The other was from a triangular junction with the first line on Kearsley Moss to an end on junction with the Manchester and Southport's Wardley Branch which had been authorised in 1847.

Despite an extension of time for the Clifton Branch Extension in 1852 [118], no construction was undertaken on any of these lines. It was not until some twenty five years later that the Lancashire and Yorkshire reached the area south of Farnworth by means of the Kearsley Branches, which were authorised in 1873 [119] and opened for goods traffic on 1st March 1878 [65].

The Kearsley No 1 Branch ran from a junction with the Manchester to Bolton line south of Stoneclough Station to a point near the Vitriol Works, where a junction was made with the Bridgewater Trustees' railway system at Linnyshaw Moss. The Kearsley No 2 Branch left the No 1 Branch just west of the Bolton to Manchester Road and terminated immediately to the west of the Farnworth to Worsley road.

The No 2 Branch only had a short life, being taken out of use following the closure of Stonehill Colliery early in 1888. Subsequently there were moves by local industrialists to have the branch reinstated [120], but these were unsuccessful.

In the meantime the cable operated incline at Unity Brook had been superseded. A line which zigzagged up the side of the valley had been built on private land and was worked by the Clifton and Kersley Coal Company's locomotives. The precise date for this change has not been recorded. The incline is still mentioned in a document of December 1865 [121] but the new alignment is shown on an L&YR Sidings Diagram of 1875 [122].

In 1876, competition was threatened when a Bill was presented in Parliament for the Bolton Junctions Railway. The intention was to provide a new route to Bolton, linking up with the Cheshire Lines Railway at Manchester Central Station, at Chorlton and at Trafford Park. The line would have run through Weaste, Swinton and Farnworth to its own terminus in Bolton [123]. Several connections were planned with the Bridgewater Trustees railway system.

The Bolton Junctions Bill, which failed to gain Parliamentary approval, came at a time when the Lancashire and Yorkshire Railway was undertaking a number of new projects at Bolton and elsewhere.

The Astley Bridge Branch was authorised in 1871 [68] from a junction with the Blackburn line south of the Croal Viaduct to a point 365 yards west of the Bolton to Blackburn road, opposite Sharples Bleach Works. The line was opened on 15th October 1877 [65] as far the Blackburn road, the section beyond not being built. Although the branch was primarily intended to serve public goods yards at Halliwell and Astley Bridge, there was a short lived passenger service which ceased on 1st October 1879.

A south curve, connecting the Bury line with the Bolton to Manchester line at Burnden, was opened for traffic on 27th March 1881 [65,124] and a north curve from the Blackburn line to the Bolton and Preston line was opened on 26th March 1888 [65,125].

In 1872 an Act [126] for a line from the former East Lancashire Railway at Radcliffe North Junction through Whitefield and Prestwich to Manchester was passed by Parliament. Also authorised was a spur from Radcliffe South Junction to the Bolton and Bury line at Black Lane. An extension of time was granted in 1876 [121] and a short spur from Radcliffe West Junction to Radcliffe North Junction was authorised in 1877 [127]. The line from Radcliffe North Junction to Cheetham Hill Junction at Manchester was opened for all traffic on 1st September 1879 [65], although goods trains had been using the portion south of Whitefield since 1st August [65]. The spurs from Radcliffe South Junction to Black Lane and between Radcliffe West and North Junctions were opened on 1st December of the same year [65].

Meanwhile, a short branch from the Bury to Heywood line to Heap Bridge, authorised in 1871 [125], had been opened on 8th Sept 1874 [65]. This was primarily intended to serve the paper mills at Heap Bridge, where there was also a small public goods yard. A passenger service was never provided.

North of Bury, the nominally independent Bury and Tottington District Railway was incorporated in 1877 [128] to construct a line from a junction with the former East Lancashire Railway north of Bolton Street Station to Holcombe Brook. The original proposals included a west to north curve to the East Lancashire line and branches at Woolfold to Olive's Paper Mill and to Olive's wagon works [129]. Of these only the branch to "Messrs John Olive and Sons wagon building shed" was authorised. A continuation of the Woolfold Branch for just over 1 mile to Bury Gas Works was proposed in the 1880 Parliamentary Session [130], but the line was not sanctioned.

A 1950s view of the terminus of the branch at Astley Bridge Goods Yard. The ex-L&YR saddle tank has completed its work for the day and is coupled to a brake van ready for the return journey to Bolton.

Neville Knight

The branch goods train waits to leave Heap Bridge with a rake of empty coal wagons. The siding on the left leads to the paper mill of Yates Duxbury and Sons. Across the river can be seen the remains of the paper mill of Thomas Wrigley and Sons, which at one time also provided traffic for the branch.   Neville Knight

The Bury and Tottington District's line to Holcombe Brook was opened on 6th November 1882 [65]. It was worked by the Lancashire and Yorkshire Railway throughout its short independent existence, which came to an end when the company was taken over by the L&YR in 1888 [131].

The position regarding the branch at Woolfold is uncertain. The land was purchased [132] and the first edition of the 25" map shows that the earthworks, including a bridge under the Bury to Tottington road, were completed. It is not clear, however, whether the track was ever laid as the wagon works which the branch was intended to serve closed in the early 1880s.

A major addition to the L&YR system took place in the 1880s with the construction of a new main line to provide a faster and less circuitous route between Manchester and Liverpool. This represented the culmination of plans going back to the 1840s for a direct route from Manchester towards Wigan, avoiding Bolton. Since the defeat of the Bill for a line from Hindley to Clifton Junction, described earlier, consideration had been given in 1872 to extending the Kearsley No 2 Branch to Hindley [65].

The new scheme took a more direct route through Atherton. The section from Windsor Bridge on the Manchester and Bolton line to Hindley on the Bolton and Liverpool line was authorised in 1883 [133] and was built with four tracks throughout. Powers for a link to the Hindley and Blackrod line were obtained in 1884 [134] and for additional connecting railways at Pendleton in 1885 [135]. The latter comprised a deviation to take the slow lines under the fast lines between Pendleton and Irlams o' th' Height and a connection from these low level lines to form a loop back to the Manchester and Bolton line at Agecroft.

The section between Windsor Bridge and Agecroft Junction, including the station at Pendleton (Broad Street), opened on 13th June 1887 [65]. Goods traffic between Pendleton and Swinton commenced on the same day. The goods train service was extended to Atherton on 2nd July 1888 and from there to Crow Nest Junction at Hindley on 1st October 1888 [65]. The whole line, from Pendleton to Hindley, was opened for passenger traffic on 1st June 1889 [65], on the same date as the link from Dobbs Brow Junction to the Hindley and Blackrod line.

A loaded coal train at Sandersons Siding on the Eccles, Tyldesley and Wigan line, photographed in April 1948. The bridge in the background carries the Bridgewater Collieries railway over the LNWR.

Cooper's Railway Photographs

The London and North Western Railway 1847 to 1895

In the area covered in this book, few developments took place on the London and North Western Railway from its formation in 1846 until the 1860s. As has been mentioned, the LNWR obtained an Act of Parliament in 1861 for the construction of the Eccles, Tyldesley and Wigan Railway [136]. As well as the main line linking the places named, the Bedford Leigh Branch, from Tyldesley to Pennington on the Bolton and Leigh line, and a short spur at Atherton were authorised at the same time. Construction proceeded rapidly and all three lines were opened for traffic on 1st September 1864 [30], providing connections with a number of collieries in the neighbourhood of Tyldesley not previously served by rail.

There followed a series of lines serving the territory northwards towards Bolton. A branch from Roe Green Junction on the Eccles, Tyldesley and Wigan to Little Hulton was authorised in 1865 [137]. The Deposited Plans [138] show Railway No 1 starting at Roe Green and terminating at a point a little beyond Clegg's Lane. Railway No 2 formed a continuation of Railway No 1 towards the site of the future Brackley Colliery while Railway No 3 was a branch from near Clegg's Lane to Ashton's Field. Only Railway No 1 was authorised and this in a truncated form, terminating just short of Mount Skip Lane. An extension of time was granted in 1870 [139], and the line opened for goods traffic 1st July of that year [30].

Powers were obtained in 1869 [140] to extend the Little Hulton Branch to join the Bolton and Leigh line at Fletcher Street. The same Act authorised construction of the Little Hulton Mineral Branch, from the new line to Charlton's Colliery, and alterations to the tracks near Great Moor Street Station at Bolton.

A 19" Goods Engine on a train heading in the Bolton direction, leaving Roe Green Junction, on a snowy day in February 1941.   Coopers Railway Photographs

Great Moor Street Station was closed in September 1871 [141] and trains used a temporary terminus in the goods sidings while the level crossing over Crook Street was replaced by a bridge. The reconstructed station and the new approach lines were opened on 28th September 1874 [142,143]. The Little Hulton Extension Railway was opened for goods traffic on 16th November 1874 [30] and passenger trains between Manchester and Bolton started to run between Roe Green Junction and Fletcher Street Junction on 1st April 1875. The date of opening of Little Hulton Mineral Branch seems to have escaped the notice of railway historians. It is thought to have been 16th November 1874, the same date as the extension line.

On the Bolton and Leigh line rope haulage on the two inclines had been discontinued some time previously. Although we have been unable to find when this occurred, it certainly must have been before 1858. On 27th January of that year a goods train, which had been banked from Atherton to Chequerbent by two locomotives, failed to stop properly at the top of the Daubhill incline to pin down brakes and ran away, causing considerable damage when it crashed at Great Moor Street station [144]. The winding engine house at Chequerbent had been replaced by a three-road locomotive shed by 1873 [145] and probably much earlier.

In the latter part of the 1870s moves were made to reconstruct the whole of the railway from Leigh to Bolton, which was still mainly single track. The line between Pennington and Kenyon had already been doubled [146], presumably when the Eccles, Tyldesley and Wigan railway was constructed. Widening between Pennington and a point 250 yards north of Atherton Station was authorised in 1876 [147]. The second track between Pennington Junction and Atherton Junction was brought into use on Monday 31st May 1880 [148] and that through Atherton Station on 4th July of the same year [149].

A train of hopper wagons destined for the Hilton Gravel Company's siding approaching the summit of the incline on the deviation line at Chequerbent. The train engine is 48327, with 48529 banking. The photograph was taken in May 1968, shortly before the line was closed.   Neville Fields

In 1878 powers were obtained [150] to build deviations to avoid the inclines and to widen the remaining portions of the line. A further Act in 1880 [151] permitted alterations to the course of the deviation line at Chequerbent and authorised a north to west curve to the Eccles, Tyldesley and Wigan line at Atherton. The Deposited Plans [152] for the 1880 Bill also included a connection from the Bolton and Leigh at Kenyon Junction to the LNWR West Coast main line near Winwick Junction, involving a bridge over the Liverpool and Manchester line. This last proposal was, however, dropped before the Act was passed.

The west curve at Atherton was probably brought into use in 1883 and the reconstructed line from Atherton to Fletcher Street Junction at Bolton was opened for traffic on 2nd February 1885 [30]. Several portions of the original Bolton and Leigh alignment were retained. From Pendlebury Fold to a point south of the Chequerbent Pits the old line remained in place, worked by the owner of the colliery, Mr W B Hulton, using his own locomotives. His traffic was allowed to pass free of toll against an annual payment of £1 per annum, under an agreement dated 17th August 1885 [153]. On the original line through Daubhill, about half a mile at the western end remained in use to serve a coal yard and goods depot at Adelaide Street, near the site of the stationary engine. At the eastern end, a section a little over a quarter mile in length was kept for access to a coal yard and private sidings at High Street.

Meanwhile, a number of improvements had been taking place elsewhere, mainly on the Liverpool and Manchester line. A new station, Manchester Exchange, was built to provide facilities independent of those shared with the Lancashire and Yorkshire at Victoria. At the same period, quadrupling of the lines between Manchester and Barton Moss was completed.

Authorisation to widen the line between Oldfield Road and Eccles had been obtained as long ago as 1865 [154]. It is not clear how much, if any, work was carried out at the time, as the contract for the section from Cross Lane to Eccles apparently was not let until November 1882 [155]. According to Neele [156], the new lines were opened in 1884.

Widening from Ordsall Lane to the junction with the Manchester South Junction and Altrincham Railway, together with alterations to the junction itself, were authorised in 1882 [157]. Parliamentary approval had already been obtained in 1878 for widening east of here [150]. The new lines, which were mainly on viaduct, were brought into use at the same time as the new Exchange Station, on 30th June 1884 [156].

The widening between Eccles Junction and Barton Moss was authorised in 1878 [150]. The construction contract was let in July of the same year [158] and the new tracks were opened for passenger traffic on 1st February 1883 [156].

Other work was carried out in the neighbourhood of Eccles and Patricroft at the same period. The LNWR Act of 1880 [151] authorised the construction of a bridge to take the Patricroft and Molyneux Junction line over the Eccles, Tyldesley and Wigan line, replacing the existing level crossing [159]. A curve permitting through running from Eccles to Molyneux Junction, not specifically mentioned in the Act, was also provided, though it was short-lived and closed on 31st May 1891 [160]. An additional pair of tracks was laid between Eccles Junction and Monton Green. The work here was completed before a revised Line Plan was published about 1883 [161].

East of Patricroft, a scheme was prepared in 1879 [152] for quadrupling the line from Barton Moss to Kenyon Junction, to link up with the proposed curve to the West Coast main line, mentioned earlier. However, the widening proposals, like the curve, were withdrawn before the Bill became law.

The Manchester Ship Canal

In the late 1870s and early 1880s support was actively being canvassed for a canal from Manchester to the Mersey capable of accommodating sea going ships. The promoters, mainly industrialists and textile magnates, sought to break the monopoly of the port of Liverpool and the railway companies which served it. After a series of unsuccessful applications to Parliament, an Act was finally obtained in 1885 [162].

The Manchester Ship Canal opened for traffic on 1st January 1894 [1]. Its history is outside the scope of the present study, but we need to consider the influence it had on the development of the local railway network.

In an attempt by Liverpool interests to obviate the need for the canal, a scheme was put forward in the 1882 Parliamentary Session for the Lancashire Plateway. The intention was to employ a modernised form of the railway adopted for short canal feeder lines at the end of the eighteenth century, where the wheels of the wagons were flangeless and guidance was provided by an upstand on the rail [163]. Locomotives were to be used to haul the trains along the plateway. Between the docks and the plateway and from the plateway to the factories, individual vehicles could be drawn by horses through the streets.

An extensive network was planned, connecting Liverpool with every major cotton manufacturing town in Lancashire. Within the limits of the present book, there would have been a line of plateway through Leigh and Atherton, passing to the north of Farnworth, to a Bolton terminus at what is now the junction of Weston Street and Crescent Road. From a point near Fishpools a second line would have run through Little Lever, Radcliffe and Bury, and then on to Rochdale [164]. The 1882 Bill failed as did another submitted a year later and thereafter there was little support for the scheme.

A train of empty coal wagons leaving Patricroft for the Clifton Branch in May 1952. It is just starting the ascent up to the bridge built in the 1880s over the Eccles, Tyldesley and Wigan line.

Coopers Railway Photographs

With the completion of the canal, the Lancashire and Yorkshire and London and North Western Railways no doubt experienced a reduction in traffic between Liverpool and the Lancashire cotton districts. However, this was to a large extent offset by freight transported to and from the new Manchester Docks. The Manchester Ship Canal built up an extensive railway system of its own, which was linked to the lines of both companies.

The London and North Western connection with Ship Canal railway was at Weaste Junction. The branch from the Liverpool and Manchester line was authorised in 1892 [165] and opened for goods traffic on 4th November 1895 [65].

The Lancashire and Yorkshire's Dock Branch ran from Windsor Bridge on the Bolton line to a point near the then Manchester Racecourse at New Barns. The branch was authorised in 1890 [166], but there were delays in the construction. The L&YR Act of 1894 [167] granted an extension of time and also abandoned a portion of the line beyond New Barns, which was left to the Ship Canal company to build. Goods traffic commenced on 28th March 1898 [65]. The racecourse was served by special passenger trains from 1898 until it was closed in 1901 to make way for the new No 9 Dock. The racecourse station, however, continued to be used by unadvertised trains taking workmen to the docks until August 1939 [65].

To enable goods trains from Yorkshire to reach the docks without reversal, a curve was built at Bury from the Heywood line to the former East Lancashire line. This was authorised in 1891 [168] and, after an extension of time in 1896 [169], was opened on 21st November 1898 [65].

The Manchester Ship Canal was seen as providing an outlet for coal mined in South Lancashire and elsewhere and loading basins were established at Partington, on both the Lancashire and Cheshire banks. A Bill was submitted to Parliament in the 1895 Session for the Leigh and South Central Lancashire Railway, with the intention of providing direct access to Partington from the collieries. The Deposited Plans [170] show a main line running in a long loop south from the Lancashire and Yorkshire at Ince back to the Lancashire and Yorkshire at Walkden, with branches to almost every colliery in the territory traversed. A second main line, intersecting the first south of Gin Pit, ran from Tyldesley to Cadishead, where there were a series of spurs to the Ship Canal system and to the Cheshire Lines Railway. The Preamble of the Bill was not proved, bringing the project to an end.

The LNWR and the L&YR 1895 to 1923

After the opening of the Lancashire and Yorkshire's direct route from Pendleton to Hindley in 1888, there were few changes to the railway map of South Lancashire. The only new lines were those associated with the Manchester Ship Canal, described above, and a short line at Pennington, opened by the LNWR on 2nd June 1903 [30], connecting the Bedford Leigh Branch with the Bickershaw Branch. One further line, a west to south spur, connecting the Preston and Wigan lines at Lostock Junction was authorised by the Lancashire and Yorkshire Act of 1913 [171]. The junction with the Preston line was never completed [65], the tracks connecting with the Wigan line merely serving as sidings.

The period from 1890 to the outbreak of the first world war, in 1914, was one of consolidation of existing facilities rather than one of expansion. The Lancashire and Yorkshire Railway in particular carried out a number of long overdue improvements at this time.

Widening to accommodate an extra pair of tracks between Windsor Bridge and Victoria Station, Manchester, was authorised in 1890 [172]. The section from Victoria to Deal Street was passed for use on 9th December 1896 and the remainder on 10th April 1900 [65].

Reconstruction of Trinity Street Station at Bolton was taken in hand. A new station had been opened there on 8th May 1871 to replace the original Manchester, Bolton and Bury structure [173]. Further powers had been obtained in 1877 [127] for major alterations, but these had been allowed to lapse. A new scheme was authorised in 1894, which included additional tracks on the three routes leading into the station [167]. Construction started in 1899 and the new and enlarged station was brought into use on 29th February 1904 [65].

Quadruple tracks were laid between Bolton and Lostock. The work, originally proposed in 1874 [174], was deferred until the 1890s and was carried out in two parts. The portion from Lostock to Bullfield was authorised in 1892 [175] and was ready for use at the end of 1899 [65]. That from Bullfield into Trinity Street Station, which involved extra tunnels [176], was authorised in 1900 [177] and completed in 1905 [65]. Further widening at Lostock Junction was authorised in 1907 [178].

On the Bolton to Bury line, two additional tracks were laid in at Darcy Lever, between Moss Lane and Crow Nest Level Crossing, under powers obtained in 1910 [171]. Widenings were also carried out on the Bolton and Blackburn line between Bromley Cross and King William, authorised in 1897 [179] and completed in 1903 [65], and at Craddock Lane, authorised in 1900 [177].

Growing competition from electric tramways led the Lancashire and Yorkshire to consider electrification of its suburban railways. By way of experiment, the line from Bury to Holcombe Brook was converted, using 3,500 volt direct current supplied from overhead wires. The work was completed towards the end of 1912 or early in 1913, the public service being inaugurated on 29th July of the latter year [65].

For its line between Manchester and Bury, the company opted for 1,200 volt direct current using a third rail. The electric trains started to run as part of the advertised service on 17th April 1916 [65]. The overhead wire equipment on the Holcombe Brook Branch was subsequently dismantled and replaced by the third rail system, which came into use on 29th March 1918 [65].

As from 1st January 1923, the railway companies were brought together into four new groups under the provisions of the Railways Act of 1921 [180]. The Lancashire and Yorkshire and London and North Western, which had already amalgamated on 1st January 1922, became part of the London, Midland and Scottish Railway.

A 1950s scene of Bolton Street Station at Bury. An electric train formed of the original 1916 rolling stock waits in the bay platform on the right ready to depart for Manchester. A Bacup train is heading north, while a light engine passes through the station bound for the locomotive sheds. The tall building on the right hand platform is the former headquarters of the East Lancashire Railway.   Harry Townley

The Railways after 1923

From 1923 onwards the new railway companies faced increasing competition from road transport. The reduction in passenger traffic, which had started when electric tramways were introduced, continued as bus services expanded. The freight side declined as more and more firms began to employ motor lorries to carry their products.

Although in some cases facilities were reduced, only two short branch lines were closed completely in the period up to the outbreak of the second world war. The portions of the Clifton Branch which remained railway company property ceased to be used around 1929 when the colliery and the associated coal preparation plant were closed. The branch at Bolton, serving Deansgate warehouse was officially taken out of use on 25th February 1930 [181].

On 1st January 1948, the railways passed into public ownership as a result of the Transport Act of 1947 [182]. The London, Midland and Scottish lines in South Lancashire became part of the London Midland Region of the new British Railways.

From the early 1950s there was a further downturn in all classes of traffic. Passenger services between Bury and Holcombe Brook were withdrawn on 5th May 1953, after the electric trains had been replaced by steam trains a year earlier. Regular passenger trains on the former LNWR lines serving Bolton ceased on 29th March 1954.

Drastic restructuring in the 1960s in an attempt to reduce losses resulted in the closure of most of the local goods facilities and many more of the passenger train services. Those between Manchester and Wigan via Tyldesley were withdrawn on 2nd November 1964, and those using the Eccles, Tyldesley and Kenyon Junction route on 5th May 1969. On the former Lancashire and Yorkshire lines, passenger trains between Clifton Junction and Bury were withdrawn on 5th December 1966, between Bolton, Bury and Rochdale on 5th October 1970 and north of Bury on 5th June 1972. With the reduced traffic, most of the four track sections of line were replaced by double track and some of the existing double track lines were singled.

The railways now present a very different picture from what they did when they were at the height of their prosperity.

Freight services are now few and far between and mainly of a specialised nature. Greater Manchester Refuse Disposal trains from the terminal at Pendleton still run over the former Lancashire and Yorkshire lines to Wigan and, until towards the end of 1993, there were parcels trains serving a central depot at Bolton. Long distance train load freight traffic continues to make use of the Liverpool and Manchester line.

There has been a dramatic decline in the number of the through express trains, once a feature of many of the routes. In contrast, local passenger services on those lines which survive, mostly subsidised by the local authorities, are more frequent than at any time in their history. SELNEC (the South East Lancashire and North East Cheshire Passenger Transport Authority) and its successor, the Greater Manchester Passenger Transport Executive, have provided financial backing for several important developments.

The Manchester to Bury line featured in a ambitious scheme put forward by SELNEC, which, in 1972, obtained an Act [183] for an underground railway linking suburban lines on the south side of Manchester with those on the north. Through electric trains would have served Bury and it was also proposed to re-open and electrify the line from Radcliffe to Bolton [184].

Lack of finance forced the underground project to be abandoned although some work was carried out by British Railways at Bury, under an Act of 1975 [185]. A line was opened 17th March 1980 [186] from Buckley Wells to a new station, near the Market Place. It was built in part on the formation of the Ship Canal Loop, closed some years previously. Just outside the new station there was a level crossing with what had originally been the spur from Knowsley Street Station to Bolton Street Station and which was now used by an occasional freight train from Castleton to a coal yard at Rawtenstall. The section of line from Buckley Wells to Bolton Street was taken out of use when the new station opened, except for the short portion giving access to the carriage sheds.

The electric trains from Manchester (Victoria) to the new station at Bury were replaced by tram cars of the Greater Manchester Passenger Transport Executive's Light Rapid Transit System, which started running on 6th April 1991 [187]. The trams, operated by Greater Manchester Metro Ltd under a 15 year concession [188], run through the streets between Victoria Station, Piccadilly Station and the G Mex Centre, from where the service continues to Altrincham over former British Railways lines. The work was authorised in by two Acts of Parliament in 1988 [189,190], the second of which also permitted the British Railways Board to transfer the Victoria to Bury line and a portion of the Altrincham line to the Passenger Transport Executive.

A north to south railway connection was achieved by the construction of the Windsor Link, which was brought partly into use in April 1988 [191], with full operation in the following month [192]. The work involved the upgrading of the former Manchester South Junction and Altrincham track from Castlefield Junction to Ordsall Lane [193] and the construction of a new section of line from there to the former Lancashire and Yorkshire Railway's Bolton and Hindley lines [194].

The line northwards from Bury has also seen a revival, although of a rather different kind. The East Lancashire Light Railway now operates a service of trains, mainly at weekends, hauled by preserved steam and diesel locomotives. After the withdrawal of the British Railways freight service from Heywood to Rawtenstall in December 1980, the Metropolitan Borough of Bury and the Rossendale District Council purchased the sections of trackbed within their respective boundaries, which were then vested in a Trust comprising the two local authorities and the Light Railway.

The ELLR service from Bolton Street Station, in Bury, to Ramsbottom started on 25th July 1987. The line from Ramsbottom to Rawtenstall was formally opened on 27th April 1991 [195], with public services on the following day. At the time of writing, work is in progress to re-open the line from Bolton Street to Castleton. The bridge needed to carry the line over the rapid transit tracks approaching Bury Interchange was put in place early in 1993.

References to Chapter 2

1 *"The Canals of North West England"* - Hadfield and Biddle - David and Charles, Newton Abbot, 1970
2 7 Geo I cap 15; 17th June 1721
3 34 Geo III cap 37; 1794
4 10 Geo II cap 9; 1737
5 32 Geo II cap 2; 23rd March 1759
6 33 Geo II cap 2; 24th March 1760
7 *"Worsley in the Eighteenth Century"* - Helen Wickham - publ 1984
8 2 Geo III cap 11; 1762
9 LRO PDC 17
10 35 Geo III cap XLIV; 28th April 1795
11 LRO PDC 25
12 LRO PDC 30
13 LRO PDC 35
14 59 Geo IV cap cv; 21st June 1819
15 *"The Bridgewater Heritage "* - Christopher Grayling - Bridgewater Estates plc, Manchester, 1983
16 SAO CA 117
17 48 & 49 Vic cap clxxxviii;6th August 1885
18 31 Geo III cap 68; 13th May 1791
19 LRO PDC 22
20 LRO PDC 11
21 LRO PDC 14
22 34 Geo III cap 77 ; 1794
23 4 & 5 Geo VI cap xii; 22nd July 1941
24 10 & 11 Geo VI cap xxxv; 31st July 1947
25 9 & 10 Eliz II cap xxxvi; 27th July 1961
26 *"The Liverpool and Manchester Railway Project"* - R E Carlson- David and Charles, Newton Abbot 1969
27 7 Geo IV cap xlix; 5th May 1826
28 10 Geo IV cap xxxv; 14th May 1829
29 LRO PDR 270
30 *"Chronology of the Railways of Lancashire and Cheshire"* - M D Greville - Railway and Canal Historical Society, 1981
31 2 & 3 Vic cap xli; 14th June 1839
32 5 & 6 Vic cap cviii; 30th July 1842
33 8 & 9 Vic cap cxcviii; 8th August 1845
34 9 & 19 Vic cap cciv; 16th July 1846
35 8 & 9 Vic cap cxi; 21st July 1845
36 10 & 11 Viccap lxxiii; 2nd July 1847
37 8 & 9 Vic cap cxxiii; 21st July 1845
38 LRO PDR 390
39 Line Plan of Eccles, Tyldesley and Wigan Railway - 2 chains to 1 inch - LNWR, Rugby, 1868 - At GMRO A19/2/24
40 6 Geo IV cap xviii; 31st March 1825
41 LRO PDR 131
42 BC 2-8-1828
43 *Manchester Courier* 10-4-1830
44 Liverpool and Manchester Railway Minutes 7-12-1829
45 BC 10-10-1829
46 BC 28-8-1830
47 10 Geo IV cap xxxvi; 14th May 1829
48 BC 8-1-1831
49 1 & 2 Wm IV cap xi; 30th July 1831
50 LRO PDR 244
51 6 Wm IV cap liii; 20th May 1836
52 LRO PDR 143
53 LRO PDR 151
54 LRO PDR 195
55 LRO PDR 196
56 LRO PDR 197
57 1 & 2 Wm IV cap lx; 23rd Aug 1831
58 LRO PDC 42
59 2 Wm IV cap lxix; 1st June 1832
60 LRO PDR 208
61 LRO PDR 227
62 BMB ZAL 282
63 5 & 6 Wm IV cap xxx; 17th June
64 LRO PDR 444
65 *"The Lancashire and Yorkshire Railway"* John Marshall - David and Charles, Newton Abbot, 1969
66 24 & 25 Vic cap xxxiv; 17th May 1861
67 LRO PDR 1067
68 34 & 35 Vic cap clxx; 24th July 1871
69 1 Vic cap xxv; 11th June 1838
70 LRO PDR 317
71 9 & 10 Vic cap ccclxxviii; 18th Aug 1846
72 10 & 11 Vic cap clxiii; 9th July 1847
73 LRO PDR 275
74 1 Vic cap cxxi; 15th July 1837
75 1 & 2 Vic cap lvi; 4th July 1838
76 7 & 8 Vic cap ii; 10th May 1844
77 9 & 10 Vic cap ccxxxi; 27th July 1846
78 51 & 52 Viccap clxxvi; 7th Aug 1888
79 52 & 53 Viccap xcviii; 26th July 1889
80 8 & 9 Vic cap xliv; 30th June 1845
81 BMB PBO/P9
82 BMB PBO/P10
83 LRO PDR 464
84 9 & 10 Vic cap cccx; 3rd Aug 1846
85 10 & 11 Vic cap clxiv; 9th July 1847
86 9 & 10 Vic cap cclxv; 27th July 1846
87 14 & 15 Vic cap lxxxix; 24th July 1851
88 BMB PBO/P63 89 LRO PDR 649
90 21 & 22 Vic cap cvi; 12th July 1858
91 22 & 23 Vic cap cx; 13th Aug 1859
92 7 & 8 Vic cap lx; 4th July 1844
93 8 & 9 Vic cap ci; 21st July 1845
94 LRO PDR 535
95 LRO PDR 443
96 LRO PDR 598
97 17 & 18 Viccap cxvii; 3rd July 1854
98 LRO PDR 481
99 LRO PDR 411
100 LRO PDR 412
101 8 & 9 Vic cap clxvi; 31st July 1845
102 8 & 9 Vic cap liv; 30th June 1845

103	9 & 10 Vic cap cccxii; 3rd Aug 1846
104	9 & 10 Vic cap cclxxxii; 27th July 1846
105	LRO PDR 192
106	LRO PDR 193
107	LRO PDR 207
108	LRO PDR 230
109	LRO PDR 236
110	LRO PDR 493
111	LRO PDR 503
112	LRO PDR 502
113	10 & 11 Vic cap ccxxi; 22nd July 1847
114	LRO PDR 539
115	LRO PDR 592
116	LRO PDR 707
117	12 & 13 Vic cap l; 13th July 1849
118	15 & 16 Vic cap cxxxii; 30th June 1852
119	36 & 37 Vic cap clxxix; 21st July 1873
120	BMB ZBR/5/63/505
121	LRO DDX 326/7
122	*"The Clifton and Kersley Coal Company and the LYR"* - D Richardson - in *"Platform 33"*, L&YR Soc Jnl, Autumn 1990
123	BMB ABPP/15/1
124	39 & 40 Vic cap clxx; 24th July 1876
125	47 & 48 Vic capcxlv; 14th July 1884
126	35 & 36 Vic cap cxvi; 18th July 1872
1273	4 & 35 Vic cap clxx; 24th July 1941
128	40 & 41 Vic capclvii; 2nd Aug 1877
129	LRO PDR 1029
130	LRO PDR 1109
131	51 & 52 Vic cap cxl; 24th July 1888
132	Line Plan of Holcombe Brook Branch - 2 chains to 1 inch - LMSR, Euston, 1934 - At GMRO A19/1/6
133	46 & 47 Vic cap clxix; 2nd Aug 1883
134	47 & 48 Viccap cxlv; 14th July 1884
135	48 & 49 Vic cap xciv; 16th July 1885
136	24 & 25 Vic cap cxxx; 11th July 1861
137	28 & 29 Vic cap cccxxiii; 5th July 1865
138	LRO PDR799
139	33 & 34 Vic cap cxii; 4th July 1870
140	32 & 33 Vic cap cxv; 12th July 1869
141	BC 9-9-1871
142	*"The Railways of Bolton 1824 -1959"* - J P Bardsley - Bolton, reprinted 1982
143	BC 3-10-1874
144	BC 30-1-1858
145	LRO PDR 966
146	LRO PDR 1014
147	39 & 40 Vic cap clxxx; 24th July 1876
148	LNWR Locomotive Committee Minute 6745 of 18-6-1880
149	LNWR Locomotive Committee Minute 6783 of 9-7-1880
150	41 & 42 Vic cap clxxxii; 22nd July 1878
151	43 & 44 Vic cap cxlv; 6th Aug 1880
152	LRO PDR 1142
153	Line Plan of Bolton and Kenyon Railway - 2 chains to 1 inch - LNWR, Euston, 1888 - At BRPB, Manchester
154	28 & 29 Vic cap cccxxiii; 5th July 1865
155	*Building News* 10-11-1882
156	*"Railway Reminiscences"* - G P Neele - Mc Corqodale, London 1904
157	45 & 46 Viccap lxxxviii; 3rd July 1882
158	*Building News* 5-7-1878
159	LRO PDR 1128
160	Typescript notes by John Marshall on Patricroft and Clifton Branch - copy in authors' possession
161	Line Plan of Eccles, Tyldesley and Wigan Line -2 chains to 1 inch -LNWR - nd about 1883 - At GMRO A 19/4/8
162	48 & 49 Vic cap clxxxviii;6th Aug 1885
163	*"An Account of the Proposed Lancashire Plateway Company"* - Alfred Holt, Liverpool, 1883, with Appendix dated 1889
164	LRO PDR 1215
165	55 & 56 Vic cap clxviii; 27th June 1892
166	53 & 54 Vic cap clvii; 4th Aug 1890
167	57 & 58 Viccap cxlviii; 31st July 1894
168	54 & 55 Vic cap xcix; 3rd July 1891
169	59 & 60 Vic cap cxxxix; 20th July 1896
170	LRO PDR 1491
171	10 Edw VII and 1 Geo V cap cxxiv; 15th Aug 1913
172	53 & 54 Vic cap clvii; 4th Aug 1890
173	*"A History of Trinity Street Station"* - publ Bolton Environmental Project, Bolton, no date, about 1988
174	BMB PBO/P41
175	55 & 56 Vic capclxxvi; 27th June 1892
176	BMB ABPP/38/1
177	63 & 64 Vic cap lxxxix; 10th July 1900
178	7 Edw VII cap cxxv; 9th August 1907
179	60 & 61 Vic cap cxxx; 15th July 1897
180	11&12 Geo Vcap 55; 19th July 1921
181	*"Register of Closed Passenger Stations and Goods Depots - Vol II"* - C R Clinker - publ by the author, 2nd edn 1964
182	10 & 11 Geo VI cap 49; 6th August 1947
183	1972 cap xliv; 9th August 1972
184	BLN 191
185	1975 cap i; 13th March 1975
186	BLN 390
187	BLN 680
188	BLN 683
189	1988 cap i; 9th February 1988
190	1988 cap ii; 9th February 1988
191	BLN 585
192	BLN 589
193	1980 cap xvi; 30th June 1980;
194	1982 cap xxiii; 28th October 1982
195	BLN 658

RAILWAY CHRONOLOGY

LONDON AND NORTH WESTERN RAILWAY

Became LMSR	1. 1. 1923	
Became British Railways	1. 1. 1948	

Liverpool to Manchester

Originally Liverpool and Manchester Railway

Absorbed by Grand Junction Railway	8. 8. 1845	(1)
Became LNWR	16. 7. 1846	(1)

Opened:

Liverpool (Crown St) to Manchester (Liverpool Rd)	15. 9. 1830	(1)
Ordsall Lane to Manchester (Victoria)	4. 5. 1844	(1)
Exchange Station	30. 6. 1884	(2)
Ship Canal Branch Eccles to Weaste Jct	4.11. 1895	(3)

Widenings:

Barton Moss to Eccles opened for passrs	1. 2. 1883	(2)
Victoria to Ordsall Lane	30. 6. 1884	(2)
Ordsall Lane to Eccles	1884	(2)

Closed:

Ordsall Lane to Liverpool Road passengers	4. 5. 1844	(4)
Ordsall Lane to Liverpool Road goods [Note 1]	8. 9. 1975	(5)
Manchester Exchange Station	5. 5. 1969	(6)

Third and fourth tracks removed:

Deal Street to Ordsall Lane Fast Lines [Note 2]	5. 2. 1968	(7)
Barton Moss to Ordsall Lane Slow Lines [Notes 3 and 4]	26. 8. 1971	(8,9,10)

Still open:
Liverpool Lime Street to Manchester Victoria for passenger traffic
Earlestown to Manchester Victoria for goods traffic
Ship Canal Branch to Weaste Jct for goods traffic [Note 5]

Notes:
1   Connection to Liverpool Road Goods Station. Now Manchester Museum of Science and Industry. Connection restored for Liverpool and Manchester 125 celebrations, and reopened 13th April 1980 (11).
2   Date last used, officially taken out of use 15-12-1968 (12).
3   Not available for use by this date, but not officially taken out of use until 12.12.1971 (13).
4   Down slow line Eccles to Patricroft retained until about 1987 to serve Royal Ordnance Factory and roadstone sidings. Down slow line also retained east of Eccles to give access to Ship Canal Branch (8) (9) (10) (13).
5   Eccles to Weaste Jct singled 6.10. 1968 (14).

Patricroft to Molyneux Junction

Originally Liverpool and Manchester Rly
Absorbed by Grand Junction Railway   8. 8. 1845   (1)
Became LNWR   16. 7. 1846

Opened:

Patricroft to Molyneux Jct [Note 1]	2. 2. 1850	(1)
Deviation bridge at Patricroft over Eccles, Tyldesley and Wigan line, replacing a level crossing	See Note 2	
Curve at Patricroft to ET&W line	26. 5. 1884	(15)

Closed:

Throughout for regular passengers [Note 3]	5. 1850	(1)
Curve at Patricroft to ET&W line	31. 5. 1891	(15)
South end of Pendlebury Tunnel to Clifton Hall Colliery Sdgs No 1 Box	See Note 4	
Clifton Hall Colliery Sidings to Molyneux Junction [Note 5]	16. 6. 1961	(15)
Patricroft to south end of Pendlebury Tunnel	See Note 6	

Notes:
1   According to (15) the line was opened on 2-2-1850. The passenger service first appeared in Bradshaw for March 1850.
2   Probably 1884.
3   According to (15) regular passenger services ceased in June 1850, but the line was used for excursions until 1939.
4   Line closed during second world war and tunnel used to store chlorine tank wagons (14). Line reopened for through traffic 6.10. 1947 (9). Finally closed on 13th April 1953 (15) due to dangerous state of tunnel. Reference (5) states that line closed on 7. 4. 1953 and tunnel collapsed on 28. 4.1953.
5   Reference (5) gives 13. 6.1960, but this is probably wrong.
6   Used for wagon storage after April 1953. Track lifted during 1962 (15).

Bolton to Kenyon Junction

Originally Bolton and Leigh Railway from Bolton to Leigh;
    Kenyon and Leigh Junction Railway from Leigh to Kenyon Junction

Kenyon and Leigh Junction Railway leased to Bolton and Leigh Railway	See Note 1	
Bolton and Leigh Railway leased to John Hargreaves	4. 1831	
Bolton and Leigh Railway absorbed by Grand Junction Railway	1. 7. 1845	(1)
Kenyon and Leigh Junction Railway absorbed by Grand Junction Railway	1846	(1)
Became LNWR	16. 7. 1846	(1)

Opened:

Lecturers Closes to Pendlebury Fold for coal traffic	1. 8. 1828	(16)
Lecturers Closes to George Inn Coal Yard for coal traffic [Note 2]	5.10. 1829	(17)
Bolton to Leigh for goods [Note 3]	30. 3. 1830	(18)
Lecturers Closes to Deansgate for goods.	See Note 4	
Bolton to Kenyon Jct for goods	3. 1. 1831	(19)
Bolton to Kenyon Jct for passengers [Note 5]	11. 6. 1831	(1)

Widenings and Deviations:

Widening Pennington (Bradshaw Leach) to Kenyon Jct	See Note 6	
Deviation Fletcher Street Jct to Great Moor Street and New Station at Great Moor Street [Note 7]	28. 9. 1874	(20)
Widening Pennington to Atherton Jct	31. 5. 1880	(21)
Widening Atherton Jct to Atherton (250 yds nth of stn)	4. 7. 1880	(22)
Widening Atherton to Chequerbent (620 yds sth of stn)	2. 2. 1885	(1)

Deviation 620 yds south of Chequerbent Stn to Pendlebury Fold (1200 yds north of Chequerbent Stn) [Note 8]	2. 2. 1885	(1)
Widening Pendlebury Fold to Daubhill (500 yards west of St Helens Road)	2. 2. 1885	(1)
Deviation Daubhill to Fletcher Street Jct [Note 9]	2. 2. 1885	(1)

Closed:

Original alignment from south of Chequerbent to Hultons Sidings	See Note 10	
Deansgate Branch [Note 11]	25. 2. 1930	(4)
Bolton Great Moor Street to Pennington South Jct for passengers	29. 3. 1954	(4)
Atherton Jct to Pennington South Jct for goods	17. 6. 1963	(5)
Bolton No 1 to Great Moor St for goods	14. 8. 1965	(5)
Rumworth and Daubhill Coal Yard (Adelaide Street) to St Helens Road Coal Yard	2. 9. 1965	(5)
Bolton No 1 to High Street [Note 12]	13.10. 1965	(5)
St Helens Road Coal Yard to Rumworth and Daubhill Jct	30. 6. 1967	(5)
Bolton No 1 to Hultons Sidings for goods	16.10. 1967	(5)
Hultons Sidings to Atherton Jct for goods	6. 1. 1969	(5)
Pennington South Jct to Kenyon Jct [Note 13]	5. 5. 1969	(5)

Notes:

1 See text. Bolton and Leigh Railways authorised to rent tolls of Kenyon and Leigh Junction on 30.6. 1831 and authorised to lease or purchase the line on 20.5. 1836.

2 Includes the section from Lecturers Closes to Great Moor Street, which may have been brought into use for coal traffic earlier.

3 Line "considered open for the conveyance of all sorts of goods" at this date.

4 Probably in 1829 - see text.

5 There was a special train from Bolton to Newton for the races on 2nd June 1831 (23).   There may have been some form of passenger service between Bolton and Leigh at an earlier date.

6 Believed to be contemporary with the opening of the Bedford Leigh Branch on 1. 9. 1864.

7 Authorised at same time as Little Hulton Extension Railway.

8 At Chequerbent, the whole of the original alignment was retained for use by the Hulton Collieries and worked by the firm's own locomotives under an agreement with LNWR. There was a connection with the reconstructed LNWR line at Hultons Sidings, Pendlebury Fold, but no connection at the south end.

9 On the original line through Daubhill, only the section between the level crossings at Adelaide Street and High Street was taken out of use. The two stub ends were kept by the LNWR to serve goods depots and coal yards.

10 The line was possibly taken out of use following the closure of Chequerbent Colliery in 1927, but was probably retained for use by the Hulton Colliery Co Ltd until the closure of the firm's Bank Nos 3 & 4 Pits in 1934.

11 According to one source, the branch was taken out of use following the closure of the Bolton Iron and Steelworks in 1924 (24).

12 According to Clinker (25) High Street Coal Yard closed on 1. 3. 1947, but line was retained to serve private siding for Magee, Marshall's brewery. Officially taken out of use on 13.10. 1965, but traffic ceased earlier.

13 Closed to all traffic on this date. Goods trains ceased earlier.

Eccles to Springs Branch Junction and Tyldesley to Pennington Junction

Originally London and North Western Railway

Opened:

Eccles to Springs Branch Jct [Note 1]	1. 9. 1864	(1)
Tyldesley to Pennington Jct [Note 2]	1. 9. 1864	(1)
Chowbent East Jct to Atherton Jct for passengers [Note 3]	1864	(26)
Chowbent East Jct to Atherton Jct for goods	See Note 4	
Chowbent West Jct to Atherton Jct for passengers	1883	(26)
Chowbent West Jct to Atherton Jct for goods	See Note 5	

Closed:

Howe Bridge East Jct to Atherton Jct for passengers	4. 5. 1942	(4)
Tyldesley to Springs Branch Jct for passengers	2. 11. 1964	(27)
Howe Bridge West Jct to Atherton Jct for goods	18. 1. 1965	(5)
Tyldesley to Springs Branch Jct for parcels [Note 6]	6. 1. 1969	(5)
Howe Bridge East Jct to Atherton Jct for goods	6. 1. 1969	(28)
Tyldesley to Howe Bridge East Jct for goods	6. 1. 1969	(5)
Eccles to Tyldesley for passengers [Note 7]	5. 5. 1969	(5)
Tyldesley to Pennington South Jct for passengers [Note 7]	5. 5. 1969	(5)
Howe Bridge West Jct to Bickershaw Jct for goods [Note 8]	11. 2. 1975	(5)

Notes:
1   Eccles, Tyldesley and Wigan Line.
2   Bedford Leigh Branch.
3   Chowbent East Jct renamed Howe Bridge East Jct; Chowbent West Jct renamed Howe Bridge West Jct.
4   Probably 1864.
5   Probably 1883.
6   Probably closed to all traffic from Howe Bridge East Jct to Howe Bridge West Jct on this date.
    Through goods traffic between Eccles and Springs Branch Jct ceased 1. 1. 1968 (5).
7   Closed to all traffic on this date. Goods trains ceased earlier.
8   Official date for line taken out of use. Last traffic 8.1974, from Parsonage Colliery.

Roe Green Junction to Bolton

Originally London and North Western Railway

Opened:

Roe Green Jct to Little Hulton for goods [Note 1]	1. 7. 1870	(1)
Little Hulton to Bolton, Fletcher St Jct for goods [Note 2]	16. 11. 1874	(1)
Roe Green Jct to Fletcher St Jct for passengers	1. 4. 1875	(1)
Little Hulton Jct to end of branch for goods [Note 3]	See note 4	

Closed:

Roe Green Jct to Bolton Fletcher St Jct for passengers	29. 3. 1954	(4)
Roe Green Jct to Little Hulton Jct for goods	24. 10. 1960	(5)
Little Hulton Jct to Plodder Lane (Highfield Siding) for goods	11. 5. 1964	(5)
Little Hulton Jct to end of Mineral Branch (goods only)	11. 5. 1964	(5)
Fletcher St Jct to Plodder Lane (Highfield Siding) for goods	1. 7. 1965	(5)

Notes:
1   Little Hulton Branch.
2   Little Hulton Branch Extension.
3   Little Hulton Mineral Branch.
4   Probably on 16.11. 1874.

LANCASHIRE AND YORKSHIRE RAILWAY

Absorbed by LNWR	1. 1. 1922	
Became LMSR	1. 1. 1923	
Became British Railways	1. 1. 1948	

Manchester to Bolton and Branches

Originally Manchester Bolton and Bury Canal Navigation and Railway
from Salford to Bolton

Absorbed by Manchester and Leeds Railway	18. 8. 1846	(1)
Became L&YR	23. 7. 1847	(1)
Clifton Jct to Salford became L&YR and ELR joint	3. 7. 1854	(3)
Clifton Jct to Salford became sole property of L&YR	13. 8. 1859	(3)

Opened:

Salford to Bolton Trinity Street	29. 5. 1838	(1)
Kearsley Moor Branch [Note 1] - Goods only	30. 4. 1840	(3)
Salford to Manchester Victoria	1. 8. 1865	(3)
Kearsley No 1 Branch to Linnyshaw Moss - Goods only	1. 3. 1879	(3)
Kearsley No 2 Branch to Stonehill Colliery - Goods only	1. 3. 1879	(3)
Ship Canal Branch - Windsor Bridge to Manchester Docks [Note 2]	28. 3. 1898	(3)

Widening:

Farnworth Tunnel	5.12. 1880	(3)
Manchester Victoria to Deal Street	9.12. 1896	(3)
Deal Street to Salford	10. 4. 1900	(3)
Salford to Windsor Bridge [Note 3]	10. 4. 1900	(3)
Clifton Junction (Pepper Hill)	1902	(3)
North and south of Bolton Trinity Street Station and reconstruction of station	29. 2. 1904	(3)

Closed:

Kearsley No 2 Branch	See Note 4	
Clifton Branch (formerly Kearsley Moor Branch)	See Note 5	
Ship Canal Branch for passengers	See Note 2	
Ship Canal Branch for goods [Note 6]	15. 6. 1963	(3)
Kearsley No 1 Branch [Note 7]	2.10. 1970	(29)

Widened lines removed:

Deal Street to Salford	See Note 8	
Salford to Windsor Bridge	See Note 9	

Still open:

Manchester Victoria to Bolton for passengers

Notes:

1 From Unity Brook on the main line to a point about 480 yards west of the Manchester to Bolton Road. Later known as the Clifton Branch. The rope worked incline was replaced by an adhesion worked line on a different alignment between 1865 and 1875, probably built by the Clifton and Kersley Coal Company. Much of the new alignment was on land occupied by the colliery company, which also maintained the track. From the incline top to the terminus, the track was the property of the railway company and on railway company's land.

2   In addition to goods traffic, excursion trains were run to Manchester Racecourse until 1901. There was also a workman's service until August 1939 (3).

3   The work is thought to have included an extra pair of passenger lines and an extra pair of goods lines between Salford and Windsor Bridge No 1 Signal Cabin and two extra pairs of passenger lines between Windsor Bridge No 1 and Windsor Bridge No 3 Cabins.

4   Closed in 1888, following the closure of Stonehill Colliery early that year.

5   Closed about 1930, following the closure of the coal washery at Spindle Point Colliery Only part of the line remained as railway company property after the realignment of 1865 to 1875 (See Note 1). Line was worked by colliery company's locomotives after realignment.

6   Reference (5) gives closure date as 15.6. 1964.

7   This was the date of last coal traffic. The final movement was a light engine from the NCB workshops at Walkden to Agecroft Colliery on 12.10.1970 (29).

8   Down fast line lifted by December 1987, Up fast line probably taken out of use 1. 5. 1988 (30). There were further alterations to the track layout during the rebuilding of Victoria Station in 1993.

9   The tracks in the vicinity of the former Windsor Bridge Nos 1, 2 and 3 Signal Cabinsunderwent considerable modification during the period 1985 to 1987 as a result of the construction of Salford Crescent Station and the Windsor Link line. The goods lines west of Salford were retained to provide access to a roadstone siding, where they now terminate. The fast lines were slewed to join the slow lines east of the junction with the Windsor Link. They have now been taken out of use.

Bolton to Euxton Junction and Branches

Originally Bolton and Preston Railway		
Absorbed by North Union Railway	1. 1. 1844	(1)
Leased to Grand Junction and Manchester & Leeds Rlys	1. 1. 1846	(1)
Became LNWR and L&YR joint property	7. 8. 1888	(1)
Bolton to Euxton Jct became sole property of L&YR	26. 7. 1889	(5)

Opened:
Bolton to Rawlinson Bridge for passenger and goods	4. 2. 1841	(1)
Rawlinson Bridge to Chorley for passenger and goods	22.12. 1841	(1)
Chorley to Euxton Junction for passenger and goods	22. 6. 1843	(1)

Widening:
Bullfield to Lostock Junction	28.12. 1899	(3)
Bolton Trinity Street to Bullfield	10. 4. 1906	(3)

Third and fourth tracks removed:
Bolton West to Lostock Jct - Down Slow Line taken out of use	19. 9. 1971	(31)
Bolton West to Bullfield - Up Slow Line taken out of use	19.12. 1972	(32)
Bullfield to Lostock - Up Slow Line out of use by	18. 4. 1989	(33)

Still open:
Bolton to Euxton Junction for passenger traffic

Bolton to Blackburn and Branches

Originally Blackburn, Darwen and Bolton Railway		
Became Bolton, Blackburn, Clitheroe and West Yorkshire Railway	9. 7. 1847	(1)
Became Blackburn Railway	24. 7. 1851	(1)
Absorbed jointly by L&YR and ELR	31.12. 1857	(1)
Became sole property of Lancashire and Yorkshire Rly	13. 8. 1859	(3)

Opened:

Sough to Blackburn	3. 8. 1847	(1)
Bolton to Sough	12. 6. 1848	(1)
Astley Bridge Branch	15.10. 1877	(3)
Johnson Street Fork, Bolton	26. 3. 1888	(3)

Widenings:

The Oaks About	1902	(3)
Bromley Cross to King William	4. 1903	(3)
Entwistle to Waltons Sidings	1902-1904	(3)

Closed:

Astley Bridge Branch - passenger service	1.10. 1879	(3)
Astley Bridge Branch, Halliwell to Astley Bdge - goods [Note 1]	4. 9. 1961	(25)
Johnson Street Fork [Note 2]	5. 1. 1970	(34)
Astley Bridge Branch, Astley Bridge Jct to Halliwell - goods	1. 8. 1981	(35)

Third and fourth tracks removed:

The Oaks - Loops officially taken out of use	25.10. 1966	(36)
Bromley Cross to King William	26. 5. 1968	(37)
Entwistle to Waltons Sidings - Fast lines	26. 5. 1968	(38)

Line singled:

Bromley Cross to Darwen	2. 9. 1973	(39)
Bolton West to Astley Bridge Junction	Late 1985	(40)

Notes:

1   A short portion from Halliwell Goods Yard to Back o' th' Bank Power Station remained in use, probably until about 1979.

2   Reference (5) gives closure date as 26.1. 1970.

Liverpool to Bury

Originally Liverpool and Bury Railway (Portion between Hindley and Pemberton was Manchester and Southport Railway)		
Absorbed by Manchester and Leeds Railway	1.10. 1846	(1)
Became L&YR prior to opening	23. 7. 1847	(3)

Opened:

Lostock Jct to Walton Jct for passengers and goods	20.11. 1848	(1)
Bolton (East Jct) to Bury (End on junction with Manchester and Leeds Rly Heywood to Bury branch approx 10 chains east of bridge over River Irwell)	20.11. 1848	(1)
Burnden Fork (Burnden Jct to Rose Hill Jct) - goods only	27. 3. 1881	(3)

Closed:

Bolton (East Jct) to Bury - all traffic	5.10. 1970	(41)
Burnden Fork [Note 1]	4.10. 1970	(42)

Still open:

Lostock Junction to Walton Jct for passengers, with change at Kirkby since 2. 5. 1977

Note:

1   The triangle formed by Bolton East Jct, Rose Hill Jct and Burnden Jct was retained for turning coal trains from the Wigan area to Back o' th' Bank Power Station until the late 1970s (42). The tracks had been lifted by October 1983 (44).

Heywood to Bury

Originally Manchester and Leeds Railway
Became Lancashire and Yorkshire Railway before opening

Opened:

Heywood to Bury (Knowsley Street)	1. 1. 1848	(3)
Knowsley Street to junction with Liverpool and Bury line	20.11. 1848	(3)
Curve to East Lancashire Railway at Bury (Knowsley Street to Bolton Street)	20.11. 1848	(3)
Heap Bridge Branch - goods only	8. 9. 1874	(3)
Ship Canal Loop at Bury (Loop Jct to Loco Jct)	21.11. 1898	(3)

Closed:

Curve from Knowsley Street to Bolton Street - passengers	5. 2. 1968	(45)
Heywood to Bury - passengers	5.10. 1970	(41)
Heap Bridge Branch - goods only [Note 1]	5.12. 1973	(46)
Ship Canal Loop [Note 2]	24. 3. 1967	(3)
Heywood to Knowsley Street and curve to Bolton Street - goods [Notes 3 and 4]	4.12. 1980	(47)

Notes:

1   The branch points at Heap Bridge Junction were disconnected on this date (48). Traffic to the private sidings had ceased earlier in the year. The public goods yard at Heap bridge had closed on 16.10. 1967 (25).
2   Date of closure for goods traffic, following fire at Loop Junction Signal Box. No regular passenger traffic.
3   The last coal train from Castleton to Rawtenstall ran on this date. There was a special rail tour on 4. 2. 1981 and some light engine movements to the East Lancashire Light Railway subsequently. Official closure date was 8. 4 .1981 (49).
4   The trackbed was acquired in 1991 by local authorities for an extension of the East Lancashire Light Railway.

Clifton Junction to Accrington and Bacup

Originally Manchester Bury and Rossendale Railway		
Became East Lancashire Railway before opening	21. 7. 1845	(1)
Amalgamated with Lancashire and Yorkshire Railway	13. 8. 1859	(1)
Bury Loco Jct to Rawtenstall sold to local authorities for operation by East Lancashire Light Railway	See Note 1	
Radcliffe North Junction to Bury Loco Jct and new line to Bury See Note 2		
Interchange transferred to Greater Manchester Passenger Transport Executive		

Opened:

Clifton Jct to Rawtenstall	28. 9. 1846	(1)
Bury Loco Jct (Buckley Wells) to Bury Interchange new passenger station [Note 3]	17. 3. 1980	(50)

Electrified (for passenger services only):

Bury Bolton Street to Tottington Junction [Note 4]	29. 7. 1913	(3)
Radcliffe North Junction to Bury Bolton Street [Note 5]	17. 4. 1916	(3)

Closed:

Clifton Jct to Radcliffe North Jct - All traffic	5.12. 1966	(3)
Bury Bolton Street to Rawtenstall - Passengers	3. 6. 1972	(5)
Bury Loco Jct to Bolton St [Note 6]	14. 3. 1980	(50)
Bury Bolton Street to Rawtenstall - goods [Note 7]	4.12. 1980	(47)
Radcliffe North Junction to Bury Interchange [Note 8]	16. 9. 1991	(51)

Converted to single track:		
Bury to Rawtenstall	19. 3. 1970	(52)
Re-opened by East Lancashire Light Railway		
Bury Bolton Street to Ramsbottom	25. 7. 1987	(30)
Bury Loco Jct to Bury Bolton Street	See Note 9	
Ramsbottom to Rawtenstall [Note 10]	28. 4. 1991	(53)
Re-opened by Greater Manchester Metro Ltd on behalf of		
Greater Manchester Passenger Transport Executive:		
Radcliffe North Junction to Bury Interchange [Note 11]	6. 4.1992	(54)

Notes:

1. Trackbed was purchased in 1983. Operation by East Lancashire Light Railway was authorised by Ministry of Transport Light Railway Orders of 20. 2 1986 and 12.1986.
2. Probably 1991.
3. Partly on formation of Ship Canal Loop line (Bury Loco Jct to Bury Loop Jct).
4. Date of introduction of experimental 3500 volt DC system with overhead current collection from Bury Bolton Street to Holcombe Brook. Converted to third rail 1200 volt DC system on 29. 3. 1918. Steam trains replaced electric trains on passenger service 25. 3. 1951 (3).
5. Date of introduction of third rail 1200 volt trains from Manchester Victoria to Bury Bolton Street via Whitefield.
6. Closed to all traffic on this date.
7. The last coal train from Castleton to Rawtenstall ran on this date. There was a special rail tour on 4. 2. 1981 and some light engine movements to the East Lancashire Light Railway subsequently. Official closure date was 8. 4 .1981 (49).
8. For conversion to Light Rapid Transit System.
9. No public service. Used only for access to carriage sidings. Also used for transfer of stock to and from British Railways line until summer 1991.
10. Date of opening of public service. A special train ran on 27. 4. 1991 (53)
11. Manchester Victoria to Bury Interchange opened on that date as Light Rapid Transit System.

Manchester (Victoria) to Radcliffe North Junction via Whitefield

Originally Lancashire and Yorkshire Railway		
Transferred to Greater Manchester Passenger Transport Executive	See Note 1	
Opened :		
Manchester to Whitefield for goods	1. 8. 1879	(1)
Manchester to Whitefield for passengers	1. 9. 1879	(1)
Whitefield to Radcliffe North Junction for all traffic	1. 9. 1879	(1)
Electrified (for passenger services only):		
Throughout [Note 2]	17. 4. 1916	(2)
Closed :		
Manchester Victoria to Crumpsall [Note 3]	13. 7. 1991	(51)
Crumpsall to Radcliffe North Junction [Note 3]	16. 8. 1991	(51)
Re-opened by Greater Manchester Metro Ltd on behalf of		
Greater Manchester Passenger Transport Executive :		
Manchester Victoria to Radcliffe North Junction [Note 4]	6. 4. 1992	(54)

Notes:
1   Probably 1991.
2   Date of introduction of third rail 1200 volt trains from Manchester Victoria to Bury Bolton Street via Whitefield.
3   For conversion to Light Rapid Transit System.
4   Manchester Victoria to Bury Interchange opened on that date as Light Rapid Transit System.

Connecting Lines at Radcliffe

Originally Lancashire and Yorkshire Railway

Opened:

Bradley Fold Junction to Radcliffe South Junction and Radcliffe West Junction to North Junction	1.12. 1879	(3)

Closed:

Radcliffe West Junction to South Junction - passengers	21. 9. 1953	(3)
Bradley Fold Junction to Radcliffe North Junction - passengers	6. 2. 1956	(55)
Bradley Fold Junction to Radcliffe South Junction and Radcliffe West Junction to North Junction - goods	2.11. 1964	(3)

Tottington Junction to Holcombe Brook

Originally Bury and Tottington District Railway

Taken over by Lancashire and Yorkshire Railway	24. 7. 1888	(1)

Opened :

Tottington Junction to Holcombe Brook	6.11. 1882	(1)
Woolfold Branch	See Note 1	

Electrified (for passenger services only):

Throughout [Note 2]	29. 7. 1913	(3)

Closed :

Tottington Junction to Holcombe Brook - passengers	5. 5. 1952	(5)
Tottington to Holcombe Brook - goods	2. 5. 1960	(5)
Tottington Junction to Tottington - goods	19. 8. 1963	(5)

Notes :
1   It is not clear if the Woolfold Branch was actually completed. The earthworks were constructed, but if any track was laid it had been lifted again by 1890.
2   Date of introduction of experimental 3500 volt DC system with overhead current collection from Bury Bolton Street to Holcombe Brook. Converted to third rail 1200 volt DC system on 29. 3. 1918. Steam trains replaced electric trains on passenger services 25. 3. 1951 (3).

Pendleton (Windsor Bridge No 3 Cabin) to Hindley (Crow Nest Jct) and connecting line at Agecroft (Brindle Heath Jct to Agecroft Jct)

Originally Lancashire and Yorkshire Railway

Opened:

Pendleton to Swinton - Slow Lines for goods	13. 6. 1887	(3)
Agecroft Connecting Line (Brindle Heath Jct to Agecroft Jct)	13. 6. 1887	(3)
Swinton to Atherton - Slow Lines for goods	2. 7. 1888	(3)
Atherton to Crow Nest Jct - Slow Lines for goods	1.10. 1888	(3)
Pendleton to Crow Nest Jct - Slow Lines for passengers	1. 6. 1889	(3)
Pendleton to Crow Nest Jct - Fast Lines	1. 6. 1889	(3)

Closed:

Agecroft Connecting Line	See Note 1	

Third and fourth tracks removed:

Windsor Bridge No 3 to Crow Nest Jct - Fast Lines [Note 2]	6. 9. 1965	(56)

Still open:
Windsor Bridge No 3 (Now Salford Crescent) to Crow Nest Junction
for passengers

Notes:
1   The intended date of closure was 10. 5. 1987, but the line is believed to have been used after that date, probably up to about February 1988 (57).
2   The fast lines were taken out of use on this date, but were probably closed to traffic wef 6. 9. 1965 (30). The slow lines between Moorside and Walkden were slewed into the position of the fast lines by the end of 1965 (30).

Windsor Link Connecting Line

Provided by British Railways

Opened:

New Station at Salford Crescent	11. 5. 1987	(58)
Ordsall Lane to junction with Manchester and Bolton line [Note 1]	1. 5. 1988	(30)
MSJ&A line from Ordsall Lane to Castlefield Jct reopened for regular passenger traffic [Note 2]	1. 5. 1988	(30)

Still open:
Throughout

Notes:
1   The down line from Ordsall Lane to Salford Crescent had been brought into use on 10 or 11. 4. 1988 for trains travelling from Manchester Victoria to Bolton and Wigan.
2   Another version states that the up line from Salford Crescent to Ordsall Lane was brought into use on 30. 4. 1988 for trains to Manchester Victoria on and also that the services to Manchester Piccadilly via Castlefield Junction did not start until 16. 5. 1988 (59, 60).

LONDON AND NORTH WESTERN AND GREAT CENTRAL JOINT LINE

Castlefield Junction to Ordsall Lane

Originally property of Manchester and Birmingham and Sheffield,
    Ashton under Lyme and Manchester Railways and Lord Francis Egerton
Became joint property of London and North Western and Manchester,
    Sheffield and Lincolnshire Railways before opening   2. 7. 1847
Became joint property of London and North Western and Great Central
    Railways   1. 8. 1897
Became joint property of London, Midland and Scottish and London
    and North Eastern Railways   1. 1. 1923
Became British Railways   1. 1. 1948

Opened:
    Castlefield Junction to Ordsall Lane   1. 8. 1849   (1)

Still open:
    See under Windsor Link above

References to Chronology

1   *"Chronological List of the Railways of Lancashire, 1828 -1939"* - M D Greville - Railway and Canal Historical Society, revised edition, 1981

2   *"Railway Reminiscences"* - G P Neele - McCorquodale, London, 1904

3   *"The Lancashire and Yorkshire Railway"* - John Marshall - David and Charles, Newton Abbot, 1969

4   *"LNWR Chronology 1900 - 1960"* - C R Clinker - David and Charles, Newton Abbot, 1961

5   *"Register of Closed Railways 1948 to 1991"* - Geoffrey Hurst - Milepost Publications, Worksop, 1992

6   BLN 130

7   BLN 101

8   BLN 205

9   BLN 207

10   BLN 214

11   BLN 394

12   BLN 121

13   BLN 192

14   BLN 118

15   Typescript notes on Patricroft and Clifton Branch by John Marshall- copy in authors' possession

16   BC 2-8-1828

17   BC 10-10-1829

18   Man Cour 10-4-1830

19   BC 8-1-1831

20   BC 3-10-1874

21   LNWR Loco Committee Minute 6745

22   LNWR Loco Committee Minute 6783

23   *"The Liverpool and Manchester Railway"* - R H G Thomas - B T Batsford Ltd, London, 1980

24   *"The Railways of Bolton 1824 - 1959"* - J R Bardsley - Bolton, reprinted 1982

25   *"Clinker's Register of Closed Passenger and Goods Depots in England, Scotland and Wales 1830-1970"* - C R Clinker and J M Firth - Published by the authors, new edition, 1971

26   Information supplied by Mr Cobb

27   Circulars of the GLO Organisation, various dates

28   Note on Line Plan of Eccles, Tyldesley and Wigan Railway - LNWR, 1892 - At BRPB Manchester Office

29   BLN 165

30   Information supplied by Mr H D Bowtell

31   BLN 273

32   BLN 194

33   BLN 609

34   BLN 147

35   BLN 327

36   BR Signal & Telegraph Notice Feb 1964

37   Information supplied by Mr John Ryan

38   BR Signal & Telegraph Notice Oct 1966

39   BLN 223

40   BLN 533

41   BLN 160

42   Line Plan of Liverpool, Bolton and Bury Rly 16 mp to 10 mp - BR Euston 1948, - at BRPB Manchester Office

43   BLN 331

44   BLN 510

45   *"Passengers No More"* - Daniels and Dench - 3rd Edition - Ian Allan, London, 1980

46   BLN 263

47   BLN 407

48   BLN 240

49   BLN 416

50   BLN 390

51   BLN 660

52   BLN 154

53   BLN 658

54   BLN 680

55   BLN 634

56   BR Signal & Telegraph Notice Nov 1965

57   BLN 645

58   BLN 563

59   BLN 585

60   BLN 589

CHAPTER 3

BOLTON

We start our explorations in and around Bolton town centre. The textile industry, which dominated the industrial scene in the nineteenth century and the first part of the twentieth, has little to interest the railway historian. The chapter opens with two firms engaged in the manufacture of iron and steel and we then go on to the gas works and the electricity works and other sidings used by Bolton Corporation.

As with the cotton mills, the numerous engineering works which were located in Bolton are mostly outside the scope of the present work. We deal with two which operated narrow gauge railway systems within their premises. We then turn to locomotive manufacture, which was firmly established in Bolton in the early years of the nineteenth century.

With the pioneer Bolton and Leigh Railway close at hand to provide a test bed, it perhaps not surprising that several established engineering firms tried their hand at locomotive building. Two of them soon decided that it was not for them and reverted to the production of stationary steam engines and general mill work. Two others included railway engines among their main products and, between them, turned out some 300 locomotives up to the middle of the century.

We conclude with a description of the activities of John Hargreaves Junior. Hargreaves was lessee of the Bolton and Leigh Railway and also contracted to work the goods traffic on other neighbouring lines. He employed a varied and interesting collection of locomotives, operating from the depot which he established in Bolton.

THE IRON AND STEELWORKS

Bolton Iron and Steel Works

An iron forge was established at the corner of Moor Lane and New Street in the early part of the nineteenth century, probably by the firm of Webster and Yates. It is shown as being worked by their assignees in 1824 [1] and in 1828 [2]. William Platt had taken over by 1829 [3] and it remained in his possession until his death in the mid 1830s. His executors are shown here in 1836 [4].

By 1838 the works had been acquired by Rushton and Eckersley [5], who made considerable extensions. The puddling furnaces, installed for the manufacture of wrought iron, probably date from this period. The firm is said to have purchased the first steam hammer produced by James Nasmyth [6,7].

The Bolton and Leigh Railway's branch to the Deansgate Warehouse ran alongside the eastern boundary of the works. No direct rail connection is shown on the Ordnance Survey 1/1056 Town Plan, published in 1849, although one was provided later.

Rushton retired at the end of 1859 [8], the firm then becoming Sharp and Eckersley. By the early 1860s the partnership included Henry Sharp, John Hick and William Hargreaves. There were further extensions to the works. Bessemer furnaces were installed for the manufacture of steel and the firm changed its name to the Bolton Iron and Steel Company [9].

Two Siemens Marten open-hearth furnaces were added in 1867 [10]. By 1873 the plant included two plate mills, one with a 60 HP reversing engine; a rail mill with a 55 HP reversing engine; a sheet mill; a tyre mill; two bar mills. In the older part of the works there were eight puddling furnaces and their associated forge trains as well as eight steam hammers. 700 men were employed [11].

The Bolton Iron and Steel Co Ltd was incorporated on 9th June 1876 to take over from the partnership. Shareholders included William Hargreaves, Henry Sharp, Thomas Lever Rushton, Francis Hargreaves, John Henry Hargreaves, and Benjamin Hick [12].

Steel making capacity was increased and the manufacture of wrought iron was run down. The puddling furnaces were shown last in the Mineral Statistics for 1878. In 1882 [10] or 1883 [8] the firm took over the premises of Rothwell and Company's Union Foundry, located on the opposite side of the Deansgate Branch, which had been derelict for several years. Subsequently there was what was described as an end-to-end reconstruction of the works [10].

A decision was made towards the end of 1905 to dispose of the works [13]. Plans [14,15] drawn up in connection with the sale show the premises extending from Railway Street in the north to New Street in the south. There were sidings serving the two portions of the works on each side of the Deansgate Branch and at two places the firm's tracks passed from one side to the other, crossing those of the LNWR on the level.

The works was eventually sold to Henry Bessemer and Co Ltd, which took over as from 6th November 1906 [16]. The Bolton Iron and Steel Co Ltd was liquidated on 20th December of the same year [17].

The Bolton Iron and Steel Company's locomotive had run over the Deansgate Branch to reach the various parts of the works and permission for this to continue under the new ownership was contained in an agreement with the LNWR dated 13th May 1907 [18]. Henry Bessemer and Co Ltd acquired extra land south of New Street and the arrangements were extended to enable the firm's locomotive to reach the sidings which were laid in there. Two connections on the east side of the Deansgate Branch were provided under an agreement dated 23rd November 1911 and one on the west side under an agreement dated 5th July 1913 [18].

The works seems to have been quite busy, particularly during the first world war. Then, in March 1924, it was announced that production was to be run down and the works gradually closed [19]. The plant was purchased for dismantling by T W Ward Ltd of Sheffield in July 1924 [16] and the site was acquired subsequently by Bolton Corporation. In May 1926 five chimneys were felled in the presence of the Mayor and Mayoress [20]. By 1927 the site had been completely cleared [21].

The trackbed of the Deansgate Branch of what was now the London, Midland and Scottish Railway was purchased by Bolton Corporation on 25th February 1930 [22] and the way was now clear for a complete redevelopment of the area. A new market hall was later built at the south end of the site and the rest was used for a bus station and a car park.

Little information has survived about the locomotives employed by the Bolton Iron and Steel Company. The Industrial Locomotive Society lists suggest that a four coupled saddle tank had been built by the company in its own workshops. While we have been unable to find independent confirmation of this, it must be remembered that John Hick and William Hargreaves were partners in the firm and it is possible that parts were supplied from their Soho Foundry.

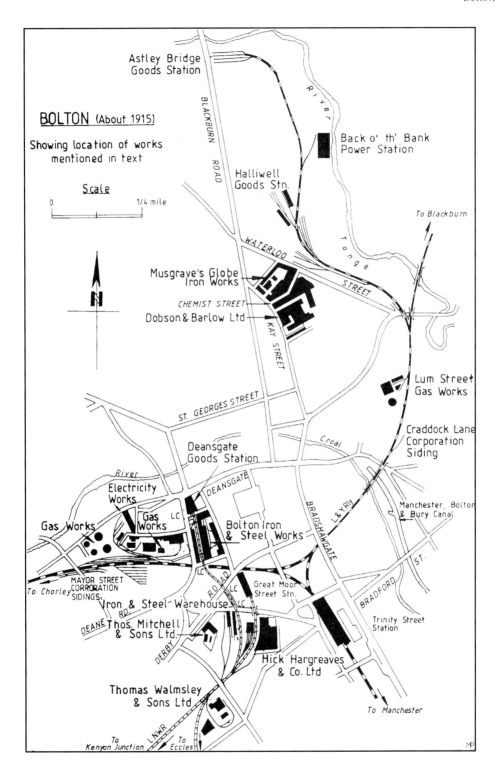

BOLTON (About 1915)

Showing location of works
mentioned in text

Scale

0   1/4 mile

Astley Bridge
Goods Station

BLACKBURN ROAD

River

Back o' th' Bank
Power Station

Halliwell
Goods Stn.

To Blackburn

Tonge

WATERLOO STREET

N

Musgrave's Globe
Iron Works

CHEMIST STREET

Dobson & Barlow Ltd

KAY STREET

Lum Street
Gas Works

ST. GEORGES STREET

Croal

Craddock Lane
Corporation
Siding

River

Deansgate
Goods Station

Electricity
Works

DEANSGATE

LC

Gas
Works

L & Y Rly

Manchester, Bolton
& Bury Canal

Gas Works

BRADSHAWGATE

Bolton Iron
& Steel Works

LC

BRADFORD ST.

MAYOR STREET
CORPORATION
SIDINGS

To Chorley

RD.

LC

LC

Great Moor
Street Stn.

BRADFORD

Trinity Street
Station

Iron & Steel Warehouse

DEANE

Thos. Mitchell
& Sons Ltd.

DERBY

LC

Hick Hargreaves
& Co. Ltd

Thomas Walmsley
& Sons Ltd

LNWR

To Manchester

To
Kenyon Junction

To
Eccles

MP

We have records of two other locomotives owned by the firm. One, a four coupled saddle tank, stated to have been built by Henry Hughes and Company of Loughborough, was sold to Thomas Mitchell and Sons, the machinery dealers, in July 1902. The other was a four coupled saddle tank, built by Manning Wardle in 1874. The manufacturer's records show that this engine had been supplied new to the Coatham Ironworks at Redcar and had come second hand to Bolton. It was sold by the Bolton Iron and Steel Company and saw further service with Kirk, Knight and Company on their contracts at Essendine and Sleaford.

Another four coupled saddle tank was hired from Thomas Mitchell and Sons for a short period from November 1904. This had been built by the Hunslet Engine Company of Leeds in 1890 and had been acquired by Mitchells second hand around 1900.

During the first world war, no doubt to cope with the increased output from the works, two new four coupled saddle tanks were obtained from Andrew Barclay, Sons and Company of Kilmarnock. BESSEMER 1 came in 1916 and BESSEMER 2 in 1917. It was presumably these two engines which were advertised for sale by T W Ward Ltd on 6th September 1924 [16].

The Atlas Forge

The first mention that we have found of Thomas Walmsley, founder of the Atlas Forge, is in 1845 [23]. He then had premises in Oxford Street and was described as a wholesale and retail iron agent, tin plate worker and cutler. He was still there in 1854 [24] but by 1869 [25] he had moved to the Phoenix Iron Works in Crook Street. This was presumably a warehouse rather than a factory, since he was stated to be "an iron merchant and sole consignee for the Grosmont pig iron and the Bowling Iron Company and the Low Wood Gunpowder Company".

It was at this period that he decided to enter the iron making business himself and established the Atlas Forge, at the corner of Bridgeman Street and Fletcher Street. Although it has been suggested that the works was built in 1866 [26], the alternative date of about 1869 [27] is possibly more correct.

Some 16 or 20 puddling furnaces [28], along with the associated forging and rolling mills, were installed to manufacture wrought iron. The works continued in operation for more than a hundred years, although latterly much of the production took the form of re-rolled wrought iron scrap. When it finally closed down in September 1975 [29], the plant was the last in Britain, possibly the last in Europe, to manufacture wrought iron. It was the subject of great interest to industrial historians and is fully described in a publication by Bolton Metropolitan Borough Council [26]. The puddling furnaces and the rolling mills, still steam driven, were acquired for preservation and re-erected at the Ironbridge Gorge Museum. One of the steam hammers is now preserved in front of the Bolton Technical College.

The founder of the firm, Thomas Walmsley, died on 13th September 1890 and the business was taken over by his son Richard and later by his grandsons Reginald and Ernest [26]. The firm was turned into a limited liability company with the title of Thomas Walmsley and Sons Ltd on 12th July 1939 [30]. In later years, the company had also acted as steel stockholders and this side of the firm's activities carried on after wrought iron production had finished at the works. The business finally closed about 1984, the firm last appearing in Trade Directories [31] in November of that year. The site was subsequently cleared and is now occupied by the Mill View Nursing Home.

The Atlas Forge appears to have been provided with a siding from the Bolton and Leigh line shortly after the works opened. The connection was altered when the Little Hulton Extension line was built in the 1870s [32]. In October 1874, the firm applied to the London and North Western Railway to run its own locomotive and wagons between its works and its warehouse, the latter presumably being the Phoenix Iron Works at Crook Street, mentioned previously. This was refused on the grounds that it was too dangerous, but the firm was quoted a rate of 4d per ton using its own wagons with LNWR locomotive power [33].

An inventory of plant dated 1877 [34] shows that the firm owned two locomotives, valued at £1500. We presume that these were the engines named ATLAS and PHOENIX which survived at the works until after the second world war. ATLAS was built by Barclays and Company of Kilmarnock in 1874 and carried plates to that effect.

ATLAS, built by Barclays and Company of Kilmarnock in 1874, and still at work at the Atlas Forge in 1947.
Alex Appleton

PHOENIX was of unknown origin. There has been some speculation that it may have been supplied second hand in the 1870s by I W Boulton of Ashton under Lyne, although we have found no evidence to support this. It was extensively rebuilt at the Atlas works at a date which has not been recorded, when its appearance was altered considerably.

ATLAS was broken up in 1948. It was replaced by a four coupled saddle tank, built by Hawthorn, Leslie and Company of Newcastle on Tyne in 1916 and purchased second hand from the Daimler Car Co Ltd of Coventry in April 1948. This, in turn, was scrapped following the acquisition, in August 1965 , of ATHERTON from the Wigan works of the North Western Gas Board. This was a four coupled saddle tank, built by Andrew Barclay Sons and Company of Kilmarnock in 1925.

Rail traffic ceased in 1967 and ATHERTON was cut up at the works by George Sweetlove and Sons Ltd, Bolton, in June of that year. The old PHOENIX, which had been lying in a dismantled state since 1960, was finally broken up in the middle of 1970.

THE CORPORATION'S RAILWAY SIDINGS

Bolton Gas Works

The Great Bolton Gas Light Company was established on 4th March 1818 and the town was first lit by gas in May 1819 [1]. The company's works were located in Gas Street off Moor Lane [1,4], although we note that the 1/1056 Town Plan, published in 1849, also shows two other works. One was at the corner of Blackhorse Street and Weston Street on a site adjacent to the Deansgate Branch of the Bolton and Leigh Railway. The other was in Little Bolton, at the corner of Bow Street and Bridge Street.

We have been unable to confirm the statement made in Clegg's history of the Bolton Gas Company [35] to the effect that in 1828 Mr Hulton, who supplied the firm with most of its coal, laid down a railroad from the Bolton and Leigh Railway to what he calls the Bullfield Works, but presumably means the one at Gas Street.

An Act of Parliament was obtained in 1820 [36], governing the affairs of the company and changing its name to the Bolton Gas Light and Coke Company. There was a further Act of Parliament in 1843 [37], when the area of supply was extended. In 1853, a new works was opened at Lum Street, adjacent to the Bolton and Blackburn line [35].

A revised issue of the first edition of the 6" map, published at about this date, suggests that a railway connection was provided to the Lum Street works from the outset. Later large scale maps, including the official sidings diagram [38], show several short branches leading into the retort houses from sidings adjacent to the main line. The railway system remained very much in this state until the works closed in March 1950 [39] and there is no record of a locomotive ever having been used.

The name of the undertaking was changed to the Bolton Gas Company in 1854 [40] and in 1872 Bolton Corporation took over [41].

There was a major extension to the Gas Street works, probably late in the nineteenth century, when a new retort house and new gas holders were erected on a site adjacent to Spa Road. A rail connection was provided with the adjacent Bolton and Preston line, under an agreement with the Lancashire and Yorkshire Railway, dated 11th August 1880 [42]. The railway layout at that time was only of modest extent. A diagram of 1903 [43] shows a single lead from the main line sidings passing into the works, where turntables gave access to the retort house. We presume that either horses or capstans were employed to shunt the incoming wagons of coal, as the layout was too small to justify the use of a locomotive.

Towards the end of the first decade of the present century, the old Gas Street works was reconstructed and the railway layout was enlarged to serve the new plant. The sidings at the Spa Road site were altered at the same time to provide a double track entry to the works. The turntables were replaced by pointwork and the sidings were extended to serve the adjacent corporation electricity works [44]. A new agreement between the Lancashire and Yorkshire Railway and Bolton Corporation in respect of the revised connections with the main line was signed on 29th June 1911 [45].

Top Left
The only known photograph of PHOENIX in its original condition, printed from an old and damaged plate negative lent to the authors.
Collection Frank Smith

Bottom Left
What a contrast! PHOENIX as it appeared in later years, with Fletcher Street Junction Signal Box in the background. The locomotive had been at the Atlas Forge for eighty years when this photograph was taken in April 1953.
Frank Jones

To operate the new railway system, a four coupled saddle tank was purchased from Hawthorn, Leslie and Company of Newcastle on Tyne. This arrived in 1911 and, with due ceremony, was named ALDERMAN WEBSTER after the then chairman of the Gas and Lighting Committee [46]. In 1928 a second, similar locomotive was purchased from the same makers and named GLAISTER.

These two engines, working one at a time, carried out all the shunting at the gas works until 1947. In that year a four wheeled locomotive with a vertical boiler and vertical cylinders was purchased from the Sentinel Wagon Works Ltd of Shrewsbury and named GRADWELL.

The records of Greenwood and Batley of Leeds show that two four wheeled battery locomotive were supplied to Bolton Gas Department in 1947, for use on 2'6" gauge track. We have been unable to find anyone who can remember these engines, nor do we know for certain where they were used . We presume that they were used on a narrow gauge system about the yard at one of the works, perhaps drawing coke from the retort houses. They are said to have been replaced by battery operated road vehicles.

The Corporation's Gas Undertaking was nationalised as from 1st May 1949 [46] and the locomotives passed to the North Western Gas Board.

The Sentinel was sold in January 1953 to work on the Whittingham Hospital railway, near Preston. The other two engines were laid aside in 1960, when a four wheeled diesel mechanical locomotive was purchased from Ruston and Hornsby of Lincoln. Prior to that, an ex-L&YR saddle tank, 51232, had been hired for a period in 1957 and 1958 from British Railways.

GLAISTER was cut up for scrap at the works in January 1961 by Rainers of Farnworth. ALDERMAN WEBSTER was scrapped in December 1963.

Production was run down as a result of the introduction of natural gas and the works closed in April 1968 [39]. The diesel locomotive was transferred to Board's St Helens works in 1969 and the agreement in respect of the main line sidings was terminated by British Railways as from 30th June of that year [47].

The gas holders at Spa Road remain in use, but the site of the exchange sidings with the main line and much of the original Gas Street works are now occupied by housing. The Lum Street works has been demolished.

Back o' th' Bank Power Station

The first steps towards providing an electricity supply in Bolton were taken in 1889 when the Corporation's Gas and Street Lighting Committee appointed an Electricity Sub Committee [48]. A Provisional Order was obtained from the Board of Trade in November 1890 and on 13th December 1890 a memorial stone was placed to commemorate the commencement of construction of the power station at Spa Road, adjacent to the gas works. The supply was inaugurated on 31st October 1894 [48]. New plant was installed over the period from 1895 to 1898 to keep pace with the increase in demand and there were further extensions in 1902, 1907 and 1908 [48].

It appears that coal was originally taken by road to the Spa Road works, possibly from the adjacent gas works siding. As described above, the railway system at the gas works was reorganised around 1910 and a siding was laid in to serve the electricity works [44].

In 1912 contracts were let for the construction of a new power station at Back o' th' Bank. Work commenced in February 1913 and the first turbo alternator set was started on 3rd

GLAISTER, one of the two identical locomotives supplied to Bolton Gas Works by Hawthorn, Leslie and Company. It is seen here, in August 1954, smartly turned out with the North Western Gas Board logo on the cabside.
Frank Smith

September 1914. The earlier power station at Spa Road ceased generating in January 1916, but the site was retained as a sub station [48]. Additional plant was installed at Back o' th' Bank in 1918, 1921, 1922 and 1923. In 1938 an extension to the power station was authorised, the plant being commissioned in November 1941 and January 1942 [48].

There were further extensions after the second world war and cooling towers were erected in 1946 and 1947 [49]. As a result of nationalisation of the industry, the power station was taken over British Electricity Authority as from 1st April 1948. Subsequent reorganisations meant that it passed to the Central Electricity Authority on 1st May 1955 and to the Central Electricity Generating Board on 1st January 1958.

Back o' th' Bank power station was located alongside the Lancashire and Yorkshire Railway's Astley Bridge Branch and siding connections were provided under agreements dated 18th November 1912 and 8th July 1913 [50]. The internal siding layout was quite straightforward and shunting was performed by means of capstans and ropes.

In 1951 it was proposed to replace this system with a steam locomotive and a four coupled saddle tank, named BOLTON No 1, was obtained from Robert Stephenson and Hawthorn Ltd. However, the engine did not see much use at Back o' th' Bank. It was sent to work at Chadderton Power Station from January 1952 to March 1954. On its return it only stayed until September 1954, when it was transferred permanently to Agecroft Power Station.

The next and more successful attempt to replace the capstans and ropes was in 1972, when a four wheeled battery electric locomotive was transferred from Upper Boat Power Station in South Wales. It had been built by the English Electric Company in 1944 and arrived at Bolton in May 1972.

BOLTON No 1, the Robert Stephenson and Hawthorn locomotive photographed in May 1952 at Chadderton Power Station, shortly after its transfer from Back o th' Bank.   Alex Appleton

The battery locomotive which was transferred from Upper Boat Power Station in South Wales, seen here at Back o' th' Bank in March 1979.   Jim Peden

One of the double bogie electric locomotives from Kearsley Power Station, built by Hawthorn, Leslie and Company, was also sent to Back o' th' Bank, about July 1978. It was intended to convert it to battery power for use at the Llanberis Power Station in Gwynedd.

Back o' th' Bank Power Station closed in 1979 or 1980. The English Electric battery locomotive went to the Greater Manchester Museum of Science and Industry about June 1980. The Hawthorn Leslie locomotive was returned to Kearsley Power Station at about the same time, with the modifications still not started.

Bolton Corporation Sidings at Craddock Lane and Bullfield

As well as those serving the gas works and the electricity works, two other sidings were operated by Bolton Corporation.

On the east side of the Bolton to Blackburn line at Craddock Lane, the Manure Sidings had been provided under an agreement dated 11th July 1867 [51]. Night soil, collected from the privies then in general use in the town, was despatched by rail for agricultural use.

One destination, perhaps the principal one, was the Corporation's siding at Lostock where the material was unloaded for delivery to local farms. The siding here was established under an agreement dated 13th June 1867. Traffic ceased towards the turn of the century and the siding was taken out in July 1900 [52]. We think that the Craddock Lane Siding probably ceased operation at about the same date, although we have been unable to confirm this.

Sidings were provided under an agreement of 16th May 1860 [53], on the south side of the Bolton to Preston line at Bullfield, to serve the Corporation's Mayor Street and Wellington Street Yards. The main traffic seems to have been road-making and building materials for use by the Borough Engineer's Department. With the increasing use of road transport after the second world war, need for the sidings diminished. The agreement was cancelled as from 18th September 1964 [54].

THE ENGINEERING WORKS

John Musgrave and Sons' Globe Works

We turn now to two factories which employed narrow gauge railways to transport materials and heavy components around the works, from shop to shop. The railway system at the Globe Works was certainly in existence by the late 1880s and is shown in some detail on the first edition of the 25" map. Subsequent large scale maps show that it was still in place when the works closed in 1927. We think it extremely unlikely that locomotives were ever used. The wagons are more likely to have been moved manually or by animal power.

The Globe Foundry had been established by John Musgrave, in partnership with his son Joseph, in 1839 [55]. In 1845 [23] and 1848 [56] the firm was known as John Musgrave, Son and Heaton, but by 1854 [24] had reverted to the title of John Musgrave and Son.

The Globe Foundry manufactured a wide range of engineering products including steam engines and equipment for cotton mills and coal mines. It later went into the business of making boilers. The firm also branched out into the cotton trade and two mills were erected on a site adjacent to the foundry. John Musgrave and Sons Ltd was registered on 5th February 1881 [57,58] to take over the textile factory and the engineering works from the previous partnership.

The firm set up a new boiler works at Westhoughton in 1900, but seems to have overstretched itself financially in doing so. As we have described in *"Industrial Railways of the Wigan Coalfield"*, the Westhoughton works was put up for sale on 2nd July 1912 [59], as the result of a chancery court judgement, and was later taken over by the Admiralty as a Royal Naval Gun Factory.

A financial reorganisation resulted in the formation of a new company, John Musgrave and Sons (1913) Ltd, which retained the Bolton works. After a period of prosperity during the first world war, when the factory was involved in munitions work, trade began to drop off.

A standard gauge railway siding to serve the Globe Works was planned in 1914. Bolton Corporation sanctioned a level crossing over Waterloo Street, so that a line could be laid in to the nearby Halliwell Goods Yard. It is said that the materials for the work had actually been purchased but that the project was abandoned due to the outbreak of the first world war [60].

By 1927, the workforce had dropped from 1400 to 300 and a creditors meeting was called in March [55,60]. The works was offered for sale on 10th May [61], but there was no acceptable offer. The firm's goodwill and drawings, together with those of John and Edward Wood, were later transferred to Galloways Ltd, of Knott Mill Ironworks, Manchester [62].

After the second world war part of the premises was used as a garage by British Road Services and part as a furniture saleroom. Traces of the narrow gauge railway were still visible in the factory yard.

Dobson and Barlow Ltd, Kay Street Works

The Kay Street Works of Dobson and Barlow was on the opposite side of Chemist Street to Musgrave's Globe Works. The narrow gauge railway system here seems to have to come into operation in about 1900; it is not shown on the 25" map, surveyed in 1889 and 1890, but appears on the second edition, published in 1910. Few details have survived, although correspondence in 1953 revealed that horses and ponies had been used as motive power [63].

There was no standard gauge rail connection and incoming materials and outgoing finished products were carted by road between the works and the nearby Lancashire and Yorkshire Railway's Halliwell Goods Yard. Local enquiries suggested that a siding had been planned but that it had not been possible to obtain permission to cross Waterloo Street [30].

Dobson and Barlow's association with Kay Street goes back to 1846, when the firm, then known as Dobson and Metcalfe, moved from smaller premises in Blackhorse Street into what had been a chemical factory [64]. The Blackhorse Street workshop had been set up in 1790, by Isaac Dobson and Peter Rothwell [8] to make spinning mules. The move to Kay Street enabled the firm to expand into the manufacture of many other types of textile machinery [65], although mules remained the backbone of the business.

The firm changed its name to Dobson and Barlow, following the admission of Edward Barlow to the partnership in 1850 [64]. A private limited company, Dobson and Barlow Ltd, was registered on 1st September 1891 to acquire the business, which was then being carried on by T H Rushton and B A Dobson [66].

As we shall see in Chapter 5, a start was made in 1907 on the construction of a new factory on a green field site at Bradley Fold. To coincide with this development, a public company with the same name was formed in 1907 [64]. The Kay Street works was retained by the firm until the mid 1930s; it is shown in a directory of 1934 [67], but not one of 1938 [68]. The buildings were subsequently demolished and the site was redeveloped.

Bolton Model Poultry Farm

Before leaving Dobson and Barlow Ltd, we must mention a narrow gauge railway which, although it was not owned by the firm, belonged to one of the principals, Darrell S Dobson.

The 18" gauge line was built in 1909 at Poplars Farm at Lostock, where Mr Dobson had started a part-time business as a poultry farmer. It is described in an article by one of the authors which appeared in the Industrial Railway Record [69]. The wagons, used to convey the eggs from the fifty two hen houses, were built by Dobson and Barlow Ltd and there was also a saloon coach for the use of visitors. To operate the line a small four coupled saddle tank was purchased from W G Bagnall of Stafford and delivered towards the end of 1909. The name SCOUT implies that the railway was intended as much for the amusement of local groups of Boy Scouts as it was for commercial purposes.

The enterprise was short-lived. SCOUT was sold to Thomas Mitchell and Sons Ltd, the Bolton machinery merchants, in December 1911. It was re-sold to John Knowles and Co (Wooden Box) Ltd for use at that firm's brick and tile works at Woodville, near Burton on Trent. The chickens and hen house were advertised to be sold on 14th June 1913 [70] and the farm itself, including the 18" gauge railway, on 4th March 1914 [71]. In 1955, some of the trackwork still remained in situ in the farm yard.

Thomas Mitchell and Sons Ltd

This old established firm of machinery merchants was founded by Charles Mitchell [72], who is described in directories for 1845 [23] and 1851 [73] as an earthenware dealer, with an address in Oldhall Street. By 1861 [74] he had an additional line of business, as a machine broker. He died on 3rd January 1865 [75] and his effects at his premises at Oldhall Street and Howell Croft, which were put up for sale on 7th, 8th and 9th March 1865 [76], included seven stationary steam engines from 1 to 15 HP.

The business was taken over by his son, Thomas Mitchell, who, in 1869 [25], was quoted as being an "iron merchant and buyer of all kinds of cotton machinery for breaking up". In 1874 [77], he was advertising as a dealer in new and second hand locomotives as well as portable and horizontal and vertical steam engines, boilers, machine tools and contractors plant.

In 1878, with the business expanding, he moved to purpose built premises in Edgar Street [72]. A limited liability company, Thomas Mitchell and Sons Ltd, was registered on 31st October 1898 [78]. The firm continues to trade under this title today, from the premises in Edgar Street, and is one of the area's leading machinery merchants.

In the course of the firm's history, many locomotives have passed through its hands. Fortunately the company catalogues from 1891, together with the plant ledgers from 1901, survived long enough to be examined by one of the authors. Such information as we have been able to piece together from these sources and from advertisements in the technical press is given in Appendix 1.

MAUDIE, one of the two narrow gauge Bagnall locomotives purchased by Thomas Mitchell and Sons Ltd from the cement works of Greaves, Bull and Larkin at Harbury in Warwickshire in 1915. Seen here loaded on a Foden steam wagon in Mitchell's yard, it was sold in 1917 to a firm of bobbin makers at Forres in Scotland. Collection Frank Smith

LOCOMOTIVE BUILDING IN BOLTON

Rothwell, Hick and Rothwell, later Rothwell and Company, Union Foundry

The Union Foundry, in Blackhorse Street, was established about 1801. Peter Rothwell, a leading Bolton timber merchant and contractor, appears to have been a principal partner from the beginning, although the company traded initially as Smalley, Thwaites and Company [8]. It changed its name to Thwaites, Cochrane, Hick and Company after Benjamin Hick joined the firm in 1814 [8]. He became managing partner in 1821 [8] and it was his influence which later led to the construction of locomotives.

In 1816 Thwaites, Cochrane, Hick and Company, were stated to be iron and brass founders, engineers, manufacturers of steam engines, patent water presses, weighing machines, gas apparatus, boilers and mill machinery in general, and constructors of fireproof buildings, wrought iron boats and bridges [79]. Shortly afterwards, there was further change of name to Thwaites, Hick and Rothwell. Thwaites retired in 1822 and was replaced by Peter Rothwell Junior, the firm now trading as Rothwell, Hick and Rothwell [8].

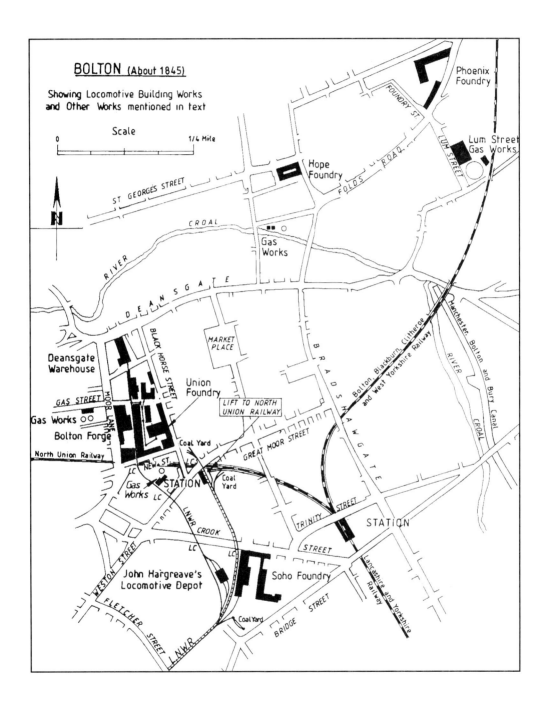

BOLTON (About 1845)

Showing Locomotive Building Works
and Other Works mentioned in text

A railway connection was provided when the Bolton and Leigh built its branch to Deansgate Warehouse, which ran along the western boundary of the firm's property. This was in use by 1829 as an engraving of that date [80] shows a series of short sidings in the works yard. As is shown on the later 1/1056 Town Plan, access was gained by means of a turntable located in the single line leading to the warehouse.

The first locomotive was turned out in 1830 and was bought by the Bolton and Leigh Railway. Named UNION, it was tried out on the Bolton and Leigh line in December [81]. A contemporary newspaper account [82] gives a detailed description of the engine. It had a vertical boiler with a spiral flue, by which a large surface of water was exposed to the heat and avoided the difficulty with burst tubes, as occurred in engines with horizontal boilers. The cylinders were mounted horizontally and "by a curious contrivance a great saving in steam was effected". The newspaper goes on to say: "The success of the experiment far outweighed the expectations of the builders of the engine and at one time it travelled at a rate of thirty miles per hour".

Despite its unusual design, UNION must have proved satisfactory as it was used, on 2nd June 1831, on a special train from Bolton to Newton le Willows for the races, following the opening of the line from Leigh to Kenyon [83]. It was also used to haul the first through train to run from Bolton to Liverpool on 13th June 1831 [83].

A contemporary engraving, dated 1829, of the Union Foundry of Rothwell, Hick and Rothwell. Note the waggon boiler on the horse drawn vehicle in the centre and the collection of large gear wheels. Also note the coal wagon and the railway track in the yard, with the turntable in the foreground.

Harry Townley collection

Before Benjamin Hick left the firm in 1833 to set up business on his own at the Soho Foundry in Crook Street [8], four more locomotives were built, three of which were sold to railways in North America. They were, however, all to conventional designs and the novel ideas incorporated in UNION were not perpetuated.

In 1836, the firm, which had by now changed its name to Rothwell and Company, seems to have decided to make locomotive building one of its main activities and new shops were erected for this purpose. About 190 engines were turned out during the next 25 years. Further information, probably neither complete nor fully accurate, can be found in articles by Stretton [84] and Ahrons [85] and in Lowe's more recent book on British Locomotive Builders [86].

In the first few years, engines were exported to North America, Germany, France and Russia, but after 1842 orders were confined to those from British railway companies. In 1841, a batch of 7 ft gauge engines was built for the Great Western Railway. Construction of broad gauge engines continued until 1860, with further orders from the Bristol and Exeter Railway, the South Devon Railway and the Great Western [87]. These were interspersed with quite large contracts for standard gauge engines from other companies - 28 for the London and South Western Railway in 1846 to 1848 [88] and twenty five for the Lancaster and Carlisle railway in 1857 [89], for example.

Rothwell and Company also appear to have dealt in second hand locomotives from time to time, some perhaps taken in part exchange for ones supplied new. In November 1844, the firm was advertising for sale a six wheeled, four coupled locomotive and tender made by Nasmyth, Gaskell and Company. It was stated to have 5ft driving wheels, 3'6" trailing wheels and 14"x18" cylinders [90].

Locomotive production seems to have ceased with the completion of two six coupled goods engines for the South Devon railway in 1860. In April 1861 it was announced that the Union Foundry was to be put up for sale [91]. The auction was held on 25th September of that year [92], but there must have been no acceptable bid. Documents were prepared, probably in September 1862, which included an inventory and plan of the works, which was then offered for sale by private treaty [93-97].

What happened next is not entirely clear. Either a new company trading under the same name took over, or the original firm was refinanced. The Union Foundry of Rothwell and Company features in an article of June 1873 [98] when the main products included hydraulic presses, corn and sugar mills and all kinds of stationary steam engines and steam hammers.

The final closure came in 1875 [99] and, after a period of disuse, the works was put up for sale on 8th and 9th June 1882 [99]. The premises were taken over in 1883 by the neighbouring Bolton Iron and Steel Company [8].

Benjamin Hick and Son, later Hick, Hargreaves and Company, Soho Foundry

Following Benjamin Hick's withdrawal from the partnership with the Rothwells at the Union Foundry, he set up in business with his son John in 1833. Their Soho Foundry was situated on the south side of Crook Street, adjacent to the branch of the Bolton and Leigh Railway leading to Great Moor Street Station. The firm traded initially as Hick and Company and later as Benjamin Hick and Son.

In 1834 [100], the Hicks were described as engineers, manufacturers of condensing, high pressure and locomotive engines and general millwrights. By 1836 they had added equipment for metal mines and smelters in Spain to their list of products [8]. Locomotive building only formed a relatively small part of the firm's general engineering activities, with some eighty or ninety turned out over the fifteen year period up to 1850.

John Hargreaves Junior, whose railway operations we describe later, married Benjamin Hick's daughter, Mary, in 1836 and later became a partner in the firm. Following Benjamin Hick's death on 9th September 1842, at the age of 52, the business was carried on by John Hick and John Hargreaves. John Hargreaves' brother William joined the partnership on 1st January 1847 [101] and John retired on 1st April 1850 [101].

Although very little has been preserved in the way of order books, many of the firm's locomotive drawings have survived and are now in the Bolton Museum. They formed the subject of special exhibitions which were held in 1974 and 1994. The catalogue [102] which was produced at the time of the 1974 exhibition provides a useful summary of the collection. Unfortunately, the majority of the drawings are undated and do not specify the customer. Many have had these details added later, but it is not possible to verify the authenticity of the information.

The drawings include several proposed designs which were never built. One was for a vertical boiler locomotive, evidently a development of the UNION, which Benjamin Hick had designed while with Rothwell, Hick and Rothwell. This later design was covered by Patent 6889 granted to Benjamin Hick on 8th October 1834 [102]. The surviving drawing shows that it was intended to be of the 2-2-0 wheel arrangement, with a vertical boiler. The three cylinder simple expansion engine was also mounted vertically and was coupled through a two speed gear to a single driving axle.

Hick was obviously interested in the potential of three cylinder locomotives, as a model was made a few years later of a more conventional engine with a horizontal boiler, in which the three cylinders were mounted under the smokebox. The model still exists in the Bolton Museum, but it seems unlikely that the proposal was ever put into practice.

What was possibly the first locomotive to be completed by the firm was supplied to John Hargreaves Junior. Appropriately named SOHO, it was of the 0-4-2 wheel arrangement, with inside cylinders and inside frames. There is some doubt about when it was actually constructed. The surviving drawings have had the date 1834 added, possibly in the 1890s. As we mention later, when dealing with John Hargreaves Junior, other sources suggest 1838 as the building date.

Between 1834 and 1838, the firm supplied five engines to railways in North America, but evidently the export trade did not develop. All subsequent orders came from railways in the United Kingdom, with the exception of two 2-2-2 engines delivered in 1840 to the Paris and Versailles Railway.

A number of 2-2-0 locomotives, of the design developed by Edward Bury, were constructed between 1837 and 1841, nine going to the Midland Counties [103], seven to the London and Birmingham [89] and four to the North Union [89]. Three 4-2-0 engines of the Norris type were supplied to the Birmingham and Gloucester Railway during 1841 and 1842 [103].

Two goods engines with an 0-4-2 wheel arrangement were built for the Liverpool and Manchester Railway in 1839 [89]. Subsequently the firm pioneered the development of six coupled goods engines with inside frames and inside cylinders. Two went to the Midland Railway in 1844 [103], three to the Taff Vale Railway in 1846 [104] and four to the Birkenhead Railway in 1849 [87]. The Midland engines had bar frames, while the remainder had plate frames.

A passenger engine with a 2-2-2 wheel arrangement was supplied to the West Hartlepool Harbour and Railway in 1841 [105] and a further two went to the Joint Locomotive Committee of the London and Croydon, South Eastern and London and Brighton Railways in 1844 [106]. Five further 2-2-2s, with inside frames and outside cylinders, were supplied to the South Eastern Railway between 1845 and 1847 [106]. Two more of a similar type were purchased by the Edinburgh and Glasgow Railway in 1847 [105].

The firm also built a number of 2-4-0 passenger engines. Two were delivered to the West Hartlepool Harbour and Railway in 1841 and 1843 [105]. Six more, with outside cylinders and inside frames were built, in 1847 and 1848, under sub contract from Robert Stephenson and Company of Newcastle, for the Eastern Counties Railway. Four further outside cylinder 2-4-0s were supplied to the North Staffordshire Railway in 1848 [107].

The last locomotives which are known to have been built at the Soho Foundry were six 2-2-2 engines with outside cylinders and inside frames. It would appear that the railway company which had placed the order subsequently cancelled it, as the firm was advertising all six engines for sale in May 1850. They were stated to have 6ft driving wheels, 3'6" leading and trailing wheels and 15"x20" cylinders [108]. They were eventually purchased by the Birkenhead Railway, which took them into stock in 1851 [87].

Drawings were made around 1849 for what appears to have been a series of standard designs, which included several different types of 2-4-0 passenger engine, an 0-6-0 goods engine based on those supplied to the Birkenhead Railway and a 2-4-0 tank engine. The impression is that the firm was intending to expand its locomotive building activities, but that did not happen.

More information about the locomotives built by the company can be found in the article by Ahrons [85] and the book by Lowe [86], mentioned earlier, although like that provided about Rothwell and Company's products, it may not be entirely accurate or complete.

Following the retirement of John Hick in 1868 to become Member of Parliament for Bolton, the title of the firm was changed to Hick, Hargreaves and Company [8]. It was at this period that a series of stationary engines of the Corliss type was developed and over two hundred of these had been turned out by 1873. Compound beam engines and Jonville turbines also featured amongst the firm's products [109]. From the mid 1870s the firm began to specialise in refrigeration machinery [8] and towards the end of the century a number of high speed steam engines were built for electric power stations.

William Hargreaves, who had been a partner since 1847, died in October 1888 [8] and a private limited company, Hick, Hargreaves and Co Ltd, was formed on 29th March 1892 [110]. Stationary steam engines continued to feature as one of the firm's main products, although in the present century there was a not very successful venture into the manufacture of petrol and oil engines. From 1930 onwards the firm has specialised in compressors, vacuum equipment, condensers and auxiliary plant for power stations [8].

A public company was formed in 1936 or 1937 [8]. The firm became a member of the EIS Group in 1969 and is still in business under the name of Hick, Hargreaves and Co Ltd.

Thompson, Swift and Cole, later Thompson and Cole, Hope Foundry

Two other Bolton firms made a brief excursion into locomotive construction. Both were located in Little Bolton, some distance from the railway, which may have accounted for the decision to discontinue this line of business.

The Hope Foundry in St George's Street, had been founded in 1807 [30] by Messrs Thompson and Swift. The proprietors were described as iron and brass founders, manufacturers of steam engines, hydraulic presses, weighing machines and mill machinery [79,111]. By 1818 the firm had become Thompson, Swift and Cole [112].

According to the *Bolton Chronicle* of 3rd October 1829, a reporter inspected a locomotive which had just been completed by Thompson, Swift and Cole. It was expected to be tried out during the following few days [113]. Apart from this brief mention, no other details have survived. Nor do we know if any other engines were built at this time.

William Swift retired from the partnership as from 18th December 1832 [114], when the firm was described as Brass and Iron founders at Little Bolton and Delfmen and Stone Getters at Halliwell. William Swift also retired on the same date from the Bradshaw Colliery Company in which he had been in partnership with Thomas Thompson, Joseph Cole, Robert Barlow and James Cross [114]. The proprietors of the Hope Foundry subsequently traded as Thompson and Cole.

In 1838 the works expanded to occupy the site of what later became the Cooperative Dairy [115] and there are records of further locomotive construction in the early 1840s. All appear to have been 0-4-2 tender engines. According to Baxter [103] two were supplied to the North Midland Railway and two to the Birmingham and Derby Junction. One further engine seems to have been built for stock, as it was advertised for sale at the works in December 1842 [116,117]. It was described as six wheeled, with 13"x18" cylinders, 5'0" driving wheels, 3'0" hind wheels and weighing 12½ tons.

The Hope Foundry premises in the 1980s, much as they had been built 150 years or so earlier.
Courtesy of the Bolton Museum and Art Gallery

The partnership was dissolved on 1st September 1848, following the death of Thomas Thompson [118], and for the succeeding thirty years the firm was known as William and Joseph Cole. The partners retired in 1878 and the works and the nearby boiler yard were put up for auction on 8th October [119,120]. Although the sales particulars refer to a locomotive shop 70ft 4in x 33ft 4ins, there is no evidence that railway engines were built during this later period. It seem likely that the firm had confined its attentions to the manufacture of stationary engines, small boilers and general millwork.

Part of the premises was taken over by Thomas Moscrop, who established his Lion Oil works here, while part became the property of the local co-operative organisation for use as a dairy [115]. The Lion Oil Works closed in 1978 and the foundry buildings were then purchased by the Borough Council. The intention was to establish an industrial museum to complement the local history museum situated in the former Little Bolton Town Hall, across St George's Street. Although Thompson and Cole's premises were given a thorough repair in 1986 [121] and restored externally to their original appearance, the museum scheme fell through for lack of finance. In March 1993, the premises were up for sale.

Crook and Dean, later William Dean, Phoenix Foundry

The firm of Crook and Dean, of the Phoenix Foundry in Folds Road, first appears in a Bolton Directory for 1824-5 [1]. The partners comprised John Crook, who appears as a millwright in earlier directories [111,112] and William Dean. In 1829 [3] they were described as brass and ironfounders, millwrights and manufacturers of steam engines, and of apparatus for gas, hydraulic, paper machines and all descriptions of mill work. William Crook died on 31st May 1831, aged 57 [122]. The Phoenix Foundry was advertised for sale on 8th July [123] and was taken over by the surviving partner, William Dean. By 1835 an additional works had been erected at the bottom of Waterloo Street [30].

In the 1830s a small number of locomotives were built at the Phoenix Foundry, although there is considerable uncertainty about the precise number and their dates of construction.

The first locomotive for which there is authentic information was tried on the Bolton and Leigh Railway at the beginning of June 1831, a day or two after the death of William Crook. A contemporary newspaper report [124] stated that the engine, which was named PHOENIX, had hauled twelve carriages and 300 people at 18 miles per hour.

It was presumably this engine which is mentioned in the Liverpool and Manchester Board Minutes [83]. John Hargreaves Junior asked if he could operate a locomotive built by Crook and Dean over that line and, if so, he would buy it. He was apparently granted permission to run the engine over the Liverpool and Manchester in October 1831. However, it is not certain that he actually made the purchase, as the next we hear of PHOENIX is in January 1832, when it was involved in an accident on the Bolton and Leigh line and was then stated to belong to William Hulton [125].

On 29th May 1832, BOLTON, built by William Dean, was tried on the Bolton and Leigh line [126]. It was said to have run up the incline at Leigh with 30 wagons, weighing no less than 150 tons. It was also stated that the engine was intended to be employed during the summer on passenger trains between Bolton and Liverpool.

There are also fragmentary references to other Phoenix Foundry locomotives working on the Bolton and Leigh Railway. We go into more detail later in the chapter when we deal with John Hargreaves Junior.

William Dean died 12th Jan 1840 [30] and his widow, Alice took control until her son, Adam, was old enough to manage the firm. Part of the premises, described as the lower foundry, was sold by auction on 24th December 1845 [127]. The rest continued to be occupied by Alice Dean until Adam Dean took over about 1850 [56,73]. By 1856, Adam Dean was bankrupt and his part of the Phoenix Foundry was sold by auction on 23rd January 1856 [128].

The site was subsequently occupied by a number of firms. James Eckersley and Sons, engineers and manufacturers were here in 1859, while what was described as the Phoenix boiler works of Thomas Sykes was offered for sale on 7th March 1863 [129]. A mill for Thompson and Gorse was built on another part in 1864 [30].

JOHN HARGREAVES JUNIOR

John Hargreaves Junior and his Locomotives

The Hargreaves family of Westhoughton had been engaged in the carrying trade since the middle of the eighteenth century and had built up a large business, transporting goods by road and by canal. The founder of the firm, James Hargreaves, died in April 1766 and the business was carried on by his son, John Hargreaves (1739-1796). He was succeeded, in turn, by his son, also named John (1778-1860), but usually referred to later as John Hargreaves Senior. Our story mainly concerns John Hargreaves Junior (1800-1874), son of John Hargreaves Senior, who was responsible for the rail transport side of the family's business affairs [130].

In April 1831, one of the John Hargreaves (it is not clear whether Junior or Senior) entered into a contract with the Bolton and Leigh Railway Company [131]. He was to lease the line and to work both the passenger and goods trains, including the through services to Manchester and Liverpool over the Kenyon and Leigh Junction line. Operation of the railway seems to have been very much in the hands of John Hargreaves Junior and certainly later documents refer to him as the lessee [132].

Goods depots were established at Manchester Liverpool Road, Liverpool Crown Street and Bolton Deansgate. To accommodate the locomotives needed for the business, sheds and repair shops were built on a plot of land at Crook Street, Bolton, in the fork between the lines leading to Deansgate and Great Moor Street. According to Whishaw [133] there was also an engine shed at Kenyon Junction.

After the opening of the line from Parkside in September 1832, Hargreaves began running his own trains to Wigan. The railway beyond there to Preston was brought into use in October 1838 and the North Union company, which had taken over the whole of the line from Parkside to Preston, awarded a contract to Hargreaves to handle its goods traffic. He subsequently acted in a similar capacity on the Lancaster and Preston Junction Railway, opened for traffic in June 1840. It is said that he built a small locomotive depot at Preston to house the engines used on these lines.

The Grand Junction absorbed the Liverpool and Manchester, Bolton and Leigh and Kenyon and Leigh Junction Railways in July 1845 and took a lease of the North Union, jointly with the Manchester and Leeds Railway, on 1st January 1846. The contracts with John Hargreaves were terminated as from 31st December 1845, when the Grand Junction assumed responsibility for handling the whole of the traffic.

John Hargreaves Junior advertised that he was withdrawing from the carrying trade and from his interest in the Bolton and Leigh Railway and that he was giving up all his buildings, offices and yards at Bolton, Chequerbent, Atherton, Kenyon, Wigan, Leyland, Horwich, Chorley and Preston [134]. He continued to play an active role in the local business community. He had already become a partner in Benjamin Hick's Soho Foundry, where he was later joined by his younger brother William. Since about 1841, he had also been proprietor of Coppull Colliery on the North Union line. As we have described in our earlier book, *"The Industrial Railways of the Wigan Coalfield"* [59], he continued to operate his own coal trains from here to Preston until the colliery closed in the early 1860s.

Some original material has survived relating to the engines employed by Hargreaves on the Bolton and Leigh line and elsewhere. A list was published in 1842 in Francis Whishaw's *"The Railways of Great Britain and Ireland"* [134], which appears to have been compiled a year or two earlier. Another list was submitted to the Board of Trade by Henry Bradshaw, principal clerk to John Hargreaves, and is dated 25th October 1841 [132]. Finally, there is the list compiled by Bradshaw and sent to Henry Booth of the Grand Junction Railway. This is dated 21st November 1845, after Hargreaves had been given notice to discontinue his carrying business and was attempting to sell off his stock [135].

The Board of Trade had originally written to the Bolton and Leigh, as they had to all the other railway companies then open to traffic. Peter Sinclair, the Treasurer of the Bolton and Leigh had replied that all the locomotive engines employed on the line were the property of and under the exclusive control of John Hargreaves and that he had handed the Board of Trade letter to Hargreaves for reply. Sinclair went on to say that " Mr Hulton has two engines upon the line, one or other of which is used from time to time in the removal of his own coal upon a small portion of the line, about two miles in length only" and went on to explain that these engines were not employed in public traffic.

The submission to the Board of Trade in 1841 by Bradshaw on behalf of Hargreaves contains some interesting comments. He stated that "Mr Hargreaves, the lessee of the Bolton and Leigh line, has 13 locomotives; but he finds his own power for the conveyance of merchandise &c on the Liverpool and Manchester, North Union and Lancaster and Preston railways, and the greater number of his engines are employed upon those lines". He continued "From practical experience of various descriptions of locomotive engines, Mr Hargreaves prefers a six-wheeled engine with straight axles and outside cylinders, there being much less liability of an axle of this description breaking than a crank axle; this kind of engine is also kept in repair at less cost than engines with crank axles, the working parts being got at with greater facility, and any slight derangement of the working parts being much sooner detected". He then qualified this by saying "Mr Hargreaves has not found any particular description of engine peculiarly dangerous".

Despite the amount of information available, the full story of Hargreaves' locomotives is far from clear. The wheel and cylinder dimensions quoted by Whishaw are sometimes difficult to reconcile with later lists. The dates of construction given in the two lists drawn up by Bradshaw in 1841 [132] and 1845 [134] do not always correspond with information available from other records. It appears that the dates given by Bradshaw are, in many instances, those of a major rebuild or of a re-boilering rather than those when the locomotives were originally built. The confusion has not been removed by several recent publications [89,131,] which, although helpful, contain a number of speculations which are sometimes in conflict with the primary sources.

In April 1831, the Bolton and Leigh appears to have owned two locomotives, LANCASHIRE WITCH and UNION, with a third, SANS PAREIL, on hire from the Liverpool and Manchester. The first two were presumably included in the plant and equipment leased to Hargreaves, but it seems likely that they remained the property of the railway company.

LANCASHIRE WITCH, a four coupled locomotive, was built by Robert Stephenson and Company in 1828. It had been used to open the first section of the Bolton and Leigh line on 1st August of the of that year, when it had been officially named by Mrs Hulton [136]. Shortly afterwards, it had been borrowed by the Liverpool and Manchester. The Bolton and Leigh was seeking its urgent return in January 1830 , when the Liverpool and Manchester Board instructed that it was to be sent back forthwith [137]. Its subsequent career on the Bolton and Leigh must have been fairly short, as it not included in Whishaw's list.

UNION, the 2-2-0 vertical boilered engine, built by Rothwell, Hick and Rothwell in 1830, was, as we have recounted earlier, used by Hargreaves to work a special train from Bolton to Newton for the races on 2nd June 1831 [83]. On 13th June 1831 UNION and two first class coaches ran the first through passenger train from Bolton to Liverpool [83]. Although UNION appears in the list by Whishaw, it is not shown in that provided by Bradshaw for the Board of Trade. Therefore, we presume that it was taken out of service around 1840.

SANS PAREIL, a four coupled locomotive built in 1829 by Timothy Hackworth of Shildon for the Rainhill trials, had been lent to the Bolton and Leigh by the Liverpool and Manchester as a replacement for LANCASHIRE WITCH. It was used to work a special train for the directors on the completion of the line to Leigh on 30th March 1830 [138].

Following the return of LANCASHIRE WITCH, early in 1830, SANS PAREIL was hired to the Bolton and Leigh for £15 per month [139,140]. It was here when John Hargreaves Junior took over the working of the line, although it is said to have remained the property of the Liverpool and Manchester company until it was sold to Hargreaves in September 1832 for £110 [83]. It was sent to his colliery at Coppull about 1840, where it was converted to a pumping engine. When the colliery closed in 1863 or 1864, it was rescued by John Hick. It was restored and presented to the Patent Office Museum, the forerunner of the Science Museum.

Two other locomotives are known to have been used on the Bolton and Leigh line at this period - DREADNOUGHT and LIVERPOOL.

DREADNOUGHT was involved in an accident at Lecturers Closes on 13th June 1831 [141], the day that the line to Kenyon Junction was opened for regular passenger traffic. It is assumed to have been the engine built by Edward Bury in 1829, the first turned out from his works. Bury's DREADNOUGHT was of a somewhat unusual design, further details of which can be found in Dendy Marshall's *History of Railway Locomotives* [142]. It apparently had a chain drive, although another version is that the piston rods were connected to the crank axle through rocking levers. It had six wheels, but the actual wheel arrangement is not known.

DREADNOUGHT was tried out on the Liverpool and Manchester line, but its performance was unsatisfactory. There is no evidence to show that it was actually purchased by Hargreaves and may have remained the property of Edward Bury. If it was taken into Hargreaves stock, it did not last long on the Bolton and Leigh line, as it is not shown in Whishaw's list.

LIVERPOOL suffered a serious derailment at Bag Lane, at the turn out to Colonel Fletcher's collieries, in July 1831, when hauling a train of five wagons from Liverpool to Bolton [143]. It seems certain that this was Edward Bury's second locomotive, completed in 1830, as the report of the accident makes reference to the unusually large wheels and that the engine was restricted to working goods trains.

LIVERPOOL was a four coupled engine with 6ft diameter driving wheels [142]. It had been also been tried on the Liverpool and Manchester line, but was found unsuitable because of the size of its wheels [83]. As with DREADNOUGHT, there is no evidence to show that it was actually purchased by Hargreaves, neither does it appear in Whishaw's list.

In July 1831, the Liverpool and Manchester Board agreed that the Bolton and Leigh, or perhaps more accurately Hargreaves, could purchase one of the locomotives then being built by Robert Stephenson and Company [144]. This was one of the maker's standard 2-2-0s of the period and was named NELSON by Hargreaves. It was given a major rebuild before

1841, when an extra pair of trailing wheels were added. It may also have been given a new boiler, as the weight was increased from 10 tons to 12 tons 5 cwt. It was disposed of before November 1845.

According to Thomas [83] several locomotives were hired by the Liverpool and Manchester Railway to the Bolton and Leigh Railway, presumably to be used by John Hargreaves Junior to deal with the increased traffic which followed the opening of the Kenyon Junction line. ARROW and METEOR, both similar to ROCKET, with an 0-2-2 wheel arrangement, but with larger cylinders and driving wheels, were said to be there in August 1831. They were followed, a few months later by PLANET, a 2-2-0, and ATLAS, an 0-4-0.

Two more four coupled locomotives, originally ordered by the Liverpool and Manchester Railway, were purchased from Edward Bury and named BEE and CLARENCE. The railway company agreed, in January 1832, that Hargreaves could buy one of them [83]. The second engine was rejected by the railway a few months later [145] and was also purchased by Hargreaves.

BEE is shown in Whishaw's list, still as an 0-4-0. It does not appear in Bradshaw's list of 1841. We think, although we lack proof, that it may have been sold to William Hulton. If Hulton was, at this time, still using PHOENIX, the Crook and Dean engine of 1831, this could account for the two locomotives mentioned in Sinclair's letter to the Board of Trade.

Whishaw's list shows that CLARENCE was subsequently rebuilt with an additional trailing axle. It was still in Hargreaves' ownership in 1841, as it is shown in Bradshaw's first list, but had been disposed of by 1845.

At this period, Hargreaves acquired two 0-4-0 locomotives, stated both by Whishaw and Bradshaw as having been built by William Dean. Whishaw gives the names as SALAMANDER and VETERAN, while Bradshaw's 1841 list gives LIVERPOOL and VETERAN. We think it possible, but have found no confirmatory evidence, that SALAMANDER may have been renamed LIVERPOOL, following the withdrawal of the earlier Bury engine of that name.

No construction dates are given by Whishaw or by Bradshaw in his list of 1841. Bradshaw's list of November 1845 quotes 1838 for VETERAN, but this may refer to a major rebuilding. One locomotive, possibly SALAMANDER, must have been completed towards the end of 1831, as in October of that year Hargreaves was granted permission for a locomotive built by Crook and Dean to run over the Liverpool and Manchester line [83]. We think that VETERAN might have been the engine which was tried out on the Bolton and Leigh line in May 1832 and which a contemporary newspaper account says was named BOLTON [126]; however, we have no real proof.

VETERAN was rebuilt with a trailing axle before October 1841 and remained in Hargreaves' possession until the end of 1845. LIVERPOOL, still shown as an 0-4-0 in 1841, does not appear in the 1845 list.

The next acquisition was an 0-4-2 tender engine, named SOHO and supplied by Benjamin Hick and Son. The 1845 list states that it was built in 1838. However, as we have noted earlier, a note added to the original drawings suggests that been may have been built in 1834.

Three further 0-4-2 tender engines were purchased from Tayleur and Company of the Vulcan Foundry, Newton le Willows, named WELLINGTON, MARQUIS OF DOURO and PANDORA. According to Whishaw the first was built in 1836 and the other two in 1838. Bradshaw's list of 1841 shows that they had outside frames and inside cylinders.

Three 0-4-2 tender locomotives were constructed by Hargreaves himself at this period; at least that is what is claimed in Bradshaw's list of 1841. The engines were, for that date, of an advanced design. The boilers were unusually large and there were also a number of other novel features such as outside cylinders and outside steam pipes. Although it is likely that the boilers and some other items came from outside suppliers, Hargreaves' workshops at Bolton were quite capable of doing much of the work. According to Whishaw, the locomotive establishment included, in addition to four drivers and four firemen, five smiths, eight fitters, two spring makers, six machinists and a supporting staff of apprentices and labourers. Another twenty six men were employed in the wagon shops.

The first of the Hargreaves built engines, named UTILIS, was completed in 1836, according to the 1845 list. At 15½ tons it was banned from running on the Liverpool and Manchester Railway in February 1837. An additional pair of carrying wheels was added at the front, making it one of the first 2-4-2 locomotives in the country. Shortly after the alteration, UTILIS was derailed at Newton Racecourse Station. The accident happened on 16th June 1837, at the points where five lines diverged and several other special trains were trapped all night. The engine does not seem to have been at fault as a pointsman was held to be responsible [146].

Some saving in weight was achieved on the two engines which followed and they kept the 0-4-2 wheel arrangement throughout their working lives. Named VICTORIA and CASTLE, the 1845 list says that they were built in 1837 and 1838 respectively.

Two single driver engines were obtained about 1840 for working passenger trains. Neither appears in Whishaw's list, but both are shown in Bradshaw's 1841 list.

ST DAVID, with a 2-2-2 wheel arrangement and outside frames, is stated by Bradshaw to have been built by Bourne and Bartley. This was presumably the engine which was to be auctioned at their premises at Mason Street, Manchester on 17-3-1840 [147], as the wheel dimensions quoted in the advertisement tally with the data given by Bradshaw. It evidently remained unsold until it was re-advertised in September of the same year by Oswald Stephenson [148], who appears to have taken over Bourne and Bartley's works. It is doubtful whether Bourne and Bartley were the actual builders; according to Lowe [86] ST DAVID was one of two locomotives constructed by Summers, Grove and Day of Southampton, but we do not know his authority for this statement. It was disposed of before November 1845.

The other passenger engine acquired by Hargreaves was named PEEL According to Bradshaw's 1841 list, it had been built by Edward Bury as a 2-2-0 but had been altered to a 2-2-2. Baxter [89] states that it was new in 1840. It lasted in Hargreaves ownership until the end of 1845.

It has been suggested [86,131] that one other engine, a 2-4-0 built by Mather Dixon in 1836, was owned by John Hargreaves. It does not appear in any of three lists and we have been unable to find any other evidence to support the suggestion.

By the time the third list was drawn up in November 1845, there remained eight of the four coupled engines, mainly used for goods traffic, comprising WELLINGTON, MARQUIS OF DOURO, PANDORA, UTILIS, VICTORIA, CASTLE, SOHO and VETERAN.

Four additional single driver engines, VIXEN, VICTORY, No 1 and PRINCE had been purchased to supplement PEEL on the passenger trains. According to Bradshaw's 1845 list, VIXEN was a 2-2-0 while the remainder were of the 2-2-2 wheel arrangement. All seem to have come second hand and it has not proved possible to identify their origins unequivocally.

VICTORY was possibly the engine of that name built by Robert Stephenson and Company for the Liverpool and Manchester Railway in 1831. The story about No 1 is more complicated.

No 1 eventually became the property of the Midland Railway and Baxter [103], presumably quoting from that company's records, states that it was built by Nasmyth, Gaskell and Company in 1840, their works number 9. Information provided by Cantrell in his history of the Nasmyth's Bridgewater Foundry [149] shows that two locomotives, works numbers 9 and 10, were delivered to Messrs H and E Hilton in October and November 1841 respectively.

The Hiltons, as we have described in *"Industrial Railways of the Wigan Coalfield"* [59], as well as being proprietors of a paper mill at Darwen, owned collieries at Ince, Coppull and Burgh and had apparently purchased the engines to work their own traffic over the North Union Railway to Preston. The Hiltons were both bankrupt by the middle of 1842. The Coppull and Burgh Collieries were put up for auction and were purchased by John Hargreaves Junior. It seems quite likely that he took over one, if not both, of the locomotives at the same time. Presumably they were numbered 1 and 2 by their previous owners.

When John Hargreaves disposed of his stock at the end of 1845, four of the locomotives were purchased by the Grand Junction in January 1846, along with 200 wagons, 14 coaches and sundry other equipment at a total cost of £21,203.6s. SOHO, VICTORY and PEEL were retained on the Bolton and Leigh line, while MARQUIS OF DOURO was used on the North Union line [135]. All four later passed to the London and North Western Railway.

At least two locomotives were retained by Hargreaves for use on his coal trains from Coppull Colliery to Preston. One of these was certainly VICTORIA, which was mentioned in connection with an accident at Preston in August 1846 [150]; another was probably CASTLE.

According Baxter [103] WELLINGTON, PANDORA and No 1 were bought by the Joint Board of Management of the Birmingham and Gloucester and Bristol and Gloucester Railways. They subsequently became the property of the Midland Railway. The fate of the remaining engines has not been recorded.

Hargreaves' premises in Bolton were taken over by the Grand Junction Railway. A sale was advertised for 27th May 1846 at the Luggage Depot, Crook Street, on instructions from John Hargreaves. Items for disposal included "smiths tools lately used by him in the construction of locomotive engines and waggons. Connecting rods and side-rod ends, locomotive engine springs, steam and water gauges together with an assortment of locomotive engine and other patterns" [151].

LOCOMOTIVE SUMMARY

Bolton Iron and Steel Works

Rushton and Eckersley until 1859
Rushton and Sharp until 1863
Bolton Iron and Steel Company until June 1876
Bolton Iron and Steel Co Ltd from 9th June 1876
Henry Bessemer and Co Ltd from 6th November 1906
Works closed early 1924 and purchased by T W Ward Ltd July 1924

	0-4-0STOC	HH			8½"x15"	

Sold to Thos Mitchell and Sons Ltd, 7-1902

	0-4-0STOC	MW	456	1874	10"x16"	2'9"

New to Downey and Company, Coatham Ironworks, Redcar, as COATHAM No 2
Second hand to Bolton Iron and Steel Company
Sold and later with Kirk, Knight and Company, contractors, and used at Essendine and Sleaford

	0-4-0STOC	HE	238	1880	10"x15"	2'9"

Hired from Thos Mitchell and Sons Ltd, 11-1904 for a short period

BESSEMER 1	0-4-0STOC	AB	1485	1916	10"x16"	2'10"

New
Taken over by T W Ward Ltd, 1924
Sold to Crowley and Russell, Derby

BESSEMER 2	0-4-0STOC	AB	1559	1917	10"x16"	2'9"

New
Taken over by T W Ward Ltd, 1924
Scrapped or sold

The list prepared by the Industrial Locomotive Society makes reference to a four coupled, inside cylinder, saddle tank, built by the Bolton Iron and Steel Company. We have been unable to find independent information about this locomotive.

Atlas Forge

Works built 1866 or 1869
Thomas Walmsley and then Thomas Walmsley and Sons
Thomas Walmsley and Sons Ltd from 12th July 1939
Rail traffic ceased 1967
Works closed about 1984

13 ATLAS	0-4-0STOC	Bs	222	1874	11"	3'0"

Scrapped 1948

14 PHOENIX	0-4-0STIC					

Rbt Walmsley
Dismantled 10-1960 Scrapped on site about 6-1970

	0-4-0STOC	HL	3182	1916		

Ex Daimler Car Co Ltd, Coventry 4-1948
Scrapped 9-1965

ATHERTON	0-4-0STOC	AB	1882	1925		

Ex North Western Gas Board, Wigan Gas Works, 8-1965
Scrapped on site by George Sweetlove and Sons Ltd, Bolton, 6-1967

Bolton Gas Works

Bolton Gas Company until 1872
Bolton Corporation until May 1949
North West Gas Board from 1st May 1949
Works closed April 1968

ALDERMAN WEBSTER	0-4-0STOC	HL	2855	1911	14"x22"	3'6"

New
Scrapped 12-1963

GLAISTER	0-4-0STOC	HL	3733	1928	14"x22"	3'6"

New
Name removed
Scrapped on site by Rainer, Farnworth, 1-1961

GRADWELL	4wTGVB	S	9377	1947	6¾"x9"	2'6"

New
To Whittingham Hospital Rly, 1-1953

51232	0-4-0STOC	Hor	925	1906	13"x18"	3'0"

Hired from British Railways during 1957-1958

	4wDM	RH	435492	1960	88DS Class	

New
To St Helens Gasworks, 1969

2'6" gauge

	4wBE	GB	2096	1947	5 HP

New, ex works 10-11-1947

	4wBE	GB	2097	1947	5 HP

New, ex works 10-11-1947

It is not known whether these were used at the Spa Road / Gas Street Works or at the Lum Street Works. They are said to have been superseded by battery operated road vehicles

Back o' th' Bank Power Station

Works opened Sept 1914
Bolton Corporation until April 1948
British Electricity Authority from 1st April 1948
Central Electricity Authority from 1st May 1955
Central Electricity Generating Board from 1st January 1958
Works closed in 1979 or 1980
Rail traffic worked by capstans and ropes until 5-1972

BOLTON No 1	0-4-0STOC	RSH	7681	1951	14"x22"	3'6"

New
To Chadderton Power Station, 1-1952 Returned 1-4-1954.
To Agecroft Power Station 9-9-1954

	4wBE	EE	1378	1944		

Ex Upper Boat Power Stn 5-1972
To Greater Manchester Museum of Science and Industry, Liverpool Rd, Manchester, about 6-1980

2	4w-4wWE	HL	3872	1936	230HP	

Ex Kearsley Power Stn about 7-1978 for conversion to battery power for use at Llanberis Power Station
Conversion not carried out and returned to Kearsley Power Station 6-1980

Bolton Model Poultry Farm

Darrell S Dobson in association with other members of family
Railway opened 1909
Poultry Farm advertised for sale June 1913 and March 1914

18" gauge

SCOUT   0-4-0STOC   WB   1907   1909   4"x7½"
New
Sold to Thos Mitchell and Sons Ltd, 12-1911
Hired and then sold to J Knowles and Co (Wooden Box) Ltd, 1915

John Hargreaves Junior

Lease of Bolton and Leigh Railway April 1831
Later contracts to work goods traffic on North Union Railway and Lancaster and Preston
    Junction Railways
Contracts terminated 31st December 1845

The information given below is based on the list of locomotives in Whishaw's *"Railways of Great Britain and Ireland"* [133], together with lists prepared in 1841 [132] and 1845 [135] by Henry Bradshaw, Principal Clerk to John Hargreaves. Reference has also been made to Baxter's *"British Locomotive Catalogue"* [89,103], to Thomas's *"Liverpool and Manchester Railway"* [83] and to Shill's recent work on the subject [131].

LANCASHIRE WITCH   0-4-0   RS   1828
Ordered by Liverpool and Manchester Railway, but order transferred to Bolton and Leigh Railway
Named at opening ceremony of Bolton and Leigh Railway on 1st August 1828
Borrowed by Liverpool and Manchester Railway from late 1828 to early 1830
Presumed leased to John Hargreaves Junior as from April 1831
Scrapped or sold before Whishaw's list of about 1840

UNION   0-2-2VB   RHR   1830   9"x18"   5'0"
Originally the property of Bolton and Leigh Railway
Presumed leased to John Hargreaves Junior as from April 1831
Shown in Whishaw's list of about 1840, but scrapped or sold before Bradshaw's list of 1841

SANS PAREIL   0-4-0   H'worth   1829   8"x18"   4'0"
Lent by Liverpool and Manchester Railway to Bolton and Leigh Railway late 1828 to early 1830, then
    hired at £15 per month
Presumed used by John Hargreaves Junior on Bolton and Leigh line until purchased by him from
    Liverpool and Manchester Railway in September 1832
Shown in Whishaw's list of about 1840, but transferred to Coppull Colliery before Bradshaw's list of
    1841
Converted to pumping engine and rescued by John Hick after the colliery closed about 1863. Restored
    and presented to Patent Office Museum

DREADNOUGHT   Six whld   EB   1829
According to Thomas had a chain drive, but another version is indirect drive through cranks
According to Thomas was used on Liverpool and Manchester Railway in March 1830 and then on Bolton
    and Leigh Railway late in 1830
According to Shill was purchased by John Hargreaves Junior from Edward Bury about May 1831, but no
    evidence found of sale
Scrapped or sold before Whishaw's list of about 1840

LIVERPOOL 0-4-0 EB 1830 6'0"
    According to Thomas ran trials on Liverpool and Manchester Railway in July 1830 and used for ballasting, but not purchased by railway company. Later used on the Bolton and Leigh Railway
    According to Shill was purchased by John Hargreaves Junior from Edward Bury about May 1831, but no evidence found of sale
    Scrapped or sold before Whishaw's list of about 1840

NELSON 2-2-0 RS 1831 12"x16" 5'0"
    Rbt 2-2-2
    Ordered by Liverpool and Manchester Rly, but new to Hargreaves
    Altered to 2-2-2 before Bradshaw's list of 1841
    Scrapped or sold before Bradshaw's list of 1845

ARROW 0-2-2 RS 1830 10"x16" 5'0"
    According to Thomas hired by Bolton and Leigh Railway from Liverpool and Manchester Railway, August 1831

METEOR 0-2-2 RS 1830 10"x16" 5'0"
    According to Thomas hired by Bolton and Leigh Railway from Liverpool and Manchester Railway, August 1831

PLANET 2-2-0 RS 1830 11"x16" 5'0"
    According to Thomas hired by Bolton and Leigh Railway from Liverpool and Manchester Railway, late 1831 or early 1832

ATLAS 0-4-0 RS 1831 12"x16" 5'0"
    According to Thomas hired by Bolton and Leigh Railway from Liverpool and Manchester Railway, late 1831 or early 1832

PHOENIX 0-4-0 (?) Crook and Dean 1831
    Tried on Bolton and Leigh Railway in June 1831 and presumably used by John Hargreaves Junior, who was granted permission in Oct 1831 to work it over the Liverpool and Manchester Railway
    By Jan 1832 had become property of William Hulton

BOLTON 0-4-0 (?) Wm Dean 1832
    Tried on Bolton and Leigh Railway in May 1832 with intention of using it on passenger trains. Not clear if it became the property of John Hargreaves

BEE 0-4-0 EB 1832 11"x16" 4'8"
    Ordered by Liverpool and Manchester Railway, but arrangements made for locomotive to be delivered to and paid for by John Hargreaves Junior
    Shown in Whishaw's list of about 1840, but disposed of before Bradshaw's list of 1841, perhaps sold to William Hulton

CLARENCE 0-4-0 IC EB 1832 12½"x18" 5'0"
    Rbt 0-4-2
    Ordered by Liverpool and Manchester Railway, but arrangements made for locomotive to be delivered to and paid for by John Hargreaves Junior
    Converted to 0-4-2 before Whishaw's list of about 1840
    Shown in Bradshaw's list of 1841
    Scrapped or sold before Bradshaw's list of 1845

SALAMANDER 0-4-0 Crooke and Dean 11"x16" 4'8"
    Shown in Whishaw's list of about 1840
    Not shown in subsequent lists

LIVERPOOL   0-4-0 IC   Wm Dean   4'6"
> This locomotive is shown in Bradshaw's 1841 list, but not in Whishaw' list
> There is a strong presumption that it was SALAMANDER, renamed following the withdrawal of the
>   Bury locomotive LIVERPOOL
> Scrapped or sold before Bradshaw's list of 1845

VETERAN   0-4-0 IC   Wm Dean   12"x18"   5'0"
                             Rbt 0-4-2
> In Whishaw's list of about 1840 as 0-4-0
> Rebuilt to 0-4-2 before Bradshaw's list of 1841
> Shown in Bradshaw's list of 1845, which gives building date as 1838, although the engine was probably
>   built about 1832

SOHO   0-4-2 IC   Hick   13"x18"   5'8"
> Shown in all three lists. Whishaw gives driving wheel diameter as 5'8" The 1841 and 1845 lists give 4'8"
> Bradshaw's list of 1845 gives building date of 1838, but the engine was possibly completed about 1834
> Sold to Grand Junction Railway and according to Baxter became LNWR No 125 in 1847

WELLINGTON   0-4-2 IC   Tayleur   1836   13"x18"   5'6"
> Shown in all three lists. Whishaw gives driving wheel diameter as 5'6". The 1841 and 1845 lists give 4'8".
> Whishaw gives cylinder size as 13"x18". The 1845 list gives 14"x18"
> According to Baxter was sold to the Joint Board of Management of the Birmingham and Gloucester and
>   Bristol and Gloucester Railways, becoming their No 39. Later became Midland Railway No 295.

MARQUIS OF DOURO   0-4-2 IC   Tayleur   1838   13"x18"   5'6"
> Shown in all three lists. Whishaw gives driving wheel diameter as 5'6". The 1841 and 1845 lists give 4'8"
> Sold to Grand Junction Railway and according to Baxter became LNWR No 124 in 1847

PANDORA   0-4-2   Tayleur   1838   13"x18"   5'6"
> Shown in all three lists. Whishaw gives dimensions as above. The 1841 lists gives driving wheel diameter
>   as 4'8". The 1845 list gives dimensions as 14"x20" 4'4" and notes that the engine has had new cylinders
>   and working parts.
> According to Baxter was sold to the Joint Board of Management of the Birmingham and Gloucester and
>   Bristol and Gloucester Railways, becoming their No 60. Later became Midland Railway No 297.

UTILIS   2-4-2 OC   Hargreaves   1836   14"x18"   4'8"
> Built as 0-4-2, but rebuilt as 2-4-2 after being banned from Liverpool and Manchester Railway in February
>   1837
> Shown in all three lists
> Scrapped or sold

VICTORIA   0-4-2 OC   Hargreaves   1837   14"x18"   4'8"
> Whishaw gives dimensions as above. The 1845 list gives cylinders as 14"x20"
> Retained by John Hargreaves Junior for use at his Coppull Colliery

CASTLE   0-4-2 OC   Hargreaves   1838   14"x18"   4'6"
> Whishaw gives dimensions as above. The 1841 and 1845 lists give driving wheel diameter as 4'8"
> Probably retained by John Hargreaves Junior for use at his Coppull Colliery

ST DAVID   2-2-2 IC   Summers   1839   5'0"
                              Grove and Day (?)
> Presumed purchased by John Hargreaves Junior from Bourne and Bartley, Manchester or Oswald
>   Stephenson and Co, late 1840 - see text
> Shown in Bradshaw's list of 1841 as built by Bourne and Bartley
> Scrapped or sold before Bradshaw's list of 1845

PEEL   2-2-2 IC   EB   1840   13"x18"   4'8"

     Not in Whishaw's list, but shown in Bradshaw's lists of 1841 and 1845
     Built as 2-2-0 but rebuilt before 1841
     Sold to Grand Junction Railway and presumably became LNWR No 127 in 1847

VIXEN   2-2-0   12"x18"   5'6"

     Presumably second hand
     Purchased after 1841 as not in Bradshaw's list of that date Shown in Bradshaw's list of November 1845
        as built in 1838
     Scrapped or sold

No 1   2-2-2   NG   9   1840   14"x20"   5'0"

     Purchased after 1841 as not in Bradshaw's list of that date Circumstantial evidence to suggest that it was
        built by Nasmyth, Gaskell and Company in 1841, works no 9, and acquired following the bankruptcy
        of H and E Hilton - see text
     Shown in Bradshaw's list of November 1845 as built 1839
     According to Baxter was sold to the Joint Board of Management of the Birmingham and Gloucester and
        Bristol and Gloucester Railways, becoming their No 5 CAMILLA. Later became Midland Railway
        No 104

PRINCE   2-2-2   12"x18"   6'0"

     Presumably second hand
     Purchased after 1841 as not in Bradshaw's list of that date Shown in Bradshaw's list of November 1845
        as built in 1839
     Scrapped or sold

VICTORY   2-2-2   12"x16"   4'8"

     Presumably second hand
     Purchased after 1841 as not in Bradshaw's list of that date Possibly built by RS in 1831 for Liverpool and
        Manchester Rly
     Shown in Bradshaw's list of November 1845 as "New in 1842 except for a few plates in the Boiler"
     Sold to Grand Junction Railway and presumably became LNWR 123 in 1847

References to Chapter 3

1 *"History, Directory and Gazeteer of the County Palatine of Lancaster"* - Edward Baines, Liverpool, 1824-5

2 *"National Commercial Directory for Cheshire, Cumberland, Lancashire"* - James Pigot and Co, Manchester, 1828

3 *"The Bolton Directory"* - M Wardle, 1829

4 *"General and Classified Directory Manchester and Salford, etc"* - James Pigot and Co, Manchester, 1836

5 *"General and Classified and Street Directory Manchester and Salford, etc"* - James Pigot and Co, Manchester, 1838

6 *Iron* 14-6-1873 7 BC 21-6-1873

8 *"Hick, Hargreaves and Company. The history of an Engineering Firm, 1833 to 1939"* - P W Pilling - PhD Thesis, Liverpool University, Oct 1985 -at BMB B620 HIC

9 BC 18-4-1863

10 *"Industries of Lancashire"* - Historical Publishing Co, London, 1889-90

11 Article on Bolton Iron and Steelworks - in *Iron* 14-6-1873

12 BMB ZZ/422/1

13 BMB ZJA 112/14

14 BMB ZJA 112/9

15 BMB ZJA 112/11

16 Information from Industrial Locomotive Society's lists

17 BC 4-1-1907

18 LNWR Sdgs Diag 144, 12-1916 19 BEN 17-3-1924

20 BEN 20-5-1926

21 BEN 2-4-1970

22 Line Plan of Bolton and Kenyon Railway - 2 chains to 1 inch - LNWR, Euston, 1888 - BRPB, Manchester

23 *"Directory of Bolton etc"* - J Williams, Manchester, 1845

24 *"History, Topography and Directory of Mid Lancashire"* - P Mannex and Co, Preston, 1854

25 *"Royal National Commercial Directory of Lancashire"* - Isaac Slater, Manchester, 1869

26 *"Wrought Iron - The end of an Era"* - Joseph Brough -Bolton Metropolitan Borough Council Arts Dept - nd (about 1975)

27 BC 10-1-1874

28 *Mineral Statistics*

29 Information from John Powell, Ironbridge Gorge Museum Trust

30 Notes in possession of Frank Smith

31 *"Borough of Bolton Companies Directory"* - publ Metropolitan Borough Council - Nov 1984 and Sept 1985 issues

32 BMB ZZ 395/3/5

33 BMB ZZ 395/3/16

34 BMB ZZ 395/3/15

35 *"Reminiscences of the Bolton Gas Company 1818 - 1872"* - James Clegg - Daily Chronicle, Bolton, 1872

36 1 Geo 4 cap lvii; 8th July 1820

37 6&7 Vic cap xiv; 11th April 1843

38 L&YR Sdgs Diag 96, 9th Nov 1896

39 Information from North West Gas Historical Society

40 17&18 Vic cap xx; 12th May 1854

41 35&36 Vic cap lxxviii; 18th July 1872

42 Line Plan of Liverpool Bolton and Bury Rly, 16mp to 10mp - 2 chains to 1inch - BR, Euston, 1948 - BRPB, Manchester

43 L&YR Sdgs Diag 303, 26th June 1903

44 BJ 28-1-1910

45 L&YR Sdgs Diag 303A, 6th July 1916

46 BC 20-5-1911

46 11&12 Geo VI cap 67; 30th July 1948

47 Endorsement on ref 42

48 *"Jubilee of the Undertaking"* - County Borough of Bolton Electricity Dept, Oct 1944 -at BMB B621.312 BOL

49 BEN 8-5-1957

50 L&YR Sdgs Diag 386, 31st Dec 192

51 L&YR Sdgs Diag 97, 9th Nov 1896

52 L&YR Sdgs Diag 25, 18-6-1895

53 L&YR Sdgs Diag 319, 29th April 1904

54 Endorsement on ref 53

55 BJ 18-3-1927

56 *"Royal National Commercial Directory and Topography of the County of Lancashire etc"* - Isaac Slater, Manchester, 1848

57 BEN 14-2-1881

58 *Iron* 18-2-1881

59 *"Industrial Railways of the Wigan Coalfield Vol 2"* - Townley, Smith and Peden - Runpast Publishing, Cheltenham, 1992

60 BJ20-5-1927

61 BJ 13-5-1927

62 BJ 23-12-1927

63 Letter Dobson and Barlow Ltd to Frank Smith 4-9-1953

64 *"Samuel Crompton 1753-1827"* - pub by Dobson and Barlow, Bolton, 1927

65 *Iron* 30-8-1873

66 *Iron* 11-9-1891

67 *"Bolton and District Directory and Buyers Guide"* - E F Cope and Co, Walsall, 1934

68 *"Bolton and District Directory and Buyers Guide"* - E F Cope and Co, Walsall, 1938

69 *"The Bolton Model Poultry Farm"* - F D Smith - *Industrial Railway Record* No 115, December, 1988

70   BC 31-5-1913

71   BC 31-1-1914

72   *"Bolton Annual Commercial Directory"* - H Whewell and Co, Bolton, 1889

73   *"Royal National Commercial Directory and Topography of the County of Lancashire etc"* - Isaac Slater, Manchester, 1851

74   *"Royal National Commercial Directory of Manchester and Liverpool and the Principal Manufacturing Towns in Lancashire"* - Isaac Slater, Manchester, 1861

75   BC 4-1-1865

76   BC 25-2-1865

77   *"Commercial Directory of Bolton etc"* - T Abbatt, Bolton, 1874

78   BC 5-11-1898

79   *"Annual Directory"* - William Holden, London, 1816

80   *"Lancashire Illustrated"* - Henry Fisher, Son and Peter Jackson, London, 1829

81   BC 4-12-1830

82   Manchester Courier 4-12-1830

83   *"The Liverpool and Manchester Railway"* - R H G Thomas - B T Batsford Ltd, London, 1980

84   *Preston Herald* 11-7-1903

85   *The Engineer* 11-6-1920

86   *"British Steam Locomotive Builders"* - Lowe - Goose and Sons, Folkestone, 1975

87   *"Locomotives of the Great Western Railway" - Part Three"* - Railway Correspondence and Travel Society, 1952

88   *"Locomotives of the London and South Western Railway"* - Railway Correspondence and Travel Society, 1965

89   *"British Locomotive Catalogue 1825 - 1923, Part 2A"* - compiled by late Bertram Baxter - Moorland Publishing Co, Ashbourne, 1978

90   *Herepath* 30-11-1844

91   *The Engineer* 12-4-1861

92   *The Engineer* 30-8-1861

93   BMB ZJA/112/1

94   BMB ZJA 112/2

95   BMB ZJA 112/3

96   BMB ZJA 112/4

97   BMB ZJA 112/11

98   Article on the Union Foundry of Rothwell and Company in *Iron* 21-7-1873

99   BC 10-6-1882

100 *"National Commercial Directory for the Counties of Chester, Cumberland, Durham and Lancaster"* - James Pigot and Son, Manchester, 1834

101 LG 8-4-1851

102 *"Exhibition of Early Locomotive Drawings"* - W O Skeat and John Marshall - Hick, Hargreaves and Co Ltd, Bolton, 1974

103 *"British Locomotive Catalogue 1825 - 1923, Part 3A"* - compiled by late Bertram Baxter - Moorland Publishing Co, Ashbourne, 1982

104 *"Locomotives of the Great Western Railway - Part Ten"* - Railway Correspondence and Travel Society, 1966

105 *"British Locomotive Catalogue 1825 - 1923, Part 5A"* - compiled by late Bertram Baxter - Moorland Publishing Co, Ashbourne, 1986

106 *"SE&CR Locomotive List 1842-1952"* - N Wakeman - Oakwood Press, 1953

107 *"The North Staffordshire Railway"* - Manifold - J H Henstock Ltd, Ashbourne, 1952

108 *Herepath* 27-5-1850

109 BC 21-6- 1873

110 *Iron* 8-4-1892

111 *"The Commercial Directory of Manchester"* - Wardle and Bentham, Manchester, 1814

112 *"Lancashire General Directory - Part First - Blackburn, Bolton and Preston"* - T Rogerson, Manchester, 1818

113 BC 3-10-1829

114 LG 1-1-1833

115 *"Thompson, Swift and Cole"* - D O'Connor - Bolton Industrial History Society - copy at BMB

116 *Railway Times* 3-10-1842

117 *Railway Times* 10-12-1842

118 LG p1395 1848

119 BC17-8-1878

120 BC 21-9-1878

121 BEN6-8-1986

122 BC 4-6-1831

123 BC 18-6-1831

124 BC 4-6-1831

125 BC 14-1-1832

126 BC 2-6-1832

127 BC 20-12-1845

128 BC 12-1-1856

129 BC 28-2-1863

130 Biographical notes provided by Frank Smith, based on parish records, probate records and census returns

131 *"Some Notes on John Hargreaves Junior and his Locomotives"* - Ray Shill - *Journal of the Railway and Canal Historical Society*, No 146, Nov 1990

132 Parliamentary Papers 1842, Vol XLI

133 *"The Railways of Great Britain and Ireland"* - Francis Whishaw - John Weale, London 1842

134 BC 27-12-1845

135 PRORAIL 1008/106

136 BC 2-8-1828

137 Liverpool and Manchester Railway Board Minutes 4-1-1830

138 Manchester Courier 10-4-1830

139 Liverpool and Manchester Railway Board Minutes 8-3-1830

140 Liverpool and Manchester Railway Board Minutes 15-3-1830

141 BC 25-6-1831

142 *"A History of Railway Locomotives down to the End of the Year 1831 "* - Dendy Marshall - Locomotive Publishing Co Ltd, London, 1953

143 BC 30-7-1831

144 Liverpool and Manchester Railway Board Minutes 11-7-1831

144 Liverpool and Manchester Railway Board Minutes 2-4-1832

146 MG 19-6-1837

147 *Railway Times* 14-3-1840

148 *Railway Times* 12-9-1840

149 *"James Nasmyth and the Bridgewater Foundry"* - J A Cantrell - Chetham Society, Manchester, 1984

150 *Preston Chronicle* 22-8-1846

151 *Bolton Free Press* 23-5-1846

CHAPTER 4

THE OUTSKIRTS OF BOLTON

We continue our story of the industrial railways in the Bolton area and we turn now to districts outside the town centre, but still within the present Metropolitan Borough. We have omitted reference to the numerous small landsale collieries, served only by road transport, which are outside the theme of the book. For readers who wish to pursue their history, we include in Appendix 5 such information as we have found out about them.

We start to the south-west of the town, in the old township of Over Hulton. Here, our main interest lies with the Hulton collieries and their rail system, dating back to the earliest days of the Bolton and Leigh Railway.

From the Hulton collieries we move across country through Dean Moor to Farnworth where the majority of the pits were connected to the system of underground navigable levels which led to the canal at Worsley. This was the most northerly part of the territory exploited by the Duke of Bridgewater and later by his Trustees and it is convenient here to deal briefly with the history of the mining operations in this area, leaving the main treatment of the Bridgewater Collieries to Chapters 11 and 12.

We conclude our perambulations to the south of Bolton by looking at the collieries on land belonging to the Earl of Bradford, mainly in the old Great Lever township.

We move next to Smithills Hall, where two quite long horse worked tramroads operated in the first half of the nineteenth century. We then go on to Tonge and Breightmet, where many of the early collieries made use of horse worked lines to take their coal to the nearest convenient turnpike road.

We finish the chapter with a brief account of the collieries served by the Manchester, Bolton and Bury Canal, situated in the old townships of Darcy Lever and Little Lever. Until the opening of the canal in 1796, such mining as there was seems to have been on a very small scale. Much of the development which then took place was carried out by families such as the Fletchers and the Knowles, who had been associated with the coal industry in Bolton since the middle of the previous century.

A number of schemes, which we have described in Chapter 2, were put forward in the 1830s to provide the area with rail transport, but none came to fruition. Only the Darcy Lever Coal Company's pits ever had a main line rail connection, to the Bolton and Bury line of the Lancashire and Yorkshire Railway. All the other mines had to rely, throughout their lives, on the canal to take away their coal, supplemented by road transport for local customers.

SOUTH WEST OF BOLTON

The Hulton Collieries up to 1859

Although mining appears to have been carried on in the neighbourhood of Hulton Park for several centuries, it was William Hulton, who succeeded to the property in 1800 [1,2], who was responsible for the major developments which took place in the early years of the nineteenth century. He was also one of the principal supporters, and later chairman, of the Bolton and Leigh Railway, which provided the means of transporting his coal to Bolton as well as to more distant markets in Manchester and Liverpool.

The first section of the Bolton and Leigh Railway was opened for traffic on 1st August 1828. Guests, including Mr and Mrs Hulton, accompanied by the Bolton Old Band were conveyed in a train of thirteen wagons and a coach from Pendlebury Fold to Daubhill Engine House. The engine then went back for six loaded coal wagons from one of Mr Hulton's collieries. On its return to Daubhill, it was named LANCASHIRE WITCH by Mrs Hulton. The whole train was then moved down the incline by the stationary engine to a point near the Bolton terminus [3].

Soon after this there were complaints about the damage which was caused to the coal when it was discharged from railway wagons into the carts used for delivery to customers. In February 1829 it was reported [4] that Mr Stephenson had constructed a carriage to obviate the problem. A trial had been made on the 14th, when coal was loaded at Mr Hulton's collieries and was brought down the line to Bolton. Here the carriage was placed on a cart constructed by the same engineer. Presumably the carriage was some form of box or container, adopted widely by colliery companies throughout South Lancashire for transport of coal by canal and by rail.

As mentioned in an earlier chapter, the railway was opened throughout to the canal basin at Leigh at the end of March, 1830. The connecting link with the Liverpool and Manchester Railway was opened in January 1831 for freight and in June of the same year for passenger traffic.

It appears likely that Hulton's traffic was worked originally by LANCASHIRE WITCH and other Bolton and Leigh engines. His first purchase seems to have been PHOENIX, built by Crook and Dean, which is reported to have entered service on the Bolton and Leigh line in June 1831 [5]. It was presumably an 0-4-0 tender engine, similar to those supplied by the firm to John Hargreaves Junior.

We have been unable to establish that PHOENIX was supplied new to William Hulton. It was certainly in his possession by January 1832, when it was in collision with a Hargreaves engine, NELSON, near Chip Hill Bridge in foggy weather [6].

For the first year or so Hulton's operations seem to have been confined to the Bolton and Leigh line, his coal traffic to Liverpool and Manchester being worked by James Hargreaves Junior. In March 1832 William Hulton was given permission to work his own coal trains over the Liverpool and Manchester Railway, after failing to get Hargreaves to reduce his charges [7]. As the Liverpool and Manchester agreed to provide locomotive power until Hulton could obtain an engine of his own, it appears that PHOENIX may not have been considered suitable for this work.

It is not clear whether Hulton did in fact purchase another locomotive for this traffic or whether he used his authorisation as a bargaining counter in his negotiations with Hargreaves about rates. In November 1837 a Grand Junction train ran into the back of a Hargreaves train, which had stopped on the main line at Chat Moss, and damaged some wagons belonging to William Hulton. Hulton sued Hargreaves and at the trial at Manchester in April 1839, it was stated that Hargreaves conveyed coal and coke on behalf of Hulton to destinations on the Liverpool and Manchester line [8,9].

MANCHESTER, a curious 2-2-0 machine with vertical cylinders, turned out by Galloway, Bowman and Glasgow of Manchester in 1831 is stated to have been hired to the Hulton Collieries for a time [7]. This may have been when PHOENIX was undergoing repairs.

There is also a suggestion that BEE a four coupled locomotive built by Edward Bury in 1832 may have been acquired second hand from John Hargreaves, but we have been unable to corroborate this. BEE is shown in a list of Bolton and Leigh engines, drawn up in 1839 or 1840 by Whishaw [10], and was presumably then the property of Hargreaves. It does not appear in a list of Hargreaves engines dated October 1841 [11], so if it did go to William Hulton, the sale must have taken place around 1840.

By 1841, Hulton certainly had two locomotives. Peter Sinclair the Treasurer of the Bolton and Leigh Railway, replying to Mr Laing of Board of Trade on 13th October 1841 [11], stated "Mr Hulton, a gentleman having collieries upon the line, has two engines, one or other of which is used from time to time in the removal of his own coal upon a small portion of the line, about two miles in length only, but as the locomotives are his own property and not used in public traffic, I apprehend they do not come within the scope of your enquiries ".

The Bolton and Leigh Railway and its successor, the London and North Western Railway, provided the only rail outlet for Hulton's coal and continued to do so until the collieries closed. There were, however, several schemes by competing companies to provide an alternative. As early as 1830, plans had been put forward for a railway from Manchester to Preston [12] which would have included a branch from Lostock to Pendlebury Fold. The whole project failed to obtain Parliamentary approval.

The Liverpool and Bury Railway Act of 1846 [13] authorised a branch from Chew Moor to the White Horse Public House, at the junction of the Manchester to Chorley and Bolton to Westhoughton roads. The line, however, was never built.

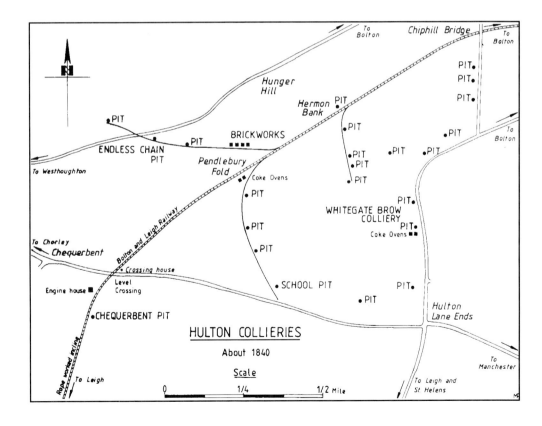

The Act of 1847 for the Manchester and Southport Railway [14] authorised a branch from the main line, north of Tyldesley, to terminate on the south side of Hulton Park [15]. However, powers for the lines east of Wigan, including the Hulton Branch, were allowed to lapse. The branch from Tyldesley was revived in the Lancashire and Yorkshire's proposal of 1860 for a direct line from Hindley to Clifton Junction [16], but the whole scheme was rejected by Parliament.

The first edition of the 6" map provides a picture of William Hulton's mining activities in the mid 1840s. The majority of the pits were in the neighbourhood of Chequerbent, served by private branches from the Bolton and Leigh line. One of these ran westwards from Pendlebury Fold past the estate brickworks and the Endless Chain Pit and then crossed the Bolton to Westhoughton turnpike to reach another, unidentified, pit. A second branch left the Bolton and Leigh line at the same point and ran south to the School Pit, alongside the Manchester to Chorley road, near Chequerbent school, passing the coke works and several other pits along its route. A third branch, which left the main line at Hermon Bank, on the Bolton side of Pendlebury Fold, gave access to several small pits to the south. There was also a colliery adjacent to the Bolton and Leigh line, near the engine house at the top of the Chequerbent incline.

Remote from the railway, the map marks other Hulton collieries alongside the Bolton to St Helens road, at Whitegate Brow and Worthington Fold. Further afield and again not rail connected, there were collieries at Halshaw Moor, east of the Bolton to Worsley Road, north of Long Causeway [17].

The Hulton Collieries 1859 to 1886

In about 1858, William Hulton formed the Hulton Colliery Company, apparently in partnership with Harwood Walcot Banner, to take over the collieries at Over Hulton and Middle Hulton. According to the Mines Lists, those at Halshaw Moor remained the property of William Hulton himself, but they closed shortly afterwards, last appearing in the Mines Lists for 1863.

William Hulton died on 31st March 1864 [1,2] and was succeeded by his son, William Ford Hulton. The partnership with Banner was dissolved at the end of 1868 [18] and the collieries became the sole property of W F Hulton, who subsequently traded under his own name.

Developments were focused on the Chequerbent area. The Park Pits were sunk south of the Manchester to Chorley road and the Arley Deep Pit to the north of it. The School Pits, the Arley No 2 Pit and the pits at Chequerbent were retained and the remainder of the older pits were abandoned.

There were consequential changes to the railway layout. The branch from Pendlebury Fold to the Endless Chain Pit was cut short at the Hulton Brickworks. A new line was built from the School Pit branch which served the Arley Deep Pit and then crossed the main road to reach the Park Pits. There was also a short spur from near the Park Pits which possibly served the Firs Pit. The branch from Hermon Bank now only ran as far a wagon works, presumably belonging to the Hultons.

The reconstruction of the Bolton and Leigh line, including the deviations to by-pass the inclines was completed in February 1885. The course of the original line past the Chequerbent pits was retained for use by the colliery locomotives. Under an agreement of 17th August 1885, the Hulton Colliery Company's traffic was allowed to pass free of toll over the this section on payment of an annual charge of £1 [19].

Records of the locomotives used at this period are sparse. The first that we know of was BEE, or possibly THE BEE, a four coupled engine which came from Sharp, Stewart and Company of Manchester in 1859. It was remembered by old employees as having a saddle tank. It has been suggested that, as originally built, it was a tender locomotive and that it was later converted. We have, however, been unable to confirm this.

A second locomotive was supplied by the same makers in 1875. It was named SQUIRE, or possibly THE SQUIRE, at a ceremony at Great Moor Street Station, Bolton, in April of that year [20]. Old employees also recalled an engine which they said was named PRINCE OF WALES, described as a 2-4-0 tank, possibly obtained second hand from the London and North Western Railway. We have been unable to confirm this statement and have found no further information about the locomotive.

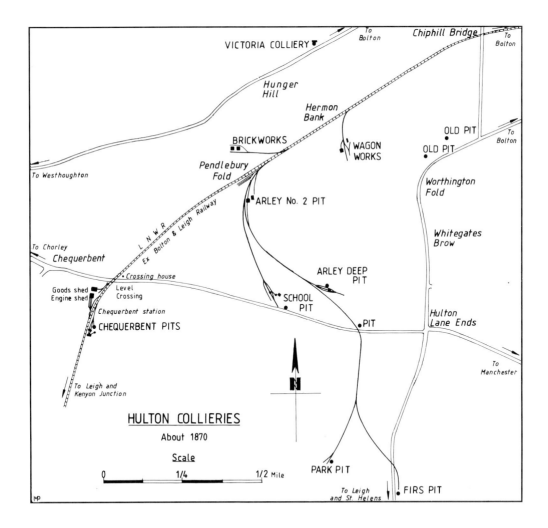

The original alignment of the Bolton and Leigh Railway at Chequerbent, showing the site of the level crossing over the Manchester to Chorley road, the present A6. Although the LNWR ceased to use this route, following the opening of the deviations in 1885, the line continued to be worked by the Hulton Colliery Co Ltd until the mid 1930s. The crossing keeper's house, dating from around 1829, can be seen in the centre of the picture. The chimney of Pendlebury Fold brickworks is just visible in the background.   Harry Townley

The Hulton Collieries 1886 to 1934

William Ford Hulton died on 18th May 1879 [21] and was succeeded by his son, William Wilbraham Brethyn Hulton [2]. Seven years later the latter disposed of his mining interests to the Hulton Colliery Co Ltd. This firm, promoted by R Brancker, G H Daglish and others, was registered on 29th March 1886 [22].

Work began in 1892 in sinking a new pit on the east side of the Bolton and Leigh line south of Chequerbent Colliery [23,24]. A further shaft was sunk on an adjacent site in 1897 and two more some half mile to the east in 1900. Known originally Atherton Pits Nos 1,2,3 and 4, they were renamed Bank Pits about 1912 to avoid confusion with the neighbouring collieries of Fletcher, Burrows and Co Ltd. The Bank Nos 3 and 4 pits were the scene of the worst colliery accident to occur in Lancashire, when 344 miners were killed as the result of an underground explosion on 21st December 1910.

The colliery company built a private line from the end of the original Bolton and Leigh incline to serve Bank Nos 1 and 2 Pits. Beyond here, a triangular siding connection with the main line was provided under agreements dated 23rd July 1900, 27th January 1904 and 14th May 1906 [25] and the colliery company's railway was extended from Nos 1 and 2 Pits, past the new exchange sidings, to Nos 3 and 4 Pits.

The mines north of the Manchester to Chorley road ceased production between 1900 and the outbreak of the first world war. The Arley No 2 Pit is shown as abandoned in the Mines Lists from 1901 to 1905, but seems to have re-opened under the name of Deep No 2 a few years later. It finally closed about 1913.

The Arley Nos 3 & 4 Pits appear briefly in the Mines Lists for 1900 to 1902, but were disused by 1904. The Arley Deep Pit is shown as discontinued in the 1913 Mines List; School Pit closed about 1914.

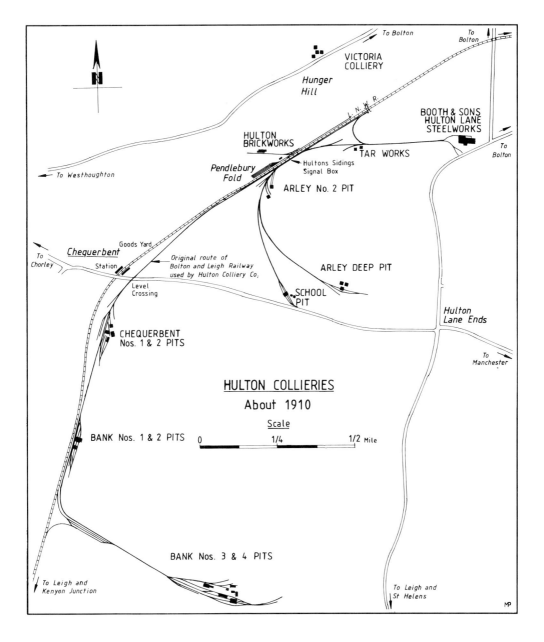

An old photograph of SQUIRE, the Sharp, Stewart locomotive delivered to the Hulton collieries in 1875. Believed to have been taken at Pendlebury Fold about 1908. Stan Garrett, the driver, is on the footplate, with fireman Almond standing alongside the engine.   Frank Smith collection

ATHERTON, the Vulcan Foundry engine of 1895, at the Hulton collieries.   Harry Townley collection

Traffic on the branches of the railway system serving these pits ceased as a result of the closures. However, the line northwards past Chequerbent Colliery to the connection with the LNWR at Pendlebury Fold remained in use. From here a new line had been built in about 1905 to give access to the constructional steelworks of John Booth and Sons Ltd, from which there was a spur serving a tar works. On the west side of the LNWR a short portion of the old Chain Pit branch was still in use as far as the brickworks.

With the falling demand for coal in the late 1920s onwards, the more modern collieries closed down. Bank No 2 pit ceased production sometime after 1921. Bank No 1 was abandoned on 30th November 1927, on the same date as the two Chequerbent pits. Finally Bank Nos 3 and 4 pits were abandoned in April 1934.

The Hulton Colliery Co Ltd took over BEE and SQUIRE from W B Hulton and also possibly the shadowy PRINCE OF WALES. A further locomotive came in 1886 from the Crow Orchard Colliery at Skelmersdale where the plant had been put up for auction on 7th April 1886 [26]. This was a six coupled saddle tank, built by the Hunslet Engine Company of Leeds in 1871. The manufacturer's records show that spares were supplied to the Hulton Colliery Co Ltd. It was remembered, still carrying the name PRESCOTT, by old employees whom we interviewed in the 1950s. It was said to have been broken up for scrap about 1898.

To cater for the increased traffic from the new Atherton Pits, a six coupled saddle tank was obtained from the Vulcan Foundry of Newton-le-Willows in 1895. It was named ATHERTON and was later numbered 3 in the Hulton Colliery stock, BEE and SQUIRE presumably being regarded as Nos 1 and 2. It was followed by three Class X six coupled saddle tanks obtained from Peckett and Sons of Bristol in 1900, 1903 and 1907. These carried the numbers 4, 5 and 6 respectively.

No 5 of the Hulton Colliery Co Ltd, photographed in NCB days at Lea Green Colliery, near St Helens, in May 1957   Jim Peden

With the arrival of these new engines, some of the older locomotives became redundant. BEE was sold to Thomas Mitchell and Sons, the Bolton machinery merchants, in August 1903. It is not entirely clear if this was the Sharp Stewart engine of 1859 or a replacement for it, as the Mitchell records quote the builder as the LNWR. A spare locomotive boiler went to Mitchells in October 1904 while THE SQUIRE, the Sharp Stewart of 1875, was purchased by them in April 1911. An old employee told us that BEE was cut up at the Tar Works and SQUIRE at Pendlebury Fold.

The plant at the Nos 3 and 4 Bank Pits was auctioned on 22nd to 27th August 1934 [27] and included a six coupled saddle tank locomotive, stated to have recently been overhauled. We presume that this was No 4, the Peckett of 1900, which later worked at the Shelton Steel Works at Stoke on Trent. The fate of ATHERTON, the Vulcan Foundry engine of 1895, is not known for certain, although we were told by an old employee that it was sold to a Yorkshire firm when the collieries closed in 1934. The other two Pecketts, 5 and 6, were transferred to the firm's Cronton Colliery, near Huyton. We were told that No 5 was the last engine to leave Chequerbent, on 26th December 1934.

John Booth and Sons (Bolton) Ltd

We have mentioned, earlier in the chapter, the constructional steelworks of John Booth and Sons which was served by the Hulton Collieries railway system. The firm was founded in 1873 by John Booth who took over premises in Mill Brow for his engine and machine smith's business. After a few months he moved to Mill Lane and then, in the early 1880s to a mill in the Croal valley, where Crompton had first spun cotton commercially [28].

Despite its poor quality, this amateur snapshot is of importance as it is the only known photograph of the diminutive Kerr, Stuart locomotive working at the constructional steelworks of John Booth and Sons Ltd.

Jim Peden collection

In 1904 the firm started to build the Hulton Steel works in St Helens Road, although the original premises in the Croal Valley were still being used in 1973. The firm, which became a limited company in 1932, specialises in structural steelwork, pressure vessels, storage tanks, fireproof doors and metal partitions.

The Hulton Steel Works was served by a private railway which connected with the LNWR at Pendlebury Fold. We think that the line, which also provided access to the Hulton tar works, was constructed by the colliery company. We assume that wagons between the LNWR and Booth's works were originally hauled by colliery locomotives.

In the late 1920s John Booth and Sons were awarded a contract for the erection of a works for the British Acetate Silk Corporation Ltd at Stowmarket in Suffolk. To assist in the construction, the firm purchased a very small four coupled saddle tank, built by Dick Kerr and Company of Kilmarnock in 1915, from Ipswich Docks [29]. On completion of the contract, about 1930, the engine was brought back to Bolton.

It proved too weak to deal with the gradients at the works and it was sold to Harry Stephenson and Sons Ltd, machinery merchants of Hindley, about 1932. It was sent to White Moss Colliery at Skelmersdale which, by this date, had closed. Here it was overhauled by the engineer in the colliery workshops, apparently as a private venture. Stephensons were unable to resell the engine and it was later broken up for scrap [30].

The Hilton Gravel Company's Siding at Pendlebury Fold

Long after the demise of the Hulton collieries, unloading facilties were provided at Hultons Sidings, Pendlebury Fold, for the Hilton Gravel Co Ltd, under an agreement with British Railways dated 14th May 1962 [31]. A siding was used for the delivery of materials for the construction of the M61 motorway. Wagons were placed in the siding by British Railways and no private locomotive was used.

Traffic ceased some time in 1968, the British Railways line from Atherton being formally closed on 1st January 1969. The agreement in respect of the siding was terminated on 28th December 1968 [31].

Jose K Holt Gordon Ltd, Chequerbent

This firm was founded in 1950, with premises at Raikes Clough, and in 1954 moved to the present site near Chequerbent Station. In the early years the principal activity was breaking up textile machinery, but, with the run down of the coal industry, the firm moved into the business of dismantling colliery plant. Contracts included work at Garswood Hall, Park and Landgate in the Wigan area and Bold, Sutton Manor, Clock Face, Ravenhead, Lea Green, Lyme and Haydock in the St Helens area [32].

A number of locomotives were purchased for scrap from the National Coal Board at this period. Those that we know about are listed in the Locomotive Summary at the end of the chapter.

Many of the engines were broken up on site, but a few were taken to the firm's yard alongside Chequerbent Station. Of these, ROBERT, a six coupled Avonside saddle tank from Garswood Hall Colliery, and HARRY an austerity saddle tank from Walkden, stood out of use for many years. HARRY was sold to the Shropshire Locomotive Society for preservation, early in 1992. ROBERT still survives in at Chequerbent at the time of writing, in a very woebegone condition.

ROBERT at the Chequerbent yard of Jose K Holt Gordon Ltd. Purchased from the National Coal Board in 1965, it was still at Chequerbent at the end of 1993.   Jim Peden

FROM DEAN MOOR TO FARNWORTH

The Bridgewater Pits at Dean Moor

We now move across the Bolton and St Helens road to Dean Moor, which formed part of the Bridgewater Estates. The mines here were opened out by the Duke of Bridgewater in the 1750s and 1760s, when a number of landsale pits were sunk, mainly to supply the Bolton market. They were later served by the system of underground navigable levels, which connected with the Bridgewater canal at Worsley. By the 1780s the upper level had been pushed forward as far as Dixon Green, from where a branch was constructed to the Dean Moor mines. The main navigable level was later extended from Walkden to Dixon Green by the Bridgewater Trustees and thence under Plodder Lane to the southern part of the Dean Moor area [33].

In the 1840s, the principal Dean Moor pits were at Eckersley's Field, Fray's Horse Field and Sappling Field [17]. There was also Watergate Pit, located to the south of Plodder Lane, which was served by a separate branch of the upper level. In the same vicinity, Delph Pit was sunk in 1848. Plans were made to link it to Watergate by a short tramroad, but these do not seem to have been carried out [33].

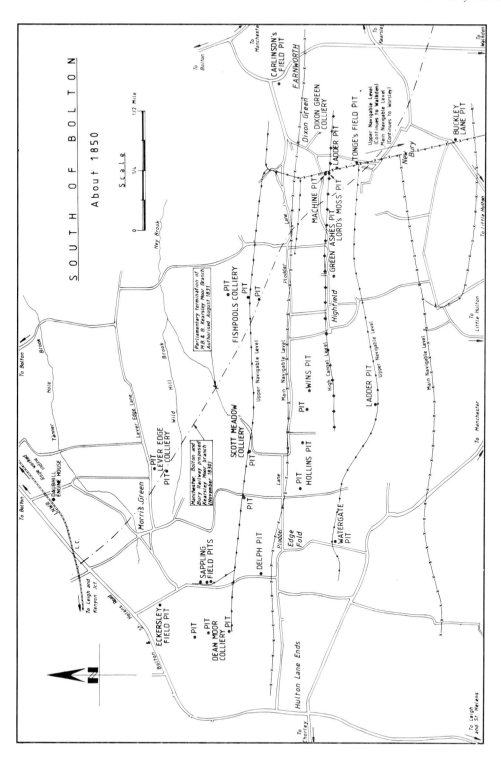

SOUTH OF BOLTON

About 1850

Scale

0   1/4   1/2 Mile

Eckersley's Field and Fray's Horse Field do not appear in the Mines Lists, which from 1858 show each of the Bridgewater pits separately; we assume that they had been closed by then. Sapling Field, now spelled with a single "p", is last shown in the Lists for 1879 and Delph in 1881. The last of the Dean Moor Mines, Watergate, does not appear after 1884.

Dixon Green and Farnworth

In 1762, the Duke of Bridgewater took a lease on land in the vicinity of Dixon Green, owned by Sir Orlando Bridgeman, grandfather of the first Earl of Bradford [34]. Adjacent lands were either bought or leased from smaller landowners [33].

Coal had been mined in the neighbourhood since the middle of the seventeenth century and initially the Duke made use of a sough which had been driven for drainage purposes in these early workings [33] . Coal was distributed by horse and cart until the upper navigable level reached the district in the 1780s. The extension of the main navigable level took place in the early years of the nineteenth century.

Coke ovens were erected at Dixon Green in about 1770 and there was also a small yard there for the repair of colliery equipment [33]. In the 1840s the principal pits were Tonge's Field, Lord's Moss Field, Howarth's Field and the Dixon Green Balance Pit. The last mentioned took its name from a water balance engine which was installed there for pumping purposes.

After 1864, the Balance Pit is replaced in the Mines Lists by the Machine Pit, which we think was probably a new name for the same place. We are not sure whether the water engine was retained or whether it was replaced by more modern equipment. Machine Pit was used for pumping until 1908.

With the new sinkings further south in the 1860s, which we describe in Chapter 11, coal production at the Bridgewater pits at Dixon Green was run down. Tonges Field was the last to close and is not shown in the Mines Lists after 1880. Howarths Field had been abandoned earlier and does not appear in the lists after 1872. Lord's Field (Moss seems to have dropped from the name latterly) was retained for pumping purposes until 1912.

In the Halshaw Moor district of Farnworth William Hulton operated a colliery on his own land. It remained in his possession until 1863 and then appears to have been closed. In 1841 discussions were underway to drain water from Hultons colliery into the Bridgewater Trustees' navigable level at Dixon Green. A plan dated May of that year, drawn up in connection with the negotiations, shows the layout of the colliery [17]. There were four pits - the Plodder, the By, the Pump Engine and the Cannel - on the east side of the Bolton to Worsley road, between King Street and Long Causeway.

The first edition of the 6" map, surveyed in 1844 to 1846, shows these pits and marks coke ovens adjacent to the By Pit. The map also marks several other pits to the east, not far from the Bolton to Manchester road, which we assume were also worked by the Hulton family. A tramroad is shown on one version of the map*, running from the more easterly pits to the coke ovens, but we have been unable to find any further information about it. It was undoubtedly narrow gauge and worked by animal power.

All traces of the Hulton pits, like those of the Bridgewater pits at Dixon Green, have long since disappeared and the sites are now mainly occupied by housing.

---

*There appears to have been a minor revision of sheet 95 of the map in the vicinity of Halshaw Moor soon after it was first published in 1850. The copy at the Lancashire Record Office does not show the tramroad, whilst an almost identical copy in the map room at Cambridge University Library does mark it.

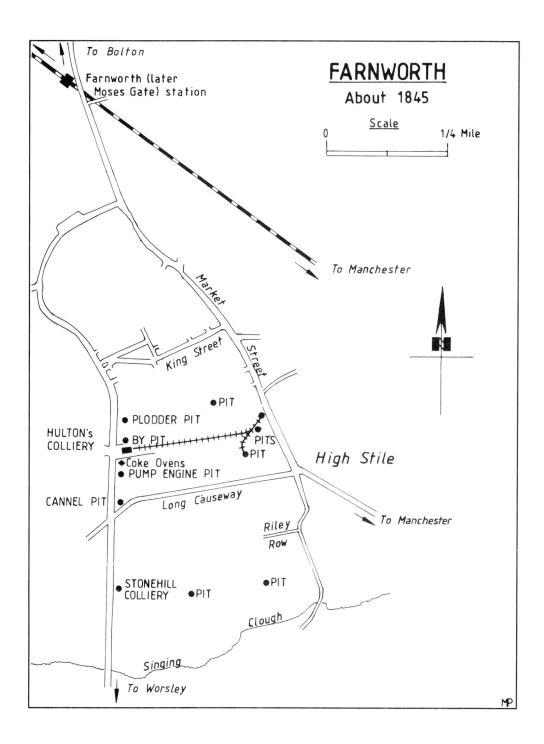

To Bolton

Farnworth (later Moses Gate) station

FARNWORTH
About 1845

Scale

0   1/4 Mile

To Manchester

Market

King Street

Street

PIT

PLODDER PIT

HULTON's COLLIERY

BY PIT

PITS

PIT

Coke Ovens

PUMP ENGINE PIT

High Stile

CANNEL PIT

Long Causeway

To Manchester

Riley Row

STONEHILL COLLIERY

PIT

PIT

Clough

Singing

To Worsley

MP

GREAT LEVER

The Earl of Bradford's Collieries

The Bridgeman family, elevated to the Earldom of Bradford in 1815 [34], had extensive estates in Great Lever and in Farnworth. From the middle of the eighteenth century onwards, mineral rights had been leased to a number of different colliery proprietors, including, as we have seen earlier, the Duke of Bridgewater. The majority of the pits were small landsale pits; some further information about them is included in Appendix 5.

Our main interest here is in events following the decision taken by the second Earl of Bradford, around 1840, to work his own coal. What was subsequently described as his Great Lever Colliery was sunk on a site at Raikes Lane. He is shown as having a coal depot at Orlando Street in directories for 1848 and 1851 [35,36].

The Act of 1845 incorporating the Liverpool and Bury Railway [37] authorised a branch from the west end of the Croal Viaduct to the colliery, to be opened at the same time as the main line, unless the Earl gave notice that it was not required. The Earl also had made an agreement with the Manchester, Bolton and Bury Canal and Railway, dated 4th April 1838, relating to the transport of his coal [38].

In the event, only the connection to the Manchester and Bolton line was constructed. On 5th May 1849, his agent, George Piggot, reported that he had nearly finished a good tramroad (ie a railway siding) to the main line. He had previously used Lancashire and Yorkshire Railway wagons to send coal to Manchester, but was now purchasing a few wagons for his lordship [39]. Presumably before this date there was a loading dock alongside the main line, to which coal from the colliery was taken either by horse and cart or, perhaps, by a short tramroad.

The second Earl subsequently expanded his mining activities. He is shown as occupier of Burnden Colliery for the first time in the mines lists for 1860. The coal here had previously been worked by the Scowcroft family, latterly from pits to the north of the Bolton to Bury railway, but the lease had reverted to the Earl.

Raikes Colliery, which appears to have been worked in conjunction with Great Lever, is also shown for the first time in the Mines Lists for 1860. There had been earlier pits here worked by John Horridge, but the Earl seems have sunk new shafts, presumably those shown on the second edition of the 6" map on the banks of the River Croal. The lease of Hacken Colliery, which we return to later in the chapter, was given up by Andrew Knowles and Sons in 1862. The Earl of Bradford took over and, again, new shafts appear to have been sunk to replace the earlier workings.

The third Earl inherited his father's property in 1865 [34] and continued the consolidation of the collieries. The Five Quarters Pit was taken over from John Smith, the proprietor of the neighbouring bleach works, and first appears under the Earl of Bradford in 1869. The Gravel Hole Pit near Moses Gate and the Aqueduct Pit at Haulgh are first shown in the Mines List for 1874, but they may have been sunk earlier.

The Gravel Hole Pit was served by a short tramroad or tubway which terminated at a landsale yard on the main road from Bolton to Farnworth. The other pits only used road transport, although, as will be seen from the maps in this chapter, they would have had rail connections if the some of the railways which were proposed in the 1830s had ever been built.

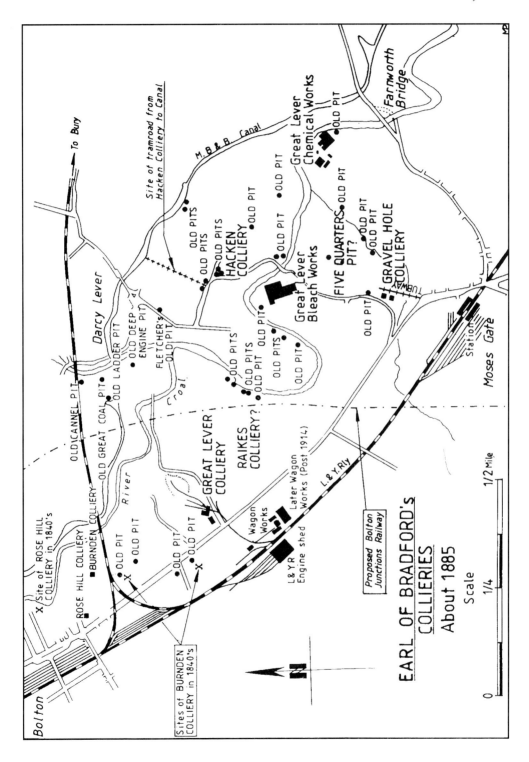

EARL OF BRADFORD's
COLLIERIES
About 1885

Great Lever Colliery was modernised in the late 1880s and the shafts were deepened to reach the lower seams. The intention seems to have been to concentrate coal production here and this resulted in the closure of the outlying pits. Burnden was the first to go and is not shown in the Mines Lists after 1884. Aqueduct and Hacken, both latterly used for pumping, closed between 1887 and 1890. Raikes is last shown in the Lists in 1890 and Gravel Hole in 1891.

We have no record of a locomotive in use at Great Lever before 1890 and it may be that one was not needed until the colliery had been redeveloped. The first reference we have found is in a letter dated 20th January 1890 from Thomas Mitchell and Co Ltd to the Earl's agent stating that they were despatching their engine ATALANTA by the Lancashire and Yorkshire Railway [40]. We have been unable to trace the identity of ATALANTA. There is a suggestion that an engine of this name had been employed by the contractors Monk and Newell on the construction of the Pendleton and Hindley line of the Lancashire and Yorkshire Railway. It may have been one of the sixteen locomotives offered for sale in July 1889 [41,42] on the completion of the work. We do not know if it was sold by Mitchell to the Earl of Bradford or if it was only on hire temporarily.

Other archive material shows that the Avonside Engine Company offered to quote for the supply of a locomotive in November 1890 [43] and two advertisements were received from Isaac Watt Boulton, the Ashton under Lyne dealer [44,45]. Quotations for an extra twenty five 10-ton wagons were obtained in July 1892 [46,47]. These provide an interesting insight into the firms which were in business at that date and the prices which were being asked; details are given in Appendix 3.

Whichever locomotive was in use at the colliery must have been giving trouble in 1894. There is a letter from the Lancashire and Yorkshire Railway at Horwich works, dated 12th January, declining to hire a locomotive and suggesting that an approach should be made to the Manchester Ship Canal Company [48]. Enquiries were also made about the supply of a new engine from the Avonside Engine Company, Peckett and Sons and Robert Stephenson and Company [49,50,51].

Nothing was done until 19th October 1896, when an order was placed with Peckett and Sons of Bristol for one of the firm's Class 632 four coupled saddle tanks. It was despatched from the works on 9th November 1896 on a Midland Railway low truck [52]. It was presumably this new engine which gave rise to a complaint of smoke nuisance on 10th, 11th and 12th November by residents at 418 Manchester Road, adjacent to the bridge taking the road over the colliery line [53,54].

From the insurance records[55-59] it seems clear that the colliery had only the one locomotive. By January 1907, the boiler pressure was reduced to 110 psi, but it was not until 1909 that repairs were undertaken. In July, the Earl's agent was again trying to hire a small locomotive from the Lancashire and Yorkshire Railway [60]. The reply must have been in the negative, as the records of Thomas Mitchell and Co Ltd, dated 12th August 1909, record an agreement to hire their locomotive WINNIE to the Earl of Bradford for not less than four weeks. The charge was £4 per week with an extra £3 for delivery and taking back.

Great Lever Colliery continued in production until after the first world war and was formally abandoned in 1922. The siding connection with the main line was taken out in the same year [61]. The Peckett locomotive was used up to the end and was included, along with 2350 yards of railway track, in the auction of plant held on 17th to 19th May 1922 [62,63]. It was later owned by the Low Beechburn Coal Company, in County Durham.

The site of the colliery was subsequently cleared and is now occupied by a greyhound racing track.

The Bolton Railway Wagon and Ironworks Co Ltd and Successor Firms

The Bolton Railway Wagon Company was established in 1885 [64] and in about 1895 changed its name to the Bolton Railway Wagon and Ironworks Co Ltd [65,66]. The original works was located on the north side of the line to Great Lever Colliery, adjacent to the Lancashire and Yorkshire Railway, and a rail connection was provided from the sidings serving the colliery [38]. The premises may have been taken over from Henry Parkinson, whose representatives were advertising a boiler and wagon works at Great Lever for sale in May 1883 [67].

A second works was erected on the south side of the line to the colliery, probably about 1914 or 1915, and a siding connection was provided with the Lancashire and Yorkshire, under an agreement dated 7th October 1915 [68].

Repair of railway wagons continued here until well after the second world war. Although an endorsement on the Siding Diagram states that the agreement was terminated on 30th November 1968 [61], the firm seems to have remained in business until 1977. It is shown in a directory of that date [69] and also appears for the last time in the Yellow Pages for that year.

An endorsement on the sidings diagram [38] records that the original premises, north of the colliery line, were used as a munitions works during the first world war. We presume that this was one of the many small machine shops set up by local munitions committees to manufacture shell casings and the like. The sidings serving the wagon works were taken up in 1915 and the munitions works sidings were completed in 1916. The site was later occupied by Bolton and Hayes Ltd, Concrete Engineers [70].

SMITHILLS

Smithills Colliery

The Smithills Estate was purchased in 1801 by the brothers Peter and Richard Ainsworth, proprietors of the nearby Halliwell Bleachworks [71]. Development of the coal mines on the estate followed shortly afterwards, to provide a supply of fuel to the factory. Peter Ainsworth died in 1807 and Richard in 1833. The business passed to Richard's sons, Peter and John Horrocks, who traded as Richard Ainsworth, Sons and Company. However there was dissolution on 30th June 1834, when Peter Ainsworth retired from the partnership to set up as a colliery and quarry proprietor and took over the mines.

There is evidence of two tramroads, both undoubtedly narrow gauge and employing horses as motive power. They must have been constructed after the Ainsworths took over the property, as they are not shown on an estate plan of 1801 [72]. We think that the northernmost one was constructed first. It appears to have terminated originally at Smithills Dean Road, as plans were drawn up in 1825 to extend it to the Upper Bleach Works [73]. The last 65 yards were on a gradient of nearly 1 in 5, which evidently was to be worked as a self acting incline.

In 1829 there were proposals for a further extension of the tramroad to the Lower or Prospect Works [74], but it seems unlikely that the work was carried out. There is nothing shown on the 2" drawings prepared around 1840 for the first edition of the 1" map.

By the 1845 to 1847 period, when the survey was carried out for the first edition of the 6" map, the more northerly tramroad appears to have fallen out of use. Only the middle section, east of Smithills Dean Road, is shown on the map.

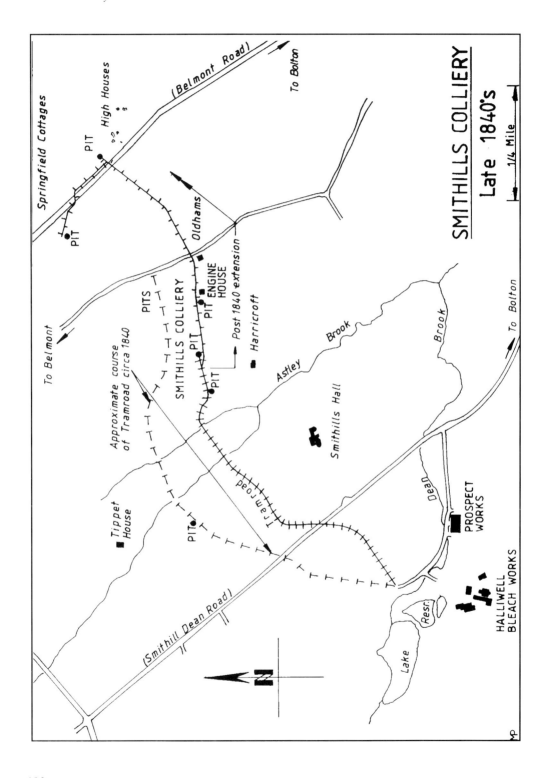

SMITHILLS COLLIERY

Late 1840's

1/4 Mile

The more southerly of the two lines is shown on the 2" drawings only between the pits north of Harricroft and the Bleach Works. We think that this may have been constructed around 1840, as, on 17th November 1841, the Halliwell Vestry gave Peter Ainsworth £40 in consideration for his making "a cartway from his coal head above Smithills Hall to Beech Clough, thereby preventing the extra expense which would have been necessary to repair the road to Smithills Mill" [71].

The first edition of the 6" map shows that the second tramroad had been extended to the Belmont Road, which it crossed on the level to reach a pit near High Houses. Another pit, near Springfield Cottages, was served by a branch which recrossed the road some distance to the north. We think that these pits may have constituted Peter Ainsworth's New Colliery, which began in the middle of 1845 and was employing 42 men in 1846 [71].

Smithills Colliery appears to have closed in 1855, the last year that it is shown in the Mines Lists. The Bleach Works was taken over by the Bleachers Association Ltd in 1900 and became part of the Whitecroft Group in the 1950s. Production ceased a few years later and the buildings have been demolished.

TONGE AND BREIGHTMET

Hardcastle's Tonge Colliery

The first edition of the 6" map, surveyed in 1844 to 1847, shows a series of pits, extending northwards from Bury Road and on the west side of the Bradshaw Brook, collectively described as Tonge Colliery. The map marks two separate tramroad systems, running to landsale yards adjacent to the main road near Turner Bridge. This suggests that the pits were originally worked by two separate firms, but we have been unable to discover anything about their early history.

The colliery became the property of James Hardcastle when he was granted leases at Crompton Fold, Breightmet and Tonge in December 1843 [75]. Hardcastle, who was proprietor of bleaching and textile printing works at Bradshaw and Firwood [76], already had mining interests in Bradshaw and Harwood. Edward Hardcastle took over from 30th September 1871, trading as the Breightmet Colliery Company [77]. From 1878 the Mines Lists record Frank Hardcastle as the occupier, although he still traded under the same title.

The tramroad system continued in use during the period that the Hardcastles worked the colliery. It was certainly still in operation in 1874 as the western portion, including the landsale yard at Turner Bridge, is shown on two plans of that date [78,79]. It probably survived until the colliery closed in 1885, the last year it is shown in the Mines Lists.

Scowcroft's Tonge Colliery

The first edition of the 6" map marks another Tonge Colliery, alongside the Bolton to Edenfield road, between Turner Bridge and Tonge Moor Gate. This was being worked by Blair and Burton in 1849 [80] and the Mines lists show that it had passed to the firm of Robert Burton and Son by 1854. By 1857, it had been taken over by Jethro Scowcroft, son of Thomas Scowcroft, who had collieries at Burnden and Kearsley.

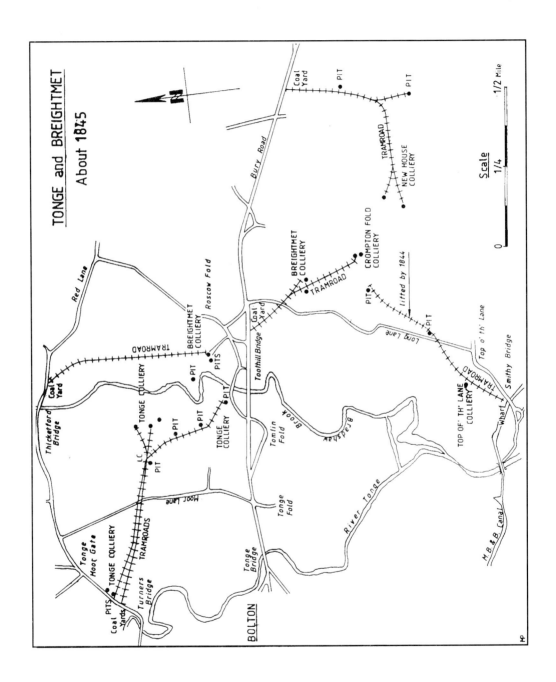

A new pit was evidently sunk in 1856 and drawings were prepared for a tramroad about 400 yards in length linking it to the Turnpike Road from Bolton to Edenfield [81]. Unfortunately, it is not possible to locate these developments precisely, but we believe that the new pit was situated to the west of the Bolton and Blackburn railway and that the tramroad ran almost due east, under the viaduct, to the main road.

Subsequently, further pits were sunk at Tonge Fold, on the north side of the Bury Road, near its junction with Moor Lane. The colliery here is first shown separately in the Mines Lists for 1874, but may have been opened a few years earlier. At this time, the there were three pits at the earlier Tonge Moor site - the Engine Pit and Air Pit on the west of the Bolton to Edenfield road and Wellington Pumping Pit on the east side [79].

Following the death of Jethro Scowcroft on 17th March 1880 [82], the property was taken over by his executors, who embarked on a programme of development. The two separate collieries were combined into a single unit, known as Tonge Colliery, of which Nos 1 and 2 Pits were located at Tonge Moor and Nos 3, 4 and 5 Pits at Tonge Fold [83]. The workings appear to have been extended to include the area previously mined from the Hardcastles' Tonge Pits.

A narrow gauge tubway, on which the trucks were moved by an endless chain, was completed before the surveys were made for the second edition of the 6" map in 1889 to 1890. This linked the pits on Tonge Fold site with the Scowcroft Street yard at Tonge Moor Gate, adjacent to Nos 1 and 2 Pits, where most, if not all, of the coal was sold.

Tonge Colliery later passed to Jethro's sons, Henry Turner Scowcroft and Thomas S Scowcroft, who are shown first as the occupiers in the Mines List for 1894. A limited liability company, T H and T Scowcroft Ltd, was formed later.

The colliery continued in production until about 1930. It was formally abandoned, according to Mines Lists, in June 1932 and it appears that the tubway was in use until the end. Some remains can still be seen, principally at Tonge Fold, where the site is now used by a car dealer.

Hardcastle's Breightmet Colliery, Roscow Fold

An estate plan of 1833 marks a colliery on the north side of the Bolton to Bury road at Roscow Fold and shows a tramroad running northwards from the pits to a landsale yard near Thicketford Bridge [84].

The colliery may have been that listed in 1829 as worked by Whitehead, Rothwell and Crompton [85]. It was taken over by James Hardcastle in December 1843, at the same time as the Tonge pits which we have noted earlier [74]. The tramroad must have been closed soon afterwards, as it is not shown on the 2" drawings of 1841. Only the trackbed is shown on the first edition of the 6" map.

As with the Tonge pits, those at Roscow Fold, now known as Breightmet Colliery, passed to Edward Hardcastle and then to Frank Hardcastle. Higher Croft Colliery, which the 1928 6" Geological map shows on an adjacent site, first appears in the Mines Lists for 1874. Breightmet Colliery is shown as "stopped" in the Mines Lists for 1879 and 1880; Higher Croft disappears from the Lists after 1881.

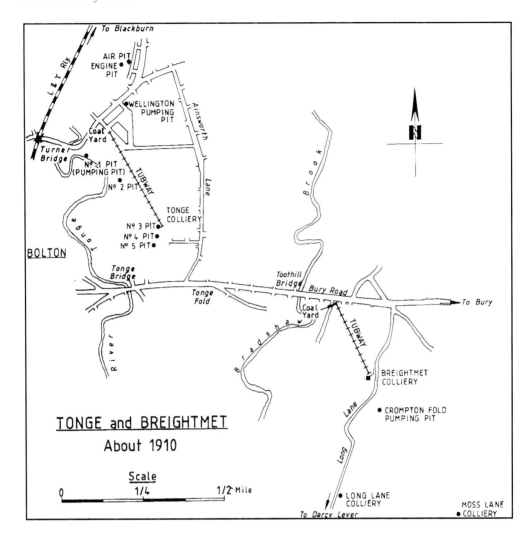

The Crompton Fold Collieries

The 2" drawings of 1841 show a tramroad running from a pit in the southern part of the Crompton Fold Estate to the Manchester, Bolton and Bury Canal, near Smithy Bridge. A second pit is shown, part way along line, in Darcy Lever township, opposite the entrance to Bradshaw Hall.

The Crompton Fold estate was inherited by Matthew Fletcher from his father, Adam. Matthew is recorded as colliery proprietor here in 1829 [84], but we do not know if the tramroad was constructed in his time. It may have been built later, by a partnership consisting of Edmund Grundy, Andrew Knowles, John Haigh and John Hudson. These four leased the coal under the estate, and possibly elsewhere in Breightmet and Tonge, on 20th June 1829 for a period of 19 years [76]. We think that it was they who sank the pit opposite the Bradshaw Hall entrance, which was on land owned by James and Ellis Fletcher [86].

By the time that the first edition of the 6" map was surveyed in 1844 to 1847 the tramroad and the pits which it served had disappeared. New pits had been sunk and a new tramroad had been built from what is described as Crompton Fold Colliery to a landsale yard on the Bolton to Bury Road. The map also marks a Breightmet Colliery alongside the tramroad, east of the point where it crossed Long Lane on the level.

We associate these developments with James Hardcastle, who obtained a lease at Crompton Fold in December 1843 [76]. The Crompton Fold Estate, together with the mineral rights, was sold by Matthew Fletcher to Frank Hardcastle, probably in the early 1860s [76]. An estate plan of 1862 [87], which we think was prepared in connection with the sale, shows that by this date the tramroad to the landsale yard on the Bolton to Bury road had been dismantled and that the pits marked on the 6" map had been abandoned.

Following the purchase of the estate, the Hardcastle family's Breightmet Colliery Company opened up new pits, two on the west side of Long Lane and one near to Bury Road, while one of the original shafts at Crompton Fold was retained for pumping purposes. The pits adjacent to Long Lane were possibly a redevelopment of an earlier colliery, the existence of which is only known from the plans, drawn up in 1856, for the extension of the Blackburn Railway to Manchester [88].

A new landsale yard was established alongside the Bolton to Bury road, adjacent to one of the new pits, and a tubway was constructed to convey coal to here from the pits at Long Lane. The layout of the line can be seen on the first edition of the 25" map, surveyed in 1889-90.

In 1900, the colliery was taken over by T and H T Scowcroft, who continued to work it until between 1912 and 1917. The Crompton Fold pumping pit was retained until 1928 to serve the Tonge Colliery of the firm [89].

John Fletcher's New House Colliery

To the south east of Crompton Fold, the 2" drawings of 1841 and the first edition of the 6" map, surveyed in 1844 to 1847, mark New House Colliery, together with a tramroad running to a landsale depot on the Bury Road.

We identify this as the Breightmet Colliery which, in 1841, was being worked by John Fletcher [90], who was probably the son of Matthew the Elder and cousin of Matthew referred to above. The colliery passed to Thomas Fletcher before 1853/4. From a mineral takings plan of 1863 [91], revised up to March 1876, it is evident that the greater part of the coal was leased from the Earl of Derby, with a smaller portion owned by Revd James Whitehead.

The Mines Lists show that Thomas Fletcher continued in occupation up to 1885, although the colliery was not in production in 1878 and 1879. As there is no evidence of any substantial roadway to the colliery site on later maps, we think that the tramroad and the associated coal depot continued in use until the colliery closed.

Bradshaw Hall and Top o' th' Meadow Collieries

We conclude the section on Tonge and Breightmet with the later developments which took place in the area south of the Crompton Fold Estate.

In the 1860s there was an attempt to reopen the pit opposite the entrance to Bradshaw Hall, mentioned earlier. The Mines Lists for 1864 and 1865 show a short lived Long Lane Colliery of Thomas Seddon. In 1908, Samuel Scowcroft and Sons Ltd were more successful. However, what they called their Bradshaw Hall Colliery proved difficult to work because of water problems and was abandoned on 31st December 1928.

A little further to the east, Thomas Seddon had his Top o th' Meadow Colliery, worked under a lease granted by the executors of Edmund Ashworth in 1860 [92 - 97]. This closed in 1870, on expiry of the lease, but was reopened by Samuel Scowcroft and Sons Ltd, under the title of Moss Lane Colliery. The first entry is in the Mines Lists for 1926, when it is noted to be "reopening and sinking shaft". Moss Lane closed in 1935, the Mines Lists recording that it was abandoned in June of that year.

DARCY LEVER AND LITTLE LEVER

The Darcy Lever Coal Company's Collieries

The first reference to the Darcy Lever Coal Company which we have found is in 1848, when the firm appeared in Slater's Directory [35]. It had evidently been in existence for a few years before that.

The mines worked by the company were in an area south of Moss Lane, Darcy Lever, and by 1841, when the survey was made for the first edition of the 1" map, they had been connected to the Manchester, Bolton and Bury Canal by a tramroad. The line, which was about 1200 yards long, started at a basin near the 9¼ mile post on the canal [98], where the firm's No 9, or New, Pit was situated [99]. It terminated at pits near Croft Side and the 2" drawings, used in the preparation of the 1" map, also show a long branch running eastwards. The branch is not marked on the first edition of the 6" map, surveyed in 1844 to 1847, and the implication is that it had been abandoned by then, together with the pits which it served.

The Darcy Lever Coal Company's plant was auctioned on 16th and 17th June 1858 due to expiry of the lease [100,101]. Items on offer included a 14 HP beam engine; a 16 HP beam engine by Musgrave of Bolton, nearly new; 2 egg ended boilers; 200 pit tubs, banking and railway wagons; 25 coal boats and 169 boxes. The pits must have closed until the leases were renegotiated a few years later, as the firm is omitted from the Mines Lists for the period from 1857 to 1860.

When the Darcy Lever Coal Company recommenced operations, it seems to have started a modernisation programme. We believe that the Davenport Colliery was sunk at this time; it was certainly working by 1874, when the Mines Lists first give details of the individual pits. Davenport Colliery was provided with standard gauge sidings which connected with the Lancashire and Yorkshire Railway's Bolton to Bury line by means of a triangular junction. The old tramroad was replaced by a tubway which ran from Davenport Colliery to the canal basin, serving the Croft Side and Victoria Pits along the way. Coal could thus be conveyed to the sidings at Davenport for loading into railway wagons or to the basin for despatch by canal. The firm's other pit, at Snow Hill, was off the route of the tubway, but was located alongside the canal, presumably with its own basin for loading boats.

The earliest agreement we have been able to trace covering the siding connection with the Lancashire and Yorkshire Railway is dated 18th February 1873 [102]. We think that the company may have had standard gauge sidings before that, perhaps as early as 1854, as on 15th December of that year there was a sale of wagons and horses [103]. Railway wagons are also mentioned in the sale of 16th and 17th June 1858 [100,101].

The firm became a limited liability company, which was registered under the title of the Darcy Lever Coal Co Ltd on 25th March 1897 [104]. Miles Settle, the Managing Director, who had over 40 years service with the firm, retired in December 1899 and his son, William Settle, took over [105]. However, the collieries did not last much longer.

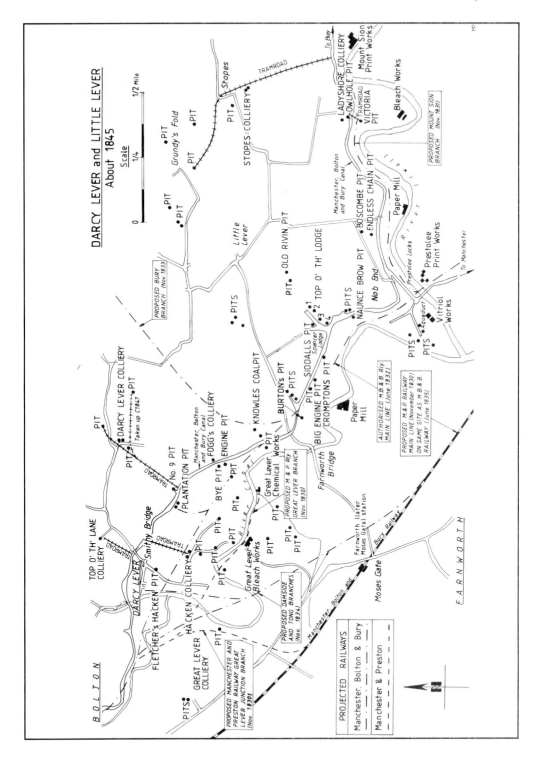

DARCY LEVER and LITTLE LEVER
About 1845

Davenport Pit had already closed and is last shown in the Mines Lists for 1890. There was an attempt to reopen Snow Hill Colliery, which had closed some years earlier. Although the Mines Lists indicate that some work was undertaken during the period from 1889 to 1897, the pit never seems to have come into production again and was finally discontinued in 1898.

Production at Croftside had virtually stopped by 1900, while at Victoria it continued for another year. Then it was announced that all the firm's pits were to cease work completely from 28th January 1901 [106,107], although the debenture holders won an action in the High Court for the business to carry on for a further six months [108]. No more coal was produced but some men were kept on to maintain the underground roadways in good condition and to look after the plant.

In January 1902 it was decided to abandon the mines. Some plant had been offered for sale on 5th November 1901 [109] and there was a further dismantlement sale on 17th to 19th September 1902, which included two tank locomotives with 10" and 13" cylinders [110,111]. The siding connection with the Lancashire and Yorkshire Railway was closed on 15th November 1902 and the points taken out in October 1909 [112].

We have only very limited information about the locomotives used by the Darcy Lever Coal Company. We know that in April 1884 the firm was advertising that it required a second hand standard gauge tank locomotive with 4 wheels and 6" to 9" cylinders [113], but we do not know what response there was.

A few years later, a four coupled saddle tank was purchased second hand. It had been built by Manning, Wardle and Company of Leeds and had been supplied to T A Walker, contractor for the construction of the Manchester Ship Canal, with the name WESTON. The manufacturer's records shows that it was in the hands of the Darcy Lever Coal Company by April 1894.

We presume that this was one of the locomotives included in the sale in 1902, but we have been unable to identify the second one.

Andrew Knowles' Little Lever and Darcy Lever Collieries

The Knowles family had leases covering a wide area of land in the southern parts of Darcy Lever and in Little Lever. Intensive mining dates from the opening of the Manchester, Bolton and Bury Canal in 1797 and Robert Knowles (1756 - 1819) and his son Andrew Knowles (1783 - 1847) were well established here in the early years of the nineteenth century.

By 1838 Andrew had taken his sons Robert (1804 ? -1871), Thomas (1807-1872), John (?- 1852) and James (1812 -1886) into the business [114,115]. The firm subsequently traded under the title of Andrew Knowles and Sons. Following the death of Thomas Knowles on 4th August 1872 [82], there was a dispute about the inheritance which resulted in a reorganisation of the family's business affairs. Robert and James retired as partners and their places were taken by Andrew and Kay Knowles, sons of Robert, by Andrew and Robert Millington Knowles, sons of James, and by John Knowles, son of Thomas [116 to 119]. Andrew Knowles and Sons Ltd was formed in September 1873 [120].

Most of the pits we describe here were situated near to the canal, on which the firm operated a large fleet of boats.

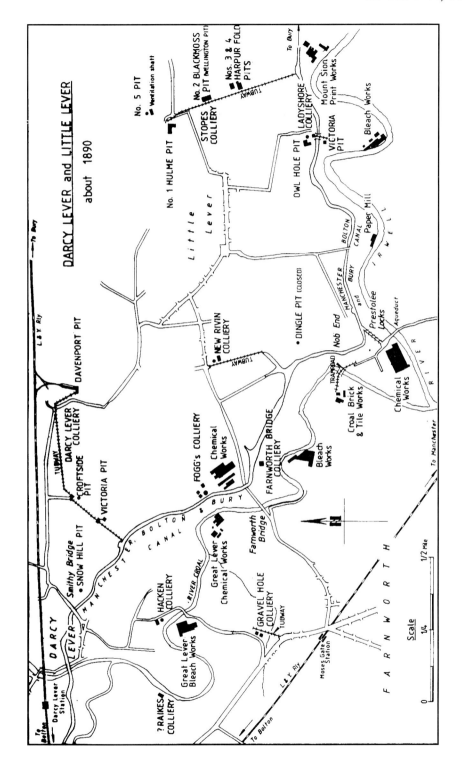

DARCY LEVER and LITTLE LEVER
about 1890

Top o' th' Lane Colliery - Little Lever

The earliest leases relating to Top o' th' Lane that we have been able to trace were granted by J E Bradshaw to Robert, Thomas, John and James Knowles in November 1836 [114]. There was a further lease[121], from Thomas and Ann Scowcroft to Messrs Knowles, in September 1846 . The Mines Lists show that by 1853/4 the property in the occupation of Andrew Knowles and Sons.

The 2" drawings of about 1840 show that Top o' th' Lane Colliery was connected to a basin on the Manchester Bolton and Bury Canal near Smithy Bridge by a short tramroad, on a course adjacent to that from the pits at Crompton Fold, mentioned earlier. Unlike this latter line, the one from Top o' th' Lane was still apparently in use when the surveys were made in 1844 to 1847 for the first edition of the 6" map.

The Liverpool and Bury Railway, opened in November 1848, passed close to Top o th' Lane Colliery. A revision of the 6" map published about 1850 suggests that the tramroad to the canal was abandoned and replaced by a loading dock on the railway. This is to some extent confirmed by an estate plan, dated March 1857 [122]. A narrow gauge tramroad is shown, running westwards from the colliery, parallel to the railway, but the area covered by the plan is too limited to locate the main line sidings.

The colliery seems to have closed around 1861 and is not shown in the Mines Lists for 1862 and subsequent years.

Hacken Colliery - Darcy Lever

Moving south along the canal, past the Darcy Lever Coal Company's Snow Hill Pit, we come to Hacken Colliery. This was situated on the opposite bank, on land owned by the Earl of Bradford. In 1820, it was being worked by Ralph Fletcher and an estate plan of that date [123] shows three pits linked by a short tramroad to the canal. A fourth pit, alongside Hacken Lane, is labelled "Fletcher's pit for getting the Hacken coal".

The lease was later transferred to the firm of Andrew Knowles and Sons, shown in occupation in the Mines Lists for 1853/4. In 1859 or 1860 the colliery was flooded when water broke through from old workings and was closed as a result. From the records of discussions between Messrs Knowles' representatives and the Earl of Bradford's agent it is clear that the tramroad had been in use up to time of closure[124 to 129] ; there is also mention of a "harbour" on the canal. An inventory [130] of 20th June 1862 shows the colliery was equipped with a lifting engine with a 16"x 7'9" cylinder and a winding engine with a 16" x 3'4" cylinder.

As Andrew Knowles and Sons did not intend to reopen the pits, the lease reverted to the Earl of Bradford, who redeveloped the colliery. Although Knowles offered to sell the rails from the tramroad at half price, the offer does not seem to have been taken up, as rent would have had to be paid to Mr Fletcher for a portion of the line which crossed his land. The tramroad was abandoned and the Earl of Bradford's new colliery seems to have relied entirely on road transport. The Hacken Sewage Works, completed by Bolton Corporation in 1886 [131], obliterated the earlier pits and the tramroad to the canal.

Fogg's Colliery - Little Lever and Darcy Lever

Continuing past the Darcy Lever Coal Company's loading basin serving the tramroad from the Croftside Pits, we arrive at the site of one of the early Fogg's Collieries. This was located in Darcy Lever Township and a take plan of 1838 [132] shows that the workings extended under the canal, with the Bye Pit and the Engine Pit situated on the west bank.

The colliery was being worked by a Mr Williams in the early part of 1835 and subsequently by his executors. We think that it passed to Messrs Knowles in 1838, as a draft lease from a Mrs Jones and a Mr Benson, dated 20th June of that year, gave the firm mining rights under Fogg's Estate in Darcy Lever and Little Lever [115].

Coal, under what is described as Fogg's Estate at Darcy Lever, was advertised to be let in April 1849 [133]. This was clearly a re-lease of an existing colliery, as the engines and machinery could be taken at valuation, but we have been unable to discover whether the advertisement refers to the colliery mentioned in the previous paragraph or to another working in the same area.

Further south, on the west bank of the canal beyond the Blackshaw Brook and over the Little Lever boundary, the first edition of the 6" map marks a number of pits, including a group labelled Knowles Coal Pits. We think that these had possibly been sunk around the turn of the century and had passed into the Knowles family occupation a result of the 1838 lease.

There was considerable redevelopment later in the century, possibly around 1868, the first year that Andrew Knowles and Sons' Fogg's Colliery is shown separately in the Mines Lists. New pits were sunk on the east bank of the canal, just south of Blackshaw Brook, to replace the earlier workings. All the previous pits had completely disappeared by the time the survey was carried out for the second edition of the 6" map in 1889 to 1891.

The new colliery, like the original ones, was so close to the canal that no tramroad of any significant extent was needed. Coal was loaded directly into boats at the pit yard. This was not always without its difficulties; output was disrupted towards the end of 1910 when a wooden bridge spanning the canal collapsed and the chute could not be used to load barges [134]. The colliery closed two years later, in May 1912 [135].

The Spencer Lodge Pits, New Rivin and Dingle - Little Lever

South of Hall Lane and stretching as far as Spencer Lodge, on both sides of the canal, mining went back to the turn of the century, if not earlier. A series of take plans [136 to 144], covering the period from 1809 to 1821, mark a number of small shafts on the east side of the canal, north of Spencer Lodge. They have names such as John Horrocks Pit, Higher Old Engine Pit, Siddalls Pit, new pit at Spencer Lodge, Old Engine Pit next canal, Crop Pit, Ladder Pit, Middle Pit.

The earlier plans refer to coal got by Mr Robert Knowles and we presume that the workings were taken over, after his death in 1819, by his son Andrew. We think that the lease dated 16th March 1807, from the Trustees of Robert Andrews to Robert and Andrew Knowles relates to mines in this area [145].

To the east of Spencer Lodge, an estate plan of 1830 marks five pits, on land owned by the executors of J Radcliffe [146]. Unfortunately, the plan gives no clue as to who was working the colliery at the time. There must have been some later developments near here, as there is a report of an accident in 1849 at Ginger Fold which was being sunk then [147].

By the mid 1840s, when the survey was made for the first edition of the 6" map, the group of pits north of Spencer Lodge had disappeared, but those to the east are still shown. Andrew Knowles and Sons subsequently sank the New Rivin and Dingle Pits, to work the coal in this area.

New Rivin Colliery was adjacent to Hall Lane, not far from Little Lever village. A tubway was constructed to transport coal to a basin at Top o' th' Lodge, near to the yard where the firm's large fleet of canal boats were repaired [98]. New Rivin Colliery closed in the mid 1890s, last appearing in the Mines Lists for 1896.

Dingle Colliery was situated on the east bank of the canal, south of Spencer Lodge. It first appears in the Mines Lists for 1874 and is last shown in 1881.

Farnworth Bridge Colliery - Little Lever

The first edition of the 6" map shows a series of shafts immediately south of Hall Lane on the west side of the canal. It describes them as the Farnworth Bridge Collieries and identifies Burton's Pit, Big Engine Pit and Crompton's Pit.

There was a major reconstruction by Andrew Knowles and Sons, probably in the late 1850s or early 1860s. The new colliery was situated on the west side of the canal immediately to the south of the aqueduct over Hall Lane. There was no need for any extensive tramroad system as the colliery had its own harbour in the pit yard, where coal could be loaded directly into boats. The colliery was sold in the early 1880s to John Fletcher and Sons, first appearing in the Mines Lists under the new owners in 1884. It was later used as a pumping station for Ladyshore Colliery.

Prestolee

Before following the Bury Branch of the canal and describing the Ladyshore and Stopes collieries which it served, it is convenient to deal with the area at the bottom of Prestolee Locks. Here, the lower level of the canal extended northwards beyond the aqueduct for some 200 yards and there was also an arm of similar length, leading off in a westerly direction.

The first edition of the 6" map shows that the western arm served a number of small coal pits and a vitriol works belonging to Benjamin Rawlinson, built in 1824 [98]. The works was subsequently extended to occupy most of the site between the canal and the River Croal. It closed towards the end of the century and was demolished soon afterwards.

The Croal Brick and Tile works was established between 1890 and 1910. In 1918 James Oakes, who also owned the Darley brickworks, was recorded as the proprietor [148]. To bring in supplies of coal and to take away the finished products, a short narrow gauge railway was built, which crossed the Croal on a bridge and terminated at the northern arm of the canal. Horses presumably provided the motive power and we have found no record of locomotives being used. The works closed in the 1940s and the centre arch of the bridge collapsed soon afterwards. The rest of the bridge was demolished in 1987 [98].

Opposite
Contrasting modes of transport at Fogg's Colliery in the early years of the present century. The upper picture shows the Manchester, Bolton and Bury Canal with a fleet of boats waiting to have their empty boxes exchanged for loaded ones. The lower picture is of a Lancashire steam wagon, which replaced horses and carts on local deliveries.   John Ryan and Alex Appleton collections respectively

Ladyshore Colliery

Ladyshore Colliery was located on the Bury Branch of the canal, a little over half a mile east of the junction at Prestolee and to the south of Little Lever village. It appears to have been started by John Fletcher, owner of the Ladyshore Estate, around 1830 [149].

In 1832, proposals were put forward to construct a branch of the Manchester, Bolton and Bury Railway which would have served both the colliery and the Mount Sion Bleachworks. However this scheme was never pursued and the colliery had to rely on water transport for the whole of its life, spanning almost 120 years. A boat yard was established at an early date, where the canal craft were built and maintained. The work which was undertaken there has been described in a booklet by Alex Waterson, who was latterly in charge of boat building for the firm [150].

Coal was carried in boxes, which were put on to the boats using a crane. The loading basin was on the north side of the canal, where the Owl Hole Pit was situated. The Victoria Pit was on the south side and was connected to the basin by a short tramway, which crossed the canal by Bridge 67. This was reputedly built in 1833 and replaced in the 1890s [98].

John Fletcher's two sons, Herbert and Walter, were later taken into the partnership, when the title of the firm became John Fletcher and Sons. On John Fletcher's death, on 24th March 1876 [82], Herbert and Walter inherited equal shares in the property. Their partnership was dissolved on 30th March 1880, when Walter retired and Herbert took over control [149].

As mentioned earlier, the Farnworth Bridge Colliery was acquired from Andrew Knowles and Sons Ltd in the mid 1880s, but was used for pumping purposes, not coal production. There were evidently two pits here, recorded separately as Farnworth Bridge Top and Bottom Pits in the Mines Lists for 1891 to 1904. A new pit was sunk at Back o' th' Barn around 1894 but was a relatively short lived venture and had closed by 1907.

By this time, the workings from Ladyshore Colliery had extended far beyond the boundaries of the Herbert Fletcher's own estate. Latterly the firm held mining leases from Lord Wilton, Lord Derby, Andrew's Trustees, Radcliffe's Trustees, Fletcher's Trustees, Andrew Knowles and Sons Ltd, the Little Lever Estates and the Lever Bank Trustees [149].

Herbert Fletcher died on 16th September 1895 [82,149] and a limited liability company with the title Ladyshore Coal Co Ltd was formed in 1906 or 1907. The company was subsequently reorganised as the Ladyshore Coal Co (1930) Ltd.

Ladyshore Colliery and its associated Farnworth Bridge pumping station were taken over by the National Coal Board on 1st January 1947, but did not survive much longer. Closure came at the beginning of June 1949 [149] and the Mines Lists show that the Owl Hole and Victoria Pits and the pumping pit at Farnworth Bridge were formally abandoned in September of the same year. Some of the original buildings remained at Ladyshore up to the end [151], bearing 1837 date stones.

Until the closure, the Ladyshore Coal Company and its successor, the National Coal Board, continued to despatch coal to Bury on what had become an isolated section of the canal. It is recorded that, in 1941, 53000 tons were shipped [98]. Examples of the wooden canal boats, together with the coal boxes which they carried, are now on exhibition at the Boat Museum at Ellesmere Port. The collection includes some boats which were built after 1947, by the National Coal Board at the Ladyshore boat yard.

Thomas Fletcher's Stopes Collieries

Stopes Colliery was worked by another branch of the Fletcher family. It probably dates from 1830, when Matthew Fletcher granted a mining lease at Grundy Fold to Jacob and Thomas Fletcher [152]. Thomas Fletcher's son, also Thomas, joined the firm later and the father and son were the sole partners after Jacob retired on 25th November 1868 [153,154]. Thomas Fletcher and Sons Ltd was registered on 11th May 1898 [155] to take over the partnership's collieries at Stopes, Bradley Fold and Outwood.

The first edition of the 6" map, surveyed in 1844 to 1846, marks a series of pits on a north to south line along the boundary of Little Lever and Radcliffe. A tramroad about three quarters of a mile in length is shown, starting at a point near Grundy's Fold and terminating at a basin on the canal about a quarter of a mile east of Ladyshore Colliery.

By the late 1880s, when the second edition of the 6" map was surveyed, the most northerly portion of the tramroad had been dismantled and the remainder turned into a tubway. The tubway started at the No 1 or Hulme Pit, at the back of the Wellington Hotel on Stopes Road. It then crossed Stopes Road on the level to reach the No 2 or Black Moss Pit, also known as the Wellington Pit. It continued past the Nos 3 and 4 Harpur Fold Pits before reaching the canal. Pingot Pit and Stopes No 4 Pit were closed in 1893 and are not shown in the Mines List after that date. Stopes No 3 Pit is shown as discontinued in the 1907 list and the remaining pits as abandoned in the 1908 list.

A compulsory winding up order was obtained against the company by its creditors on 26th November 1908 [156]. The plant at Stopes and at the Bradley Fold had already been put up for auction on 9th and 10th September 1908, along with the firm's canal wharves at Radcliffe and Bury [157]. Among the plant associated with Stopes we can identify the 10" cylinder tramway hauling engine, the 1120 yards of endless chain and gearing to the canal wharf and the "strongly built double deck canal wharf landing stage". There were also 80 canal boats, with a capacity of 15 to 20 tons, and 550 28cwt boxes.

The Wellington Pits were reopened by A J Gilbert, who appears in the Mines Lists for 1911. By 1913 Wellington Colliery (Stopes) Co Ltd had been formed, but the Mines Lists show that the colliery ceased working in July 1915. In 1917 the occupier is given as J W Heaton, although the colliery is shown as disused.

It appears that the canal wharf and tubway were refurbished in connection with the reopening of the colliery. In 1913, it was agreed that the Canal Company would dredge the basin at the expense of Peter Spence and Sons, who were reconstructing the landing stage [98]. In view of the ephemeral nature of the revived mining activity we are not sure whether any coal was actually despatched by canal at this period.

William Thornley, Little Lever

We conclude with a brief reference to an advertisement placed by a Mr William Thornley of Little Lever in August 1875 [158]. He wanted a second hand 9 HP Chaplin locomotive for use on a 2'6" gauge line. We have been unable to discover any more information about Mr Thornley or why he needed a locomotive.

LOCOMOTIVE SUMMARY

Hulton Collieries

William Hulton about 1858
Hulton Colliery Company to 1868
William Ford Hulton to May 1879
William Wilbraham Brethyn Hulton to March 1886
Hulton Colliery Co Ltd from 29th March 1886
Last Colliery closed April 1934

PHOENIX   0-4-0 (?)   Crook and Dean   1831

MANCHESTER   2-2-0   Galloway, Bowman
                                        and Glasgow
    Thomas (Ref 7) states that this engine was hired to the Hulton collieries from time to time

BEE   0-4-0 IC   EB   1832
    An uncorroborated account suggests that this engine was bought by William Hulton from John
        Hargreaves Junr about 1840

BEE   0-4-0ST IC   SS   1137   1859
    It is presumed that this was the engine which was sold to Thomas Mitchell and Sons Ltd, Bolton, 8-1903
    According to an old employee it was cut up at the Tar Works

SQUIRE   0-4-0ST IC   SS   2479   1875
    Sold to Thos Mitchell and Sons Ltd, Bolton, 4-1911
    According to an old employee it was cut up at Pendlebury Fold

PRINCE OF WALES   2-4-0T IC (?)
    Recalled by old employee who stated that it was rebuilt from a tender locomotive and came from the
        LNWR. This has not been confirmed independently

PRESCOTT   0-6-0ST IC   HE   66   1871   12"x18"   3'1"
    Ex Crow Orchard Colliery, Skelmersdale via T D Swift, dealer, Ince, about 1886
    Scrapped or sold about 1898 according to an old employee

No 3 ATHERTON   0-6-0ST IC   VF   1435   1895   13"x22"   3'6"
    New
    Sold to a Yorkshire firm in 1934 according to an old employee

No 4   0-6-0ST IC   P   855   1900   16"x22"   3'10"
    Class X
    New to Chequerbent
    Was sent to Cronton Colliery according to an old employee
    Alternative version is sold to Shelton Iron and Steel Co Ltd, Stoke on Trent, in 1934

No 5   0-6-0ST IC   P   952   1903   16"x22"   3'10"
    Class X
    New to Chequerbent
    Transferred Cronton Colliery, 12-1934

No 6   0-6-0ST IC   P   1120   1907   16"x22"
    Class X
    New to Chequerbent
    Transferred to Cronton Colliery

Hulton Steel Works

John Booth and Sons (Bolton) Ltd
Works still open, rail traffic ceased about 1960

I D C No 70	0-4-0ST OC	DK		1915	6"x10"	1'8"
		Rbt 1923				

Purchased by J R Booth from Ipswich Docks for use on contract for British Acetate Silk Corporation Ltd, Stowmarket
Transferred to Hulton Steel Works on completion of contract
To Harry Stephenson and Sons Ltd, Hindley, about 1932

Jose K Holt Gordon Ltd

Scrap yard at Chequerbent established 1954
Yard still in operation at end of 1993

ROBERT	0-6-0ST OC	AE	1600	1912	16"x22"	

Purchased at Cronton Colliery, 6-1965
Still at site 11-1993

HARRY	0-6-0ST IC	HC	1776	1944	18"x26"	4'3"

Purchased at Walkden 1976
Ex Walkden Yard 14-12-1976
Sold to Shropshire Railway Preservation Society, early 1992

Other locomotive broken up by the firm include:

SHAH	0-6-0ST IC	WCI		1874	

Purchased at Clock Face Colliery, near St Helens, in 1956 or 1957

LINNET	0-4-0ST OC	MW	1543	1902	

Purchased at Huncoat Colliery, Burnley, in 1963

LARK	0-4-0ST OC	MW	1719	1907	

Purchased at Huncoat Colliery, Burnley, in 1963

PARR	0-6-0WT OC	Haydock		1886	

Purchased at The Park Colliery, Garswood, in 1963

MAKERFIELD	0-6-0WT OC	Haydock		1874	

Purchased at The Park Colliery, Garswood, in 1963

JOHN	0-6-0ST IC	P&K		1911	

Purchased at the Standish Collieries, Wigan, in 1965

No 2	0-6-0ST IC	MW	1925	1917	

Purchased at the Standish Collieries, Wigan, in 1965

NEWTON	0-6-0T IC	MW	1504	1900	

Purchased at Lea Green Colliery, St Helens, in 1965

EARLESTOWN	0-6-0ST IC	MW	1503	1900	

Purchased at Haydock in 1965

ALLENBY	0-4-0ST OC	AB	1625	1919

Purchased at Haydock in 1965

GORDON	0-6-0ST IC	RSH	7288	1945

Purchased at Bickershaw Colliery, Leigh, in 1968

BOLD	0-4-0ST OC	P	1737	1927

Purchased at Ravenhead Colliery, St Helens, in 1969

RAVEN	0-4-0ST OC	HL	3800	1935

Purchased at Huncoat Colliery, Burnley, in 1969

KESTREL	0-4-0ST OC	HL	3875	1936

Purchased at Huncoat Colliery, Burnley, in 1969

HUMPHREY	0-6-0ST IC	RSH	7293	1945

Purchased at Walkden in 1976

WEASEL	0-6-0ST IC	HE	3844	1957

Purchased at Walkden in 1976

Many of the engines were broken up where they stood, but a few, including JOHN, No 2, NEWTON, ROBERT and HARRY, were taken to the yard alongside Chequerbent Station (Refs 32 and 159).

Great Lever Colliery

Second, third, fourth and fifth Earls of Bradford
Colliery closed 1922

ATALANTA
Sent from Thomas Mitchell and Sons Ltd, Bolton, 1-1890, to Great Lever Colliery, either hired or sold

	0-4-0ST OC	P	644	1896	10"x14"	2'6"

Class M4
New
Sold 1922 to Cudworth and Johnson Ltd, dealers, Wrexham and resold to Low Beechburn Coal Co Ltd, Co Durham

WINNIE	0-4-0ST OC	MW	880	1883	9"x14"	2'6"

Hired from Thomas Mitchell and Sons Ltd, Bolton,8-1909

Darcy Lever Colliery

Darcy Lever Coal Company to March 1897
Darcy Lever Coal Co Ltd from 25th March 1897
Colliery closed January 1901

	0-4-0ST OC	HE	424	1887	10"x15"	2'9"

New to T A Walker, Manchester Ship Canal contract as WESTON
At Darcy Lever by 4-1894

Two tank locomotives, with 10" and 13" cylinders were auctioned in September 1902

William Thornley, Little Lever

Advertised in The Engineer for 13-8-1875 that he required a second hand 9 HP Chaplin locomotive for use on a 2'6" gauge line.

References to Chapter 4

1   *"The Landed Gentry"* - J B Burke, London, 1870

2   *"The Landed Gentry"* - J B Burke, London, 1894

3   BC 2-8-1828

4   BC 28-2-1829

5   BC 4-6-1831

6   BC 14-1-1832

7   *"The Liverpool and Manchester Railway"* - R H G Thomas - B T Batsford Ltd, London, 1980

8   BC 13-4-1839

9   Manchester Courier 10-4-1839

10   *"The Railways of Great Britain and Ireland"* - Francis Whishaw - John Weale, London, 1842

11   Parliamentary Papers, 1842, Vol XLI

12   LRO PDRs 195 and 196

13   9&10 Vic cap cccxii; 3rd August 1846

14   10&11 Vic cap ccxxi; 2nd July 1847

15   LRO PDR 539

16   LRO PDR 707

17   LRO NCBw 19/1

18   BC 12-1868

19   Line Plan of Bolton and Leigh Railway - LNWR, Euston, 1888 - 2 chains to 1 inch - At BRPB, Manchester

20   BC 17-4-1875

21   BC 24-5-1879

22   *Iron* 9-4-1886

23   BC19-8-1892

24   *Iron* 2-9-1892

25   LNWR Sdgs Diag 135, Dec 1916

26   WO 10-4-1886

27   CG 10-8-1934

28   BEN 5-4-1973

29   Letter John Booth and Sons (Bolton) Ltd to Frank Smith 2-8-1960

30   *"The Industrial Railways of the Wigan Coalfield - Vol 1"* -Townley, Smith and Peden - Runpast Publishing, Cheltenham, 1991

31   Endorsement on Line Plan of Bolton and Kenyon Rly - LNWR, Euston 1888 - 2 chains to 1inch - at BRPB, Manchester

32   Letter from Jose K Holt Gordon Ltd to Frank Smith 28-9-1993

33   *"The Canal Duke's Collieries"* - Glen Atkinson - Neil Richardson, Swinton, nd (about 1980)

34   *"Debrett's Peerage and Baronetage"* - Debrett's Peerage Ltd, London, 1990

35   *"Royal National Commercial Directory and Topography of the County of Lancaster"*- Isaac Slater - Manchester, 1848

36   *"Royal National Commercial Directory and Topography of the County of Lancaster"* - Isaac Slater - Manchester, 1851

37   8&9 Vic cap clxvi; 31st July 1845

38   L&YR Sdgs Diags 251, 17th Sept 1901 and 251a, 28th Aug 1907

39   BMB ZBR/5/10/7

40   BMB ZBR/5/51/7

41   CG 5-7-1889

42   Engineering 5-7-1889

43   BMB ZBR/5/51/184

44   BMB ZBR/5/51/188 45 BMB ZBR/5/51/189

46   BMB ZBR 5/53/266

47   BMB ZBR 5/53/277

48   BMB ZBR/5/54/47

49   BMB ZBR/5/54/405

50   BMB ZBR/5/54/490 51 BMB ZBR/5/57/138

52   BMB ZBR/5/57/274

53   BMB ZBR5/57/290

54   BMB ZBR 5/57/309

55   BMB ZBR 5/60/362

56   BMB ZBR 5/68/30

57   BMB ZBR 5/68/507 58 BMB ZBR 5/69/274

59   BMB ZBR 5/69/340

60   BMB ZBR 5/70/866

61   Endorsement on L&YR Sdg Diag 385 31st Dec 1921

62   MG 29-4-1922

63   WO 6-5-1922

64   *"Industries of Lancashire"* - Historical Publishing Co, London, 1889-90

65   *"Post Office Bolton Directory"* - Tillotson and Sons Ltd, Bolton, 1894

66   *"Post Office Bolton Directory"* - Tillotson and Sons Ltd, Bolton, 1896

67   BC 19-5-1883

68   L&YR Sdg Diag 385, 31st Dec 1921

69   *"Manchester Chamber of Commerce and Industry Regional Directory"* - Kemps Group (Printers and Publishers) Ltd, Birmingham, 1977

70   Line Plan of Bolton to Manchester Line - 1/1250 - BR, Euston, 1950 - at BRPB, Manchester

71   *"Smithills Hall"* - WD Billington - Halliwell Local History Society - 1991

72   BMB ZJA/1/1 Plan of Smithills Estate - 8 Cheshire Chains to 1 inch - 1801

73   BMB ZAL953 74 BMB ZAL 956

75   WRO DDX/Ap 33/7

76   *"Bradshaw Works"* - J J Francis - Turton Local History Society, 1979

77	BC 11-11-1871
78	BMB ZJA 363/7
79	BMB ZJA 442
80	BC 2-6-1849
81	BMB ZJA 98/3/96
82	Probate Records
83	BMB ZJA 302/6
84	BMB ZAL 22
85	BC 25-1-1879
86	BMB ZAL 195
87	BMB ZJA 68/1
88	BMB PBO 73
89	BEN 25-5-1959
90	BC 21-8-1841
91	BMB ZLA 16/2
92	BMB ZSH/13/6
93	BMB ZSH/13/1
94	BMB ZSH/13/2
95	BMB ZSH 13/6
96	BMB ZSH 13/7
97	BMB ZSH 13/8
98	*"Towpath Guide to the Manchester, Bolton and Bury Canal"* - Steven Parker and Richard Chester-Browne - Manchester, Bolton and Bury Canal Society, 1989
99	BMB ZLA 16/7
100	BC 5-6-1868
101	BC 12-6-1858
102	L&YR Sdgs Diag 38, 23rd Aug 1895
103	BC 9-12-1854
104	BEN 1-4-1897
105	BC 16-12-1899
106	BJ 2-2-1901
107	FJ 16-2-1901
108	BC 9-2-1901
109	BC 11-10-1901
110	MG 5-9-1902
111	CG 5-9-1902
112	Endorsement on L&YR Sdg Diag 38, 23rd Aug 1895
113	CG 25-4-1884
114	LRO DDX/29/27
115	LRO DDX/29/28
116	LRO DDX/29/39 117 LRO DDX/29/40
118	LRO DDX/29/41
119	LRO DDX/29/42
120	MJ 20-9-1873
121	LRO DDX/29/29
122	BMB ZJA 456/9
123	BMB ZJA 338/1 Plan of Raikes Hall Estate dated 22nd April 1820
124	BMB ZBR/5/22/54
125	BMB ZBR/5/22/56
126	BMB ZBR/5/22/56
127	BMB ZBR/5/22/64
128	BMB ZBR/5/23/9
129	BMB ZBR/5/23/58
130	BMB ZBR/5/23/6
131	BC 22-9-1888
132	BMB ZLA 16/1/1
133	BC 21-4-1849
134	FJ 2-9-1910
135	FJ 31-5-1912
136	BMB ZAL 390
137	BMB ZAL 391 138 BMB ZAL 395
139	BMB ZAL 397
140	BMB ZAL 400
141	BMB ZAL 402
142	BMB ZAL 403
143	BMB ZAL 404
144	BMBZAL 410
145	LRO DDX/29/26
146	BMB ZAL 394
147	BC 17-11-1849
148	*"Directory of Lancashire"* - Kelly's Directories Ltd, 1918
149	FJ 3-6-1949
150	*"Recollections of Boat Building at Ladyshore for the Manchester, Bolton, Bury Canal"*- Alec Waterson - publ by the author, 1982
151	*"Industrial Archaeology of Radcliffe and the Irwell Valley"*- K Howarth - in *Industrial Archaeology* Spring, 1974
152	SMM U65/24
153	BC 5-12-1868
154	LG 8-12-1868
155	FJ 28-5-1898
156	BJ 24-12-1908
157	BC 29-8-1908
158	*The Engineer* 13-8-1875
159	Observations communicated by Mr H D Bowtell

CHAPTER 5

RADCLIFFE AND BURY

Chapter 5 takes us to territory now within the Metropolitan Borough of Bury. Cotton textiles, engineering and paper manufacture accounted for the bulk of the district's trade until recent years. As at Bolton, there were, in relation to the size and population of the area, few private railway lines. Most firms relied on road transport to bring in raw materials from the nearest main line goods yard and to send away their finished products.

We start on the western boundary of the Metropolitan Borough, at Bradley Fold. We shall look first at the collieries dating from the middle of the nineteenth century, but which closed in the early years of the twentieth. We shall then go on to consider two factories which were established much later, both of which had main line railway connections.

From here, we move to Radcliffe, where the coal mining industry was firmly established by the 1840s, no doubt encouraged by the ever growing demand for fuel by the expanding textile industry and by the transport facilities offered by the Manchester, Bolton and Bury Canal. By 1873 virtually all the mines north of the Irwell had passed into the possession of Andrew Knowles and Sons Ltd, with production mainly concentrated at three collieries, each served by sidings connecting with the Lancashire and Yorkshire Railway.

North of the river large scale mining ceased in the 1890s. Only a few small pits and drifts continued to be worked sporadically and all these had ceased production before the second world war. South of the river, in the old township of Pilkington, Outwood Colliery, which we deal with in Chapter 6, remained at work until the early 1930s.

Before moving on to Bury, we look briefly at the narrow gauge railway system operated by A C Bealey and Co Ltd and the steam locomotives which worked on it.

Our explorations in Bury start with the railway installations belonging to the Borough Council. The sidings serving the electricity works and the corporation yard were relatively modest affairs. The railway system at the gas works was more substantial, with its own locomotives, and was one of the very few private lines which required an Act of Parliament.

We then turn to the topic of locomotive building in Bury. The East Lancashire Railway had its headquarters offices and also its principal locomotive depot here, where major repairs to the company's rolling stock were carried out. During the period from 1862 to 1877, after the amalgamation with the Lancashire and Yorkshire Railway, some 16 or 17 new locomotives were constructed. Also associated with the East Lancashire Railway was the firm of Richard Walker and Brother, which supplied twenty four locomotives during the period from 1846 to 1854. Many years later, around 1930, an old established firm, James C Kay and Co Ltd, made a brief excursion into the growing market for internal combustion locomotives.

Three paper manufacturing concerns had quite extensive internal railway systems. Two were in the vicinity of Heap Bridge, the Yates Duxbury mills actually being situated just beyond the Bury boundary. The third was at Gigg Lane.

We conclude the chapter with a section dealing with the firms served by private sidings on the Holcombe Brook Branch. Opened by the Bury and Tottington District Railway in November 1882, the branch gave access to a district not previously served by rail and several firms took advantage of the facilities which became available.

BRADLEY FOLD

Thomas Fletcher's Bradley Fold Collieries

Bradley Fold Colliery was located on the south side of the Lancashire and Yorkshire's Liverpool and Bury line. It appears to have been opened out in the 1840s by Thomas Fletcher and the first edition of the 6" map, surveyed in 1844 to 1847, before the railway was built, shows what is named as Tonge Lane Colliery on the site. The Mines Lists refer to it as Bents Colliery until the early 1860s. A siding connection was laid in at early date and a revision of the first edition of the 6" map, published about 1850, shows a triangular junction with the main line.

There seems to have been considerable expansion during the latter part of the nineteenth century and by 1890 there were four pits at work at Bradley Fold. There was also a short lived Radcliffe Moor Colliery, which according to the Mines Lists was operational from 1861 to 1872. Further north, there was the Ainsworth Red House Pit, which was later taken over by John Rylands and Son. Neither of these had a rail connection.

There were various changes in the partnership over the years, which we have mentioned in the previous chapter when dealing with Stopes Colliery. When Thomas Fletcher and Sons Ltd was formed in May 1898, all was not well at Bradley Fold. Nos 3 and 4 Pits had already stopped work in 1893 or 1894 and the men had been warned in 1897 that the whole colliery was to be closed because of lack of trade [1]. In fact, it continued in operation until 1908.

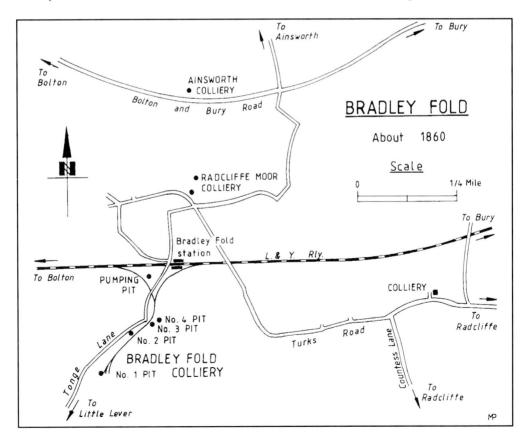

Before the firm was declared bankrupt in November 1908, the plant at Bradley Fold had already been sold on 9th and 10th September, along with that at Stopes [2]. Included in the items on offer was a locomotive shed, presumably at Bradley Fold, but no locomotive. The colliery company's sidings were taken up in September 1908, the connection at the west end in October 1909 and the connection at the east end in February 1911 [3].

Our information about the locomotives of Thomas Fletcher and Sons is far from complete and it is not entirely clear where those engines that we do know about were used. Locomotives were employed at both Bradley Fold and Outwood Collieries and it seems likely that they were moved from one location to the other as circumstances required.

The earliest locomotive we have been able to trace was supplied by Hudswell Clarke and Company, of Leeds, in 1882. According to the manufacturer's records it was delivered to Bradley Fold. It was sold in January 1902 to Thomas Mitchell and Sons Ltd, the Bolton machinery dealers, who noted that it was in need of repair. It was resold by Mitchells in 1904. We have been unable to confirm the suggestion made by some authorities that it was later used at Beeston Colliery, near Leeds.

Mitchells' records show that a locomotive named FARMERS FRIEND was hired to Thomas Fletcher and Sons Ltd in October 1901. We can identify this as a six coupled saddle tank which had been built in 1876 by Hudswell Clarke and Rodgers and used on the Garstang and Knott End Railway. It seems to have been acquired by Mitchells about 1900.

FARMERS FRIEND was presumably a replacement for the engine which Mitchells had bought from Fletchers. The hire period was to be not less than three months and may have been longer. Unfortunately, the records do not make it clear whether the engine was sent from Bolton to Bradley Fold or to Outwood.

Two new locomotives were purchased by Thomas Fletcher and Sons from Peckett and Sons of Bristol. The first to be delivered, in 1901, was a six coupled saddle tank of the maker's B1 Class. This was followed by an M4 class four coupled saddle tank in 1902. Both were acquired by the Clifton and Kersley Coal Co Ltd, following the sale of Outwood Colliery, although it seems possible that one of them may have been at Bradley Fold for a time before that.

Dobson and Barlow Ltd

We have already described the origins of the firm and the establishment of the Kay Street works in Bolton. By the turn of the century these premises had become too small to meet the firm's needs and a decision was made to erect a second factory on the north side of the Lancashire and Yorkshire Railway at Bradley Fold.

The first sod of the new works was cut on 13th November 1906 [4] and the first part of the plant was opened some months later. There were extensions in 1908, 1911 and again in 1921 and 1926 [5]. Dobson and Barlow Ltd was registered as a public company in 1907 [5,6] to take over from the private company with the same title which had been formed on 1st September 1891 [7].

The Bradley Fold works was provided with a connection with the adjacent Lancashire and Yorkshire Railway, under an agreement dated 6th April 1908 [8,9]. At this date wagons were presumably placed in the sidings by main line engines. As the factory expanded there were corresponding extensions to the railway system and it became necessary for the firm to make its own provisions for internal shunting. It was decided to use electric traction, employing overhead wire current collection. A locomotive was obtained from the British Westinghouse Company in 1911. Typical of its period, it had a central steeple cab and was equipped with two 25 HP motors, one on each axle [10].

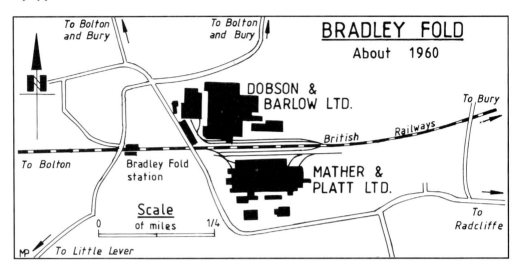

In 1931 Dobson and Barlow Ltd became a subsidiary of Platt Brothers (Holdings) Ltd, following a merger with Platt Brothers Ltd of Oldham, another old established firm of textile machinery manufacturers [11]. In the period after the second world war amalgamations in the industry led to the acquisition of Dobson and Barlow Ltd by Stone Platt Industries Ltd [11].

A new electric locomotive, very similar to the 1911 engine, was obtained in 1945 from Metropolitan Vickers Electrical Company. The original locomotive was kept in reserve for a time. It was still in existence in September 1953 [10] but is thought to have been broken up for scrap shortly afterwards.

The Metropolitan Vickers locomotive was taken out of use early in 1961, following the transfer of a small four wheeled diesel locomotive from Platt Brothers' Oldham works in March. The overhead wire system was dismantled by June of that year, but the electric locomotive seems to have remained out of use for a further two years, before being broken up in February 1963. The diesel locomotive was scrapped by April 1970. Prior to this, the railway system had been closed down, the agreement in respect of the main line connection having been cancelled as from 31st December 1968 [12].

The Dobson and Barlow name disappeared in 1970, when the Bradley Fold factory was taken over by Platt International Ltd [13] In 1973 Platt International acquired the Saco Lowell Corporation of the United States and in 1975 the firm changed its name to Platt Saco Lowell Ltd [11].

By 1977, the Bradley Fold factory was making bottle handling and cleaning equipment as well as textile machinery, with a workforce of 1200 [14]. The textile machinery plant closed in 1981 and only the foundry remained in operation. In March 1982 the parent company, Stone Platt Industries Ltd, was in liquidation [15]. The foundry at Bradley Fold, owned by the Platt Saco Lowell subsidiary, was sold to Columbus Foundries Inc of the United States, but this too closed in March 1984 [16].

The former Dobson and Barlow site is now occupied by an industrial estate and many of the original buildings survive, occupied by various firms engaged in light industry.

Radcliffe Royal Ordnance Factory, later Mather and Platt Ltd

Construction started in March 1940 [17] on a site on the south side of the London, Midland and Scottish Railway at Bradley Fold. Described as an engineering factory, the works was completed early in 1941, one of the products made there being breech blocks for anti-aircraft guns.

A siding connection was provided with the Bolton and Bury line and a four coupled diesel mechanical locomotive was supplied by the Hunslet Engine Company of Leeds in 1940 for shunting purposes within the works.

In 1946 the factory was purchased by Mather and Platt Ltd. This was an old established firm with a works at Park, near Miles Platting, manufacturing textile finishing machinery and general heavy engineering equipment. It acquired the Bradley Fold premises for post war diversification into machinery for food production and packaging.

The diesel locomotive was taken over by Mather and Platt along with the premises and continued to be used until the late 1960s, when rail traffic ceased. The agreement in respect of the main line siding connection was terminated on 30th April 1968 [12].

Mather and Platt Ltd was taken over by Wormald International Ltd towards the end of 1976 [18] and the Bradley Fold works came under the control of its subsidiary, Mather and Platt (Process Machinery) Ltd [19]. Production ceased at Easter 1983 [20]. The works was subsequently demolished and a housing estate built on the site.

THE RADCLIFFE COLLIERIES

Cockey Moor and Black Lane Collieries

The Radcliffe Tithe Map [21], dated 1841, marks three pits at Cockey Moor between the Bolton to Bury Turnpike and Starling Lane. These were on the Earl of Wilton's land and were then being worked by James Knowles (-1868), brother of Andrew Knowles (1783-1847). Black Lane Colliery, further south, alongside the Lancashire and Yorkshire Railway's Bolton to Bury line, was sunk by James Knowles in 1856 or 1857 [22], first appearing in the Mines Lists for the latter year.

James Knowles seems to have been none too successful with his colliery enterprise and the mines were mortgaged on at least two occasions to his relatives, in 1847 to his brother Andrew [23] and in 1857 to Andrew's sons, Robert, Thomas and James [24]. The plant at Cockey Moor and Black Lane, which included six steam engines, was put up for auction on instructions from John Middlehurst on 5th and 6th March 1866 [25,26,27]. The collieries were taken over by John Rylands and John Horrocks, trading as Rylands and Son, to whom the leases were transferred by the Earl of Wilton on 31st August 1868 [28].

There was a further transfer of the lease, from John Rylands and John Horrocks to Messrs Williams and Bowser through the intermediary of a Mr Charles Tattersall on 19th November 1873 [29,30]. The Mines Lists show that Williams and Bowser traded as the Cockey Moor Colliery Company until 1877, when a limited liability company with the same name was formed.

Cockey Moor Colliery, where new pits had been opened south of the Bolton to Bury road, ceased operations about 1880. Andrew Knowles and Sons Ltd took over the leases on 18th October 1880 [31] and worked the remaining coal from their pits in Radcliffe.

Cockey Moor Colliery appears to have relied on road transport throughout its life and we have found no evidence of a railway connection or a tramroad to the main line. Black Lane Colliery was adjacent to the Lancashire and Yorkshire Railway and we think it quite likely that a siding was provided. However, we lack positive proof.

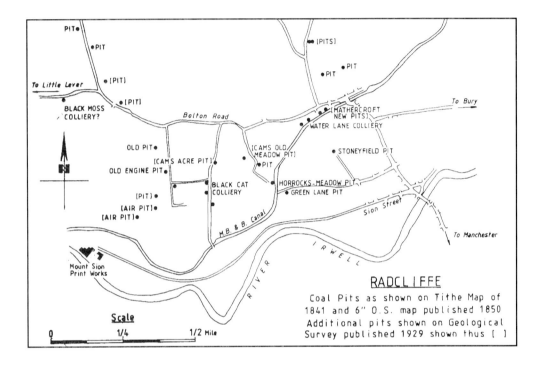

The Radcliffe Collieries of Andrew Knowles and Sons Ltd

The first edition 6" maps, surveyed in 1844 to 1847, mark a number of mines in the township of Radcliffe, in addition to those at Cockey Moor. Water Lane Colliery is shown on the north side of the Manchester, Bolton and Bury Canal at Hampson Square. Further south Green Lane Colliery and an unnamed colliery are shown on opposite sides of the canal. Black Cat Colliery is located in the fields to the west, on a lane running from the Bolton to Radcliffe Turnpike to the canal at Nickerhole Bridge. North of Hagside, there is Bank Top Colliery, again adjacent to the canal. Finally, just over the Bury boundary, Hinds Colliery is shown alongside the Bolton to Bury railway.

We know that Hinds Colliery was being worked by a Mr Robinson in 1846 [32]. Because of its proximity to the Lancashire and Yorkshire Railway we think that it must have been served by a private siding. The colliery only seems to have had a short life, as it does not appear in the Mines Lists for 1853/4.

The Radcliffe Tithe Map [21], dated 1841, shows that Water Lane and Green Lane Collieries were occupied by Knowles and Company on land owned by the Earl of Wilton. The tithe map also shows a third colliery, worked by Knowles and Company, on the south side of the Bolton and Radcliffe Turnpike, near the Little Lever boundary. It presumably closed a few years later, as it is not shown on the 6" map.

Although we have not been able to trace the occupiers of the remaining collieries, we think that they were, at least in later years, also associated with the Knowles family. The first issue of the Mines Lists, for the years 1853 and 1854, shows the firm of Knowles and Hall with collieries at Radcliffe Bridge, which we equate with Water Lane and Green Lane, and at Bank Top. Reservoir Colliery, which was possibly a new name for Black Cat, is shown in the lists from 1856 to 1860.

The partners in Knowles and Hall were Henry Hall and Robert and Thomas Knowles, sons of Andrew and nephews of James, mentioned earlier in connection with the Cockey Moor mines [33]. By the 1860s Robert and Thomas had been joined by their brother James; Henry Hall had been replaced by William Crippin. The firm continued, however, to trade as Knowles and Hall [34] until 1873.

As we have described in Chapter 4, there was a reorganisation of the firm of Andrew Knowles and Sons, which had a ¾ share in the Radcliffe mines [35,36], following the death of Thomas Knowles on 4th August 1872 [37]. Andrew Knowles and Sons Ltd was formed in September 1873 [38] and took over control at Radcliffe as it did elsewhere.

From 1874 the Mines Lists go into greater detail than previously. In that year Andrew Knowles and Sons' Radcliffe collieries were shown as Allen's Green, Green Lane, Hampson Meadow and Withins Lane. Hagside and Openshaw Fold were added to the lists in 1875, Canal Side in 1876 and Whittaker Bridge in 1879.

Hagside, Openshaw Fold and Canal Side were quite small affairs near the Bury boundary and were worked later in conjunction with Withins Lane Colliery. Neither Openshaw Fold or Canal Side seem to have had rail connections, but Hagside was served by a small bank of sidings, located on the opposite side of the East Lancashire line to the pit [39]. Canal Side seems to have replaced the earlier Bank Top Colliery and had closed by 1888. At Openshaw Fold there was a sale of plant on 4th July 1888, following the expiry of the lease [40].

Allen's Green was a relatively new sinking, located to the east of the much earlier Green Lane Colliery. The first edition of the 25" map, surveyed in 1889 to 1890, shows a private railway from the East Lancashire line at Radcliffe Bridge Station running past Allen's Green Colliery to Green Lane Colliery and to the canal. We think that this was probably constructed to coincide with the opening of Allen's Green, although we have been unable to discover a precise date.

The 25" map shows a bridge across the canal, leading to a wharf where barges could be loaded. Presumably there was some form of conveyer for taking coal from the railway wagons to the wharf. The map also shows what is apparently a small single road locomotive shed in the sidings at the west end of Allen's Green Colliery.

Withins Lane Colliery was on the east side of the L&YR at Radcliffe North Junction. Again, this seems to have been a relatively new sinking, served by sidings connecting with the adjacent main line, which appear on the first edition of the 25" map. The map also shows what appears to be a single road locomotive shed at the north end of the site.

Hampson Meadow Colliery was located to the north of the earlier Water Lane Colliery, which it presumably replaced. We assume that coal was carted by road to the nearby canal, as we have been unable to trace any tramroad or tubway connected with it. Latterly, Hampson Meadow seems to have been worked in conjunction with Whittaker Bridge Colliery which was sunk in the late 1870s on a site adjacent to the canal and to the Radcliffe to Bradley Fold line of the Lancashire and Yorkshire Railway. As well as having a loading wharf on the canal, Whittaker Bridge had an inclined tubway which led up to sidings on the main line at Radcliffe West Junction.

The last development carried out by Andrew Knowles and Sons Ltd at Radcliffe was the sinking of Coney Green Colliery, first shown in the Mines Lists in 1888. This was on a site on the north side of Cemetery Road and, although the pits were near to the Lancashire and Yorkshire line, no rail connection seems to have been provided. Coney Green Colliery was worked in conjunction with Withins Lane and it is possible that most of the coal was raised there.

The mining leases held by Andrew Knowles and Company expired in September 1895 and this led to a run down of the collieries in the mid 1890s. Withins Lane, Hagside and Coney Green are not shown after 1893 in the Mines Lists. Hampson Meadow and Whittaker Bridge are shown in the 1895 Mines Lists as abandoned and Allen's Green and Green Lane as abandoned in the 1896 list.

During the first three decades of the present century, mining continued sporadically in the district north of Irwell and did not finally cease until 1935. However, all the later ventures were on quite a small scale and none was large enough to justify a rail connection. A brief outline of their history is given in Appendix 5.

The Manning Wardle locomotive supplied to Andrew Knowles and Sons Ltd for use at the Radcliffe Collieries. After these closed it was used at other collieries owned by the firm. It is pictured here at Wheatsheaf Screens, Pendlebury, in February 1952, shortly before it was scrapped. Alex Appleton

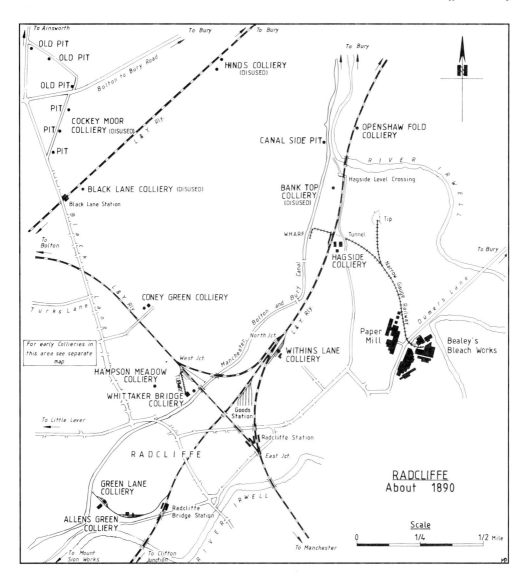

The manufacturer's records show that a six coupled saddle tank, named RADCLIFFE, was obtained from Manning, Wardle and Company of Leeds in 1890. An unnamed M4 class four coupled saddle tank was delivered from Peckett and Sons of Bristol in the same year. These engines seem to have been used at Allen's Green and Withins Lane Collieries. The sidings at Hagside and Whittaker Bridge were small enough to have been shunted by the Lancashire and Yorkshire Railway and it is unlikely that the firm employed its own locomotives there.

Following the closure of Andrew Knowles and Sons' operations at Radcliffe, the two locomotives were transferred for use elsewhere. No records of this period have survived, so it is not possible to say precisely where they went, although there were only three possibilities – the Wheatsheaf and Clifton Hall Complex, Agecroft Colliery and Pendleton Colliery.

RADCLIFFE, which was associated with Wheatsheaf and Clifton Hall at least from the 1930s, survived to pass into the hands of the National Coal Board in January 1947. The Peckett locomotive seems to have been sold in 1918. In February of that year, Andrew Knowles and Sons, writing from Pendlebury Colliery, ordered spare parts from the manufacturer. It was stated in correspondence that the engine had been out of use for some years, but that it was now to be fitted up immediately for Government use.

BETWEEN RADCLIFFE AND BURY

Richard Bealey and Company, later A C Bealey and Son Ltd

The Bealey family moved to Radcliffe in the early part of the eighteenth century and by 1732 had established a bleach works on the banks of the River Irwell in Dumers Lane. In 1796, the firm started to produce the chemicals which it needed and by 1811 had constructed Bealey's Goyt to supply water to the factory [41].

The works was owned by successive generations of the family and by 1850 had become the property of Richard Bealey and Company [42]. There was considerable expansion in the latter part of the nineteenth century and around 1870 a new chemical plant was erected, using the Leblanc process to manufacture the bleaching powder and other materials needed by the firm.

The raw materials needed for the new Leblanc plant, principally pyrites, limestone, manganese ore and coal, came by barge and a 2'6" gauge railway was constructed from the works to a wharf on the Manchester, Bolton and Bury Canal, some 3/4 of a mile away. Leaving the factory, the line crossed Dumers Lane on the level and then swung across the fields to the south of Bealey's reservoir. Beyond here, before reaching the canal, there was a short tunnel which took the line under Elton Hill Road, part of the pit yard of Knowles' Hagside Colliery and the Lancashire and Yorkshire Railway. There was also a branch, leading to a tip where waste from the chemical works was dumped. Rather surprisingly, there was no interchange siding with the Lancashire and Yorkshire line.

Several items concerning the railway have survived in the Bury Record Office. An uncatalogued plan of Dumers Field, dated 1871, shows the line in situ, all single track on this section, except for a loop on the west side of the level crossing over Dumers Lane. There is also an undated drawing [43] giving quantities of material to be excavated at the tunnel.

Of particular interest is a rough notebook containing decisions taken at management meetings during the latter part of 1871 [44]. Many of the entries relate to the erection and commissioning of equipment and to the ordering of raw materials. The alkali plant was reported, on 13th November 1871, to be working satisfactorily, but the Deacon plant, for the manufacture of bleaching powder, does not seem to have started until rather later.

The railway must have been well on the way to completion, if not actually operational, by 28th October 1871, the date of the first entry in the book. Mr Taylor was actioned to order signals and wire for the tunnel from Downham, so some way of controlling the movement of trains must have been provided. On 29th October there is the rather enigmatic entry - wagons to be like the Beverley Company, except for the mode of tipping.

Extra rails were ordered from Downham in November 1871. In December sheet iron was to be ordered for tip wagons and ordinary wagons and it was noted that the coupling chains were to be longer and stronger. These must have been to supplement the existing stock, as on 20th November it had been decided that the wagons and tipplers should be chained together every night and all (day) Saturdays. Vandalism must have been a problem even in those days.

Some consideration must have been given to the use of horses to haul the trucks from the wharf to the works. However, on 1st November 1871, Ashworth and Taylor reported that an engine would be best for the railway and one of 2 to 3 HP was to be ordered at once.

It was not obvious that anything was done at the time as in August 1874, the firm was advertising that it required a 2'6" gauge tramway locomotive of 3 to 4 HP[45]. The engine had to pass through a tunnel, with a height from rail level to the crown of the arch of 6'7" and a width of 6 feet. We do not know the outcome of the advertisement. We have no record of any locomotive owned by the firm at this period. Perhaps no one was able to provide anything to meet the rather unusual specification.

The first locomotive that we know about was delivered in 1883, from W G Bagnall and Company of Stafford, a firm which specialised in small narrow gauge engines. It was a small four coupled saddle tank named FERRET, presumably on account of its underground burrowings at Hagside. A second locomotive, FERRET II, was obtained from the same manufacturers in 1908 and the accompanying photograph shows that it was fitted with a specially low built cab and chimney.

FERRETT II, the second of the 2'6" gauge locomotives supplied by W G Bagnall for use on the railway serving Bealey's bleach works. Note the very low cab to suit the tunnel under the Lancashire and Yorkshire Railway. The photograph was taken at Easton Neston Ironstone Quarries, near Towcester, where the engine later worked,   J A Peden collection

Richard Bealey died on 3rd March 1896 [37] and was succeeded by his son, Adam Crompton Bealey, who formed A C Bealey Ltd to take over the business. The firm amalgamated with a number of others engaged in textile finishing to form the Bleachers Association Ltd, registered on 7th June 1900 [42,46], but continued to trade under its own name.

The chemical works closed down in about 1910 [47] and this meant that there was no further use for the railway. It was subsequently dismantled and at least one of the locomotives, FERRET II, was sold. It was later used by the Towcester Mineral and Brick Co Ltd in Northamptonshire.

The bleaching and dyeing side of the business continued for many years afterwards. The works, still owned by A C Bealey and Son Ltd, but now a subsidiary of Whitecroft Ltd as successors to the Bleachers Association Ltd, finally closed in September 1980 [48], after being in existence for 238 years. The buildings were demolished and the site is now occupied by housing.

Elliott's Sand and Gravel Company

The records of the Industrial Railway Society make reference to a 2'0" gauge diesel locomotive owned by Elliott's Sand and Gravel Company in the 1940s. The address is given as Dumer's Lane, Radcliffe.

The railway was presumably used to convey material from the quarry face to the lorry loading area. We have, however, been unable to trace the firm in contemporary trade directories, nor is the line marked on Ordnance Survey maps of the period.

BURY CORPORATION

Elton Gas Works

The Bury Gas Light and Coke Company was incorporated on 18th April 1828 [49] and its works, in Freetown, was opened on 29th June of the same year. A further Act in 1846 [50] changed the name to the Bury Gaslight and Coke Company and authorised additional funding. Construction of a new works at Elton was started soon afterwards [51].

The undertaking was acquired by the Bury Improvement Commissioners on 1st January 1858 [52,53] and by 1869 [54] the works at Freetown had been closed. Following the incorporation of the Borough of Bury by charter in 1876, the Elton works passed to the Mayor and Corporation.

It appears that Elton works originally received its coal by the canal, which ran on the opposite side of Bolton Road. Subsequently, when extensions to the plant were being planned, it was decided to provide a rail connection. Construction of the line, just over four furlongs in length, was authorised by Act of Parliament in 1890 [55]. The railway had to be completed within three years, locomotives or other motive power could be used, the railway was to form part of the gas undertaking but arrangements could be made with other parties to work it.

The agreement in respect of the main line connection with the Lancashire and Yorkshire's Bolton to Bury line was signed on 10th April 1890 [56]. The construction contract was let to Etheridge and Clarke of Manchester in the summer of 1891 [57] and the first sod of the new railway was cut by Alderman Burrow, Chairman of the Gas Committee, on 19th August of the same year [58]. There was a 200 yard tunnel under the main road and much of the route was in a constricted space alongside the canal feeder. A siding was laid in to serve the tar distillation plant which was built near the junction with the L&YR and provision was made to handle traffic for other businesses in the area [51].

The first train ran on 14th February 1893, when 19 wagons loaded with coal were taken to the works [59]. The railway was officially declared open on 22nd May 1895, when the extensions to the gas works were inspected by the Council. A four coupled saddle tank, purchased from Nasmyth Wilson and Company of Patricroft in 1893 and presumably delivered in time for the actual opening of the line, was named ELTON by Alderman Meadowcroft [60].

A second identical locomotive, named BURY, came from Nasmyth, Wilson and Company in 1903. ELTON was laid aside in 1924 following the purchase of a four coupled saddle tank from Andrew Barclay Sons and Company of Kilmarnock. It was subsequently broken up for scrap.

BURY and the 1924 locomotive survived to pass into the ownership of the North Western Gas Board, when the industry was nationalised on 1st May 1949. The works closed around 1970, when natural gas was introduced into the Bury area. In the last few years, the steam engines were little used and traffic was worked by a diesel locomotive which had been transferred from the Board's Oldham works.

Rail traffic ceased in the early 1960s and the siding agreement with British Railways was terminated on 6th August 1966 [61,62]. According to contemporary observations, BURY was broken up at the works in November 1962 and the Barclay locomotive in November 1965, the latter by Connel and Finnigan of Manchester. The diesel locomotive was sent to Clough Fold Gasworks, near Rawtenstall, in mid 1962.

BURY, built by Nasmyth, Wilson and Co Ltd in 1902, photographed here alongside the main line at the Gas Works Sidings in April 1956.   DL Chatfield

Chamber Hall Power Station

Electricity supply in Bury commenced on 5th November 1896, when the power station in Rochdale Road was switched on. Originally the plant consisted of two 38 HP and two 240 HP Bellis and Morcom engines, all driving Siemens generators [63]. By 1907 the smaller machines had been taken out and four 250 Kw and two 500 Kw generators installed [64].

In 1909 or 1910 it was decided to proceed with a new power station on a site adjacent to the Lancashire and Yorkshire Railway at Tottington Junction. Known as the Chamber Hall Power Station, it was completed in 1911, the supply commencing on 28th August. The plant consisted of two 2,100 Kw Musgrave turbines with Siemens alternators and Clarke Chapman boilers [64].

A railway siding was provided alongside the works for the delivery of coal, the connection with the L&YR being made under an agreement dated 10th October 1910 [65]. To lay the new siding, the bridge over Chamber Street had to be altered and this work was carried out under contract by Thomas Wrigley [64]. No locomotive was employed at the power station, electric capstans being used to position the wagons [64].

Fernhill Siding

A siding at was provided for the Bury Improvement Commissioners under an agreement with the Lancashire and Yorkshire Railway dated 28th November 1871 [66]. The siding was located on the east side of the Bury to Ramsbottom line, to the north of Bolton Street Station, and served the Commissioners yard. The property passed to Bury Corporation in 1876, on the incorporation of the Borough.

We have been unable to find further information about the siding. We think that it was mainly used for the delivery of materials for the Borough Engineer's Department. It may also have been used at first for the despatch of night soil. The siding seems to have been taken out of use before the second world war.

LOCOMOTIVE BUILDING IN BURY

Richard Walker and Brother

Richard Walker and his brother John set up business as iron founders, millwrights and general engineers in the 1820s. The firm, known as Richard Walker and Brother, appears in a directory of 1828 with premises in New Road [67]. The Soho Ironworks was established a few years later, on a site on the south side of Rochdale Road, near Whitehead Bridge [68].

The founder of the business, Richard Walker, retired from the partnership on 31st December 1839, as well as from the associated firm of Walker, Smith and Company [69]. The firm of Richard Walker and Brother was then carried on by John Walker, Richard Walker Junior and John Scholes Walker. John Walker retired on 1st January 1845 [70], leaving the others to carry on.

The firm's entry into the locomotive building seems to have arisen from family connections with the East Lancashire Railway. One of the Richard Walkers, presumably the son of the founder, was a director of the railway company and this no doubt had an influence on the matter.

Details of the locomotives, all of which were built for the East Lancashire Railway, can be found in an article in the *Journal of the Stephenson Locomotive Society* [71]. The first four, probably 2-2-2 tender engines, were turned out in 1846 and 1847. Three were used initially by the contractors building the East Lancashire line and were repaired by Richard Walker and Brother afterwards. They were rebuilt as 2-4-0 tank engines in 1853 and 1854, the work on at least three of them again being carried out by Richard Walker and Brother. Between 1848 and 1850 a further sixteen new locomotives were built, all either 2-2-2 or 2-4-0 tender engines. The final order was for a batch of four 0-6-0 goods engines which were delivered between November 1852 and February 1854.

There is no record of any other locomotive having been built by the firm. There are several advertisements in July 1869 [72,73,74], when a Mr William Clarke, of Providence Place, Rochdale Road, Manchester, was trying to sell a six wheeled tank engine with 12"x24" cylinders with 5'0" wheels, stated to have been built by Walker Brothers of Bury. This seems to have been one of the batch of four tender locomotives turned out in 1846 and 1847, which, as mentioned above, were rebuilt later with side tanks. All four had been withdrawn from service during the period 1866 to 1869 [75].

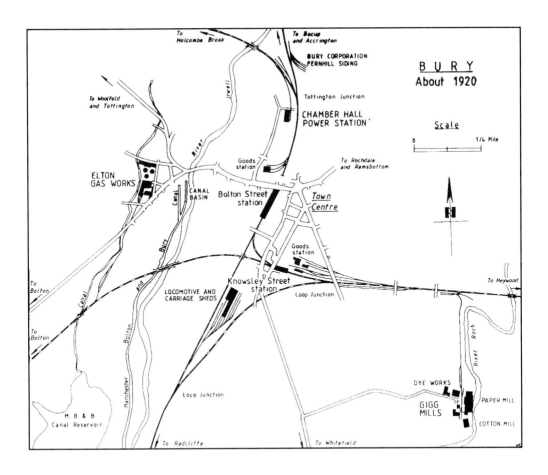

Two other locomotives are shown in Baxter's Grand Junction Railway list [76] as built by Walker and Company in 1838 or 1839. We have, however, found no evidence to suggest that this refers to the Bury firm.

After 1852, the firm settled down to its general engineering, millwrighting and iron founding activities. The business was merged in 1876 with that of William Hacking, a Bury brassfounder, and Walker and Hacking Ltd was registered on 27th June of that year [77]. Walker and Hacking Ltd, shown in 1883 as occupying the Vulcan works in Butcher Lane [78], continued in business as general engineers for a number of years.

East Lancashire Railway Workshops

The East Lancashire Railway established its locomotive depot and repair shops south of Bolton Street Station, at Buckley Wells. Following the amalgamation with the Lancashire and Yorkshire Railway in August 1859, the East Lancashire system continued to operate as a separate division. It was not until 1875 that the locomotive stock was merged with that of the parent company [75].

The workshops continued to undertake major repairs until 1888 [79]. The locomotive sheds were rebuilt and enlarged around 1876 and remained in use until 12th April 1965 [79], when steam locomotives were finally withdrawn from the area. They were later demolished. The old workshops were converted for use as the depot for the electric trains which were introduced on the Manchester to Bury line in 1916. The buildings still survive and are now occupied by the East Lancashire Light Railway.

Construction of new locomotives at the Bury workshops started in 1862 and details can be found in Baxter's *British Locomotive Catalogue* [75], and Rush's book on Lancashire and Yorkshire Locomotives [80].

The first four, or possibly five, were 2-4-0 tender engines, similar to those built by Richard Walker and Brother, and were produced over a period up to the end of 1871. They were followed, in 1873, by four engines of the same wheel arrangement, but with larger cylinders and wheels, and another four in 1876, again with different dimensions. The last locomotives to be turned out from the shops were two 2-4-0 saddle tanks. Both were completed in 1877, one being a rebuild of an 1862 tender engine.

James C Kay and Co Ltd

The 1920s saw a growing interest in the use of internal combustion locomotives for industrial use. James C Kay and Co Ltd, of the Phoenix Foundry at Heap Bridge, was one of the firms that attempted to develop this line of business, despite lack of previous experience in the railway field. Kays seem to have had little success and soon gave up their locomotive work.

The origins of the firm go back to the 1820s, when William Kay set up business as an engineer and iron founder in Bury. His Phoenix Foundry was on the south side of Bury Lane, near to the point where it became Bolton Street [68]. William Kay appears here in directories from 1828 [67] to 1854 [81]. By 1869 [54] James Clarkson Kay had taken over the business. By 1908 the firm had moved to Heap bridge, where the contemporary 25" map shows the new Phoenix Foundry on the south side of the Bury to Heywood road, immediately to the east of the underbridge for the Lancashire and Yorkshire Railway's Heap Bridge Branch.

A standard gauge example of the petrol-paraffin locomotives built by James C Kay and Co Ltd. Note the starting handle above the front buffer beam. The photograph is thought to have been taken at Heap Bridge when the locomotive was on trial. A J Booth collection

A narrow gauge petrol-paraffin locomotive built at Heap Bridge by James C Kay and Co Ltd, seen here working at Knostrop Sewage Works, near Leeds R N Redman Collection

No record remains of the locomotives which were built at Heap Bridge. Only one standard gauge and three narrow gauge locomotives are known to the authors and there is a qualified reference [82] to a second standard gauge engine. Some technical details can be found in Brian Webb's study of British internal combustion locomotives [83].

An undated catalogue [84] has the wording "Premier Petrol-Paraffin Locomotives Supplied for all Gauges: 18" to 5'6" " on the cover. The narrow gauge engines were of 30/40 Hp and weighed 4½ tons while the standard gauge engines were of 45/50 Hp and weighed 12 tons. There are illustrations of both types. There are also three photographs in the Bury Library collection showing a narrow gauge locomotive under construction in Kay's works.

The manufacture of locomotives seems to have been only a sideline and, after production ceased, the firm continued in business as general engineers. It was still in existence in 1954 [85], but closed a few years later. The buildings of the Phoenix Foundry are now incorporated into a factory owned by Jason Plastics Ltd.

THE HEAP BRIDGE AND GIGG PAPER MILLS

James Wrigley and Son Ltd, Bridge Hall Mills, Heap Bridge

The earliest private railway system in the neighbourhood of Bury was at the Bridge Hall Paper Mills. The works had been established in 1810 by James Wrigley in partnership with his younger brother, Francis, and was purchased by Thomas Wrigley, James' elder son, in 1852 [86]. The property passed through a series of family partnerships which traded under the title of James Wrigley and Son and a limited liability company of the same name was formed on 22nd July 1884 [86].

The Lancashire and Yorkshire Railway's Heap Bridge Branch was opened in 1874, terminating alongside the River Roch, opposite Bridge Hall Mills. James Wrigley and Son constructed two bridges over the river, the northernmost one being used for incoming goods and the southern one for outgoing traffic. Each carried a railway track, which led to the L&YR sidings and to a warehouse which the firm had built on the east side of the river to store raw materials. On the west bank, within the works, the tracks over the bridges connected with a line running the length of the mill yard, from which turntables gave access to the principal buildings.

The line on the west bank of the river was later extended as far as Broadoak Mill, which had been purchased in 1867 from James Hoyle. It had originally been used for cotton spinning, but had been converted to papermaking before 1890 [86].

The earliest siding agreement with the L&YR which we have been able to trace is dated 21st July 1882 [87], but we think that railway operations at Bridge Hall Mills had started somewhat before this. The firm was advertising in June 1880 that it wanted to hire a small locomotive for one month [88], which suggests that it already had an engine of its own, which was due to be repaired.

Martin Tillmans, in his history of the mills [86], relating what he had been told by old employees of the company, states that the firm owned 100 railway wagons. These were pulled by two saddle tank locos, popularly known as "Sam Weller" and "Little Kit", the latter named after Christopher J O Wrigley, son of Oswald O Wrigley Jnr.

We can identify SAM WELLER as the engine of that name supplied by Manning Wardle of Leeds in 1878 to J P Edwards for use on a contract at Saltley, Birmingham. It was a small four coupled saddle tank with 10" cylinders and, according to the manufacturer's records, it was in use at Bridge Hall Mills by August 1883. The last recorded spares were obtained in March 1909.

We think that LITTLE KIT was probably the engine supplied by Manning, Wardle and Company in 1887 to T A Walker for use on the Manchester Ship Canal contract and originally named BARTON. Like SAM WELLER, it was a class F four coupled saddle tank, with 10" cylinders. The manufacturers records show that spare parts were later supplied to Bridge Hall Mills.

The last locomotive to be purchased by James Wrigley and Son was BOBS, a class R1 four coupled saddle tank built by Peckett and Sons of Bristol in 1902. It had originally been delivered to the Derwent Valley Water Board for use on reservoir construction in the Peak District of Derbyshire. Much of the equipment passed into the possession of Bentley and Jubb, machinery merchants of Lower Ince, near Wigan, on the completion of the work, and

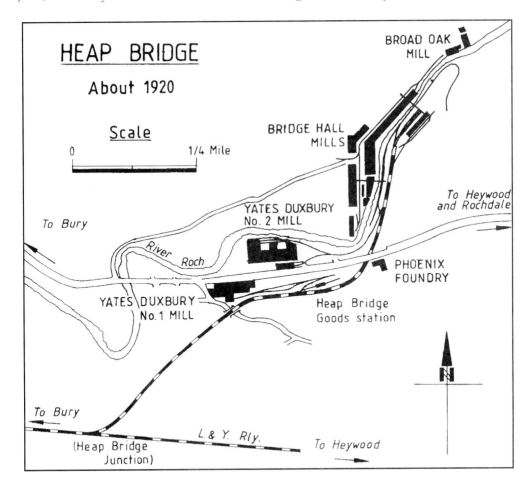

it appears that it was this firm that supplied the engine to Bridge Hall Mills, probably around 1914 or 1915. LITTLE KIT was taken out of service and sold to Thomas Mitchell and Sons Ltd, the Bolton machinery merchants, in June 1917.

After the first world war, with declining trade, the concern was sold to the National Paper and Pulp Co (1920) Ltd, but continued to trade under its original name. On 23rd January 1924 the shareholders of James Wrigley and Sons Ltd voted for voluntary liquidation. Bridge Hall Mills were put up for sale as a going concern on 19th February, but there were no bidders and the works then was closed down. The plant was sold piecemeal during 1925 and some of the buildings were dismantled [86].

The railway system evidently closed down in 1923 or 1924. BOBS remained until March 1925, when it also went to Mitchells, who resold it to the Withnell Brick Co in 1927.

The site was sold to Bridge Hall Developments Co Ltd, a subsidiary of A E Holt, and was resold, on 30th April 1928, to Transparent Paper Ltd, which had been set up a few months previously to manufacture wrapping paper and transparent film [86]. Reconstruction of Bridge Hall Mills was virtually complete by the spring of 1929, but the railway system was not reinstated.

Transparent Paper Ltd ceased operations at Bridge Hall Mills about 1980 [89]. The buildings were mainly demolished; part of the site is now occupied by Tetrosyl Ltd and part by Flexipack Ltd.

Yates Duxbury and Sons Ltd

The Heap Bridge Branch also served the paper mills of Yates Duxbury and Son Ltd. The family's association with the district dates from 1882, when Andrew Duxbury acquired a mill, formerly the property of Heap Bridge Paper Company which had been declared insolvent. Andrew was himself in financial difficulty two years later. His debts were paid by his father, Yates Duxbury and the mill, located on the south side of the Bury to Heywood road, was reopened by another son, Roger [90].

When the surveys were made for the first edition of the 25" map, in 1890, there was no direct rail connection into the works. However, one must have been provided a few years later as the firm is known to have purchased a locomotive from Peckett and Sons of Bristol in 1894. It was named MAY and was one of the maker's M4 class four coupled saddle tanks.

In 1904 it was decided to close the Duxbury family's premises at Hall i' th' Wood at Bolton and to build a new paper mill at Heap Bridge. This, designated the No 2 Mill, seems to have been completed about 1909 [90]. It was on the opposite side of the main road to the earlier works, which now became known as the No 1 Mill.

No 2 Mill had its own separate railway sidings, the connection with the Lancashire and Yorkshire Railway being provided under an agreement of 19th March 1908 [91]. A second four coupled saddle tank, ANNIE, was purchased in the same year, again from Peckett and Sons, but this time an R1 class.

The original MAY was out of service by the early 1930s and was replaced by another Peckett four coupled saddle tank, carrying the same name . This came second hand from George Cohen, Sons and Co Ltd, the machinery merchants of Stanningley, near Leeds, and had been employed previously by the English Electric Co Ltd at their Stafford works.

A further locomotive, to supplement ANNIE and the second MAY, was purchased second hand in 1944, again from George Cohen, Sons and Co Ltd. This was a four coupled saddle tank, built by Andrew Barclay Sons and Company of Kilmarnock in 1904, which had been used previously at the wagon works of S J Claye and Co Ltd, at Long Eaton in Derbyshire.

In 1960, Yates Duxbury and Sons Ltd became a member of the Tootal Group, but still traded under its own name [90]. The mills at Heap Bridge were extended to give increased capacity during this period and additional sidings were provided.

The steam locomotives continued to be used until towards the end of 1973, when rail traffic ceased [92]. The firm was sympathetic to enthusiasts who were interested in finding a good home for them. ANNIE and the Barclay of 1904 went to the East Lancashire Light Railway at Bury in 1975, while MAY went to the Steamtown Railway Museum at Carnforth in the same year.

A few years earlier Yates Duxbury had provided temporary storage for two preserved locomotives at the No 1 Mill. The former Lancashire and Yorkshire Railway six coupled saddle tank, No 11456, which had been used latterly at a number of collieries in the Wigan area, arrived at Heap Bridge in 1968. It remained here until November 1971, when it was transferred to the Keighley and Worth Valley Railway.

11456 was joined in 1971 or early 1972 by a six coupled side tank locomotive built in the 1950s by Robert Stephenson and Hawthorn, which had come from Meaford Power Station, near Stoke on Trent.

No 1 Mill, on the south side of the main road, appears to have closed in the 1970s. The buildings were demolished and the site redeveloped for the Lion Oil Works, which moved here from Bolton in 1978. No 2 Mill, on the north side, ceased production about 1980 [89] and part of the premises is now occupied by Wheeldon Waste Ltd.

The three locomotives owned by Yates Duxbury and Sons Ltd, photographed about 1970. From left to right - ANNIE, the Andrew Barclay and the second MAY. 						Alex Appleton

Bury Papermaking Company and successor firms, Gigg Mills

The Gigg Mills of the Bury Making Co Ltd were situated alongside the River Roch, some distance from the main railway line. The early history of the firm has eluded us. It appears to have been established in the 1870s or 1880s and is shown as owner of the Gigg Mills in an 1883 directory [78].

We know that in 1898 plans were well advanced for a private branch to join the Lancashire and Yorkshire Railway's Bury to Heywood line. The contract for its construction was advertised in November of that year [93] and was awarded to Thomas Wrigley of Middleton Junction [94]. The first sod was cut with some ceremony by Mr Cronshaw, Chairman of the Bury Papermaking Company, on 12th December [59,94]. The agreement in respect of the connection with the Lancashire and Yorkshire Railway was dated 22nd November 1898 [95].

We know very little about the first locomotive to have been used on the line, except that it was a four coupled saddle tank named GLADYS. It was sold to Thomas Mitchell and Sons Ltd, machinery merchants of Bolton, in June 1904. It was replaced by GIGG, a four coupled saddle tank of the maker's R1 class, which came new from Peckett and Sons of Bristol in the same year.

GIGG evidently had to be taken out of service for repairs in 1914 and it was necessary to hire a substitute. A four coupled saddle tank, built by Manning Wardle in 1883, was provided by Thomas Mitchell and Sons Ltd of Bolton. The engine was actually the property of the Pilkington Colliery Co Ltd, which had just finished the development of its Astley Green Colliery. It had been hired from that firm by Mitchells for the work at Bury and no doubt Mitchells made a profit on the deal.

A second four coupled saddle tank was purchased from Peckett and Sons in 1929, this time of the firm's M5 class. GIGG was subsequently broken up, possibly a year or two later.

The works survived a serious fire in June 1929 [96]. It passed into the hands of Standard Paper Mills Ltd in October 1930 and was then taken over by Redvales Paper Mills Ltd in 1932. In December 1935 it became the property of New Bury Paper Mills Ltd [97].

The railway continued in operation until the end of the 1930s. Its exact closure date does not seem to have been recorded, but there is a pencil note on a copy of the Line Plan of the Liverpool Bolton and Bury Railway which the authors have seen which suggests that the main line connection may have been taken out in 1939 [98]. The Peckett locomotive of 1929 was sold and was later used by Wagon Repairs Ltd at its Cardiff works.

TOTTINGTON, WOOLFOLD AND SUMMERSEAT

R K Roberts and Sons, Stormer End Bleach Works

The Stormer End Bleach Works, at Tottington Lower End, was in existence in 1824, when it appears in a directory [99] under the ownership of Hugh Roberts and Company. Hugh Roberts' sons, Henry Gordon, Robert Knowles and Joshua were later taken into the partnership. Following the death of Henry Gordon Roberts, in 1878, the partnership was dissolved in 1880. Robert Knowles Roberts and his son Hugh Porritt Roberts took control of the firm, which then changed its name to R K Roberts and Company [100].

Under the new management the works was considerably enlarged and sidings were laid in to serve the various factory buildings. The connection with the Bury and Tottington District line was provided under an agreement between the railway company and Hugh Roberts dated 6th April 1886 [101]. The work was complete by 1891 when the survey was made for the first edition of the 25" map.

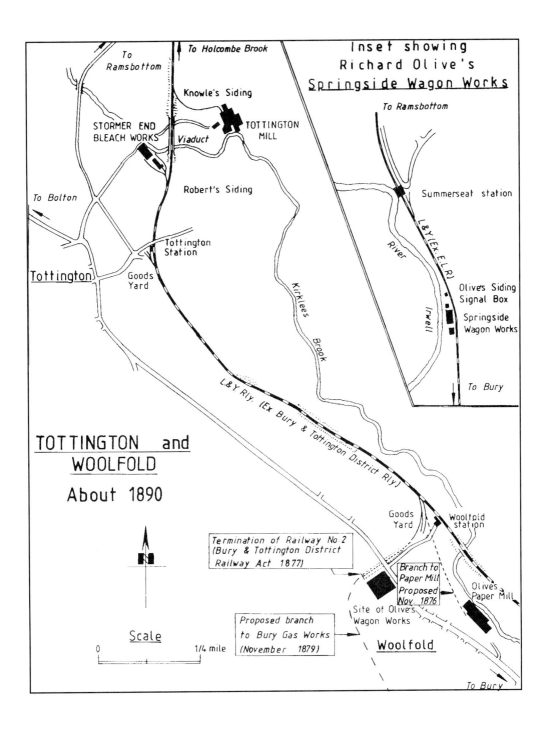

Inset showing
Richard Olive's
Springside Wagon Works

To Holcombe Brook

To Ramsbottom

Knowle's Siding

STORMER END
BLEACH WORKS

Viaduct

TOTTINGTON
MILL

To Bolton

Robert's Siding

To Ramsbottom

Summerseat station

L&Y (Ex E.L.R.)

River

Irwell

Olive's Siding
Signal Box

Springside
Wagon Works

To Bury

Tottington
Station

Tottington

Goods
Yard

Kirklees Brook

L&Y Rly. (Ex Bury & Tottington District Rly)

TOTTINGTON and
WOOLFOLD

About 1890

Goods
Yard

Woolfold
station

Olive's
Paper Mill

Termination of Railway No.2
(Bury & Tottington District
Railway Act 1877)

Branch to
Paper Mill
Proposed
Nov. 1876

Proposed branch
to Bury Gas Works
(November 1879)

Site of Olive's
Wagon Works

Woolfold

Scale

0   1/4 mile

To Bury

To shunt the internal railway system, the firm purchased a four coupled saddle tank from Hudswell, Clarke and Company, of Leeds, in 1888. It carried the nameplate ARKAYAR, based on the firm's initials. The works closed on 23rd September 1911 [102] and the locomotive was sold. The maker's records show that it went to William Underwood and Brothers, who used it on a contract for the construction of the Penderyn Reservoir in South Wales [103]. By August 1918, it had been resold to the Partington Steel and Iron Co Ltd and was used at the firm's Bodfari sand quarry in North Wales.

The Stormer End Bleach Works was taken over by Joseph Scholes and Sons Ltd in 1919 [104]. The sidings were retained, but in a much truncated form. It seems likely that the wagons were placed in position by the main line company and there is no record of another locomotive having been purchased.

We have been unable to discover when the siding was taken out. A date of around 1920 has been suggested [102], although it is still shown in situ on a Line Plan 1934 [105] and is listed in the LMSR Central Division Sectional Appendix, dated March 1937. The works itself is still occupied at the time of writing by Joseph Scholes and Sons Ltd.

S Knowles and Company, Tottington Mill

The firm of S Knowles and Co Ltd carried on business as calico printers and bleachers at Tottington Mill. The firm was established in 1821 by Joshua Knowles and by 1870 Samuel Knowles had taken over [106].

Following the opening of the Bury and Tottington District Railway in November 1882, a short private branch line was built to provide access to the works. The connection with the main line was provided under an agreement between Samuel Knowles and the railway company dated 30th June 1886 [107]. The line was complete when the survey was made in 1891 for the first edition of the 25" map. We have no record of any locomotive owned by the firm and we think that horses may have been used to move the wagons.

The mill closed down after the first world war. It is marked as disused on the 6" map revised in 1927 to 1928, although the track is still shown on the branch. The connection with the main line had been removed by the time that a new Line Plan was completed in 1934 [105], but the private siding agreement was not cancelled until 1st January 1935 [108].

The Olive Brothers and their successors at the Woolfold Wagon Works and the Springside Wagon Works

John Olive appears in a directory for 1845 [109] where he is described as a blacksmith and wheelwright at Woolfold and Tottington Lower End. By 1869 [54] the firm of Olive Brothers had been established, with a works at Woolfold making railway waggon wheels and cart wheels.

John Olive and his two brothers also moved into paper making. This side of their business had been established at Woolfold before 1850, possibly in the mill previously occupied by Samuel Coop and James Holt [109]. As papermakers, the firm continued to prosper and in 1893 Olive Brothers Ltd was formed. In 1920 the title was changed to the Olive Paper Mill Co Ltd [110] and the mill, taken over by Continental Paper Ltd in April 1990, is still at work [111].

The curiously named locomotive ARKAYAR, formed from the initial letter of R K Roberts and Company. Originally supplied for shunting at Stormer End Bleach Works at Tottington, it was later sold. After passing through the hands of William Underwood and Brothers, it was purchased by the Partington Steel and Iron Co Ltd. It is seen here working at the firm's Bodfari Sand Quarry in North Wales.

Industrial Locomotive Society - RG Pratt collection

The story of Olive Brother's engineering activities is somewhat different. By 1883, the Woolfold Waggon and Iron Co Ltd [78] had been formed to deal with that side of the business. Olive Brothers' original works was greatly enlarged, with workshops on both sides of the main road. Although the firm is described in 1883 [78] as builders of railway carriages and wagons, it is not clear whether manufacture ever really got under way. There was a series of bankruptcies in the family at this time and the firm is not shown in later directories [112]. When the first edition of the 25" map was surveyed in 1889 to 1890, the works appears to have been derelict.

The Act of Parliament [113] which authorised the Bury and Tottington District Railway included powers for a branch from Woolfold to "John Olive and Sons' wagon building shed". Rather surprisingly, a proposed branch to Olive's paper mill [114] did not obtain approval.

The main line was opened for traffic on 6th November 1882 [115], but the position regarding the branch to the wagon works is not clear. The first edition of the 25" map indicates that the earthworks, including a bridge under the main road, had been completed, but no track is shown. Perhaps none was ever laid in view of the demise of the works.

Members of the Olive family had interests in wagon works elsewhere. Since the early 1870's they had been in business at Ince, near Wigan, under the title of Olive and Sons. Richard Olive had established wagon works at Springside, on the west side of the East Lancashire line, south of Summerseat Station about 1880.

By June 1881, Richard Olive, then stated as having an interest in wagon works at Springside, Ince and Hexthorpe, near Doncaster, was declared bankrupt [116]. The Springside Works, described as newly erected, was put up for sale in January 1882 [117]. The Ince works was taken over from Olive and Sons in 1883 by the Ince Waggon and Iron Ltd, a firm in which the Olive family was not represented.

Despite his setbacks, Richard Olive was back in business again at Springside in 1883, trading as James Olive and Company. He was in the bankruptcy court again in 1885, where it was revealed that he was in partnership with Joseph Bell, who had been his works manager at the time of his previous bankruptcy [118]. James Olive appears to have had no real connection with the firm and it seems that his name was being used to give it an aura of respectability.

The firm must have been reformed as a J Olive and Company continued to run the Springside and Hexthorpe works for several more years. There was another bankruptcy and both works were put up for sale on 12th February 1894 [119].

It seems unlikely that the Springside Works reopened after the last sale. The sidings here later served J and W Tomlinson's brickworks. The agreement between the railway company and John Tomlinson was dated 2nd May 1902. It was terminated in 1919 and the sidings were taken up in the same year [120].

LOCOMOTIVE SUMMARY

Bradley Fold Colliery

Known as Tonge Lane or Bents Colliery up to early 1860s
Thomas Fletcher until about 1875
Thomas Fletcher and Sons until 11-5-1898
Thomas Fletcher and Sons Ltd from 11-5-1898
Colliery closed 1908

0-6-0STIC	HC	240	1882	12"x20"	3'3½"

New to Bradley Fold
Sold to Thomas Mitchell and Sons Ltd, Bolton, 1-1902

The following locomotives may have been at Bradley Fold for a time - see text

FARMERS FRIEND	0-6-0ST	HCR	173	1875	11"x17"	3'0"

Hired from Thomas Mitchell and Sons Ltd, Bolton, late 1901 for at least three months

0-6-0STOC	P	923	1901	14"x20"	3'2½"

0-4-0STOC	P	935	1902	10"x14"

Dobson and Barlow Ltd, Bradley Fold Works

Works opened about 1906
Electric traction ceased about 1961
Rail traffic ceased by 12-1968
Various subsequent owners
Works closed 3-1984

4wWE	British Westinghouse		1911	

New
Scrapped or sold after 9-1953

4wWE	MV	1945	

New
Scrapped by 2-1963

4wDM	RH	221649	1944	48DS Class

Ex Platt Bros Ltd, Oldham 3-1961
Scrapped or sold by 4-1970

Radcliffe Royal Ordnance Factory, later Mather and Platt Ltd

Works opened 1941
Purchased by Mather and Platt Ltd 1946
Rail traffic ceased before 12-1968
Various subsequent owners
Works closed early 1983

0-4-0DM	HE	2144	1940

New to Radcliffe Royal Ordnance Factory
Taken over by Mather and Platt Ltd, 1946
To Mather and Platt Ltd, Park Works, Miles Platting 2-1969

Andrew Knowles and Sons Ltd's Radcliffe Collieries

For details see text
Probably only Withins Lane and Allens Green/Green Lane had locomotives - closed 1893 and 1896
respectively

RADCLIFFE	0-6-0STIC	MW	1192	1890	12"x17"	3'0"

New to Radcliffe
Transferred to another Andrew Knowles and Sons Ltd's colliery (See Chapters 7 and 8)

	0-4-0STOC	P	502	1890	10"x14"	2'6"

M4 Class
New to Radcliffe
Transferred to another Andrew Knowles and Sons Ltd's colliery and apparently sold for Government
use in 1918 (See text)

Dumer's Lane Bleachworks

Various Bealey family partnerships to circa 1850
Richard Bealey and Company until circa 1897
A C Bealey and Co Ltd from circa 1897
Railway opened 1870 or 1871
Railway closed 1910 to 1914
Works closed 1980

2'6" gauge

FERRET	0-4-0STOC	WB	556	1883	7"x10"	

New

FERRET II	0-4-0STOC	WB	1853	1908	6"x12"	1'9½ "

New
To Towcester Mineral and Brick Co Ltd, via E Cornforth, dealer, in 1914

There is evidence to suggest that a locomotive might have been purchased in 1871 - see text

Elliott's Sand and Gravel Co, Dumer's Lane Sand Pits

No record of this firm has been found in contemporary directories and maps. The Industrial Railway
Society lists contain the following :

2'0" gauge

	4wDM	RH	201999	1940	20DL Class

New
Scrapped or sold about 1950

Elton Gas Works

Bury Gaslight and Coke Company until 1-1-1858
Bury Improvement Commissioners until 1876
Bury Corporation until 1-5-1949
North West Gas Board from 1-5-1949
Railway opened 2-1893
Railway closed about 1962
Works closed about 1970

ELTON	0-4-0STOC	NW	445	1893	12"x18"	3'0"

New
Scrapped about 1924

BURY	0-4-0STOC	NW	640	1902	12"x18"	3'0"

New
Name removed by 5-1957
Scrapped onsite 11-1962

	0-4-0STOC	AB	1830	1924	12"x20"	3'2"

New
Scrapped on site by Connel and Finnigan of Manchester 11-1965

	4wDM	RH	425483	1958	88DS Class	

Ex Oldham Gas Works 5-1959
To Clough Fold Gas Works about 5-1962

Bridge Hall Paper Mills

James Wrigley and Son until 22-7-1884
James Wrigley and Son Ltd from 22-7-1884
Works closed 1924

SAM WELLER	0-4-0STOC	MW	691	1878	10"x16"	2'9"

New to J P Edwards at Saltley as SAM WELLER
At Bridge Hall Mills by 8-1883
Scrapped or sold after 1909

	0-4-0STOC	MW	1029	1887	10"x16"	2'9"

Second hand, new to T A Walker, Manchester Ship Canal Contract
Sold to Thos Mitchell and Sons Ltd, Bolton, 6-1917

BOBS	0-4-0STOC	P	949	1902	12"x18"	3'0½ "

Ex Derwent Valley Water Board via Bentley and Jubb, Ince about 1916
Sold to Thos Mitchell and Sons Ltd, Bolton, 3-1925 and resold to Withnell Brick Co 3-1927

There may have been a locomotive before SAM WELLER as the firm advertised in The Engineer for 25-6-1880 that it wanted to hire a locomotive for one month with 9¼" x 15" cylinders, and weight 12 tons

Heap Bridge Paper Mills

Yates Duxbury and Son Ltd from 1884
Rail traffic ceased mid 1973
Works closed circa 1980

MAY 0-4-0STOC P 569 1894 10"x14"
Class M4
New
Scrapped or sold, probably about 1932

ANNIE 0-4-0STOC P 1159 1908 12"x18"
Class R1
New
To East Lancashire Light Railway, Bury, 6-7-1975

MAY 0-4-0STOC P 1370 1915 12"x18"
Ex English Electric Co Ltd, Stafford, via George Cohen Sons and Co Ltd, 11-1932
To Steamtown Railway Museum, Carnforth, 24-4-1975

0-4-0STOC AB 945 1904 12"x20" 3'2"
Ex S J Claye, Long Eaton, Derbyshire, via George Cohen Sons and Co Ltd, 6-1944
To East Lancashire Light Railway, Bury, 6-1975

The following locomotives were stored at the mills on behalf of railway enthusiasts :

11456 0-6-0STIC BP 1989 1881
Rbt Hor 4/1896
Ex NCB North West Area, Parsonage Colly 1968
To Keighley and Worth Valley Rly, Haworth, 11-1971

0-6-0T OC RSH
Ex Central Electricity Generating Board, Meaford Power Station
Noted at Heap Bridge 2-1971

Gigg Paper Mills

Bury Paper Making Co Ltd until 10-1930
Standard Paper Mills Ltd until 1932
Redvales Paper Mills Ltd until 12-1935
New Bury Paper Mills Ltd from 12-1935
Railway opened about 1899
Railway closed probably 1938

GLADYS 0-4-0ST 11"x22" 3'6"
Sold to Thomas Mitchell and Sons Ltd, Bolton, 6-1904

GIGG 0-4-0STOC P 982 1904 12"x18"
Class R1
New
Scrapped, probably about 1930

0-4-0STOC MW 880 1883 9"x14" 2'6"
Hired from Thomas Mitchell and Sons Ltd, Bolton, 3-1914, which firm hired it from Pilkington Colliery
Co Ltd, Astley Green

	0-4-0ST OC	P	1718	1929	10"x15"	

Class M5
New
To Wagon Repairs Ltd, Cardiff, probably about 1938

Stormer End Bleachworks, Tottington

Various Roberts family partnerships to 1880
R K Roberts and Company from 1880
Joseph Scholes and Sons Ltd from 1919

ARKAYAR	0-4-0ST OC	HC	303	1888	11"x16"	2'9"

New
Sold about 1911 to Wm Underwood and Bros, contractors, Dukinfield, and used on the construction of Penderyn Reservoir
By 8-1918 resold to Partington Steel and Iron Co Ltd, and used at that firm's Bodfari Sand Quarry

Locomotives Built by James C Kay and Co Ltd

The following locomotives are known to the authors and were all built around 1930. The list does not claim to be comprehensive and no records have survived.

All the locomotives were 4 wheeled, with petrol-paraffin engines

Gauge	Customer
1'11⅝ "	Leeds Corporation Sewage Dept, Knostrop Works
2'6"	Sandwith and Clugston Ltd, Lincoln Slag Works, Frodingham
2'8½ "	Stanton Ironworks Co Ltd, South Witham Quarries
4'8½ "	Liverpool Corporation Electricity Dept, Clarence Dock Power Station

There was possibly another standard gauge locomotive at Cyclops Engineering Co Ltd, Burton on Trent - See Industrial Railway Society's South Staffordshire Pocket Book (Ref 82)

References to Chapter 5

1	FJ 4-9-1897	46	BC 30-6-1900
2	BC 29-8-1908	47	Letter A C Bealey and Son Ltd to Frank Smith 7-8-1957
3	Endorsement on L&YR Sdgs Diag 40, 5th Dec 1895	48	RT 28-8-1980
4	BC 2-1907	49	9 Geo IV cap xxii; 18th April 1828
5	*"Samuel Crompton 1753-1827"* - Dobson and Barlow, Bolton 1927 - at BMB B 920 CRO	50	9&10 Vic cap ccxciii; 27th July 1846
		51	*"A History of the Bury Gas Undertaking 1828 - 1949"* - North West Gas Historical Society, 1993
6	BC 29-8-1908		
7	*Iron* 11-9-1891	52	20&21 Vic cap lxiii;27th July 1857
8	L&YR Sdgs Diag 372, 6th July 1916	53	*"The Bury Improvement Commissioners"* - M W Whittaker - in *Trans Lancs and Chesh Antiq Soc*, Vol XLIX, 1933
9	LMSR Sdgs Diag 4372A, nd		
10	Letter Dobson and Barlow Ltd to Frank Smith 4-9-1953		
11	LRO DDPSL	54	*"Royal National Commercial Directory of Lancashire"* - Isaac Slater, Manchester, 1869
12	Endorsement on BR Sdgs Diag 4454, June 1956		
		55	53&54 Vic cap lxix; 4th July 1890
13	BEN 24-6-1970	56	L&YR Sdg Diag 29, 17th May 1897
14	RT 21-4-1977	57	BC 20-8-1891
15	RT 25-3-1982	58	BT 22-8-1891
16	RT 2-2-1984	59	Bury Library Index
17	Schedule of Ordnance Factory Construction - copy in authors' possession	60	BT 25-5-1895
		61	Endorsement on L&YR Sdg Diag 29, 17th May 1897
18	RT 21-10-1976		
19	RT 24-8-1980	62	Endorsement on Line Plan of Liverpool, Bolton and Bury Rly - 2 chains to 1 inch - LMSR, Euston, 1936-7 - at BRPB, Manchester
20	RT 30-8-1983		
21	LRO DRM 1/83		
22	BC 11-1868		
23	LRO DDX 29/71	63	*"Electricity Supply Works"* - brochure produced for the opening on 5th Nov 1896 - Co Boro of Bury, 1896
24	LRO DDX 29/76		
25	BC 27-1-1866		
26	WO 9-2-1866	64	*"Description of Chamber Hall Power Station"* - Co Boro of Bury Elec Dept, 31st Jan 1912
27	WO 23-2-1866		
28	LRO DDX 29/78	65	L&YR Sdgs Diag 389, 31st Dec 1921
29	LRO DDX 29/83	66	L&YR Sdgs Diag 165, 26th April 1898
30	LRO DDX 29/84	67	*"National Commercial Directory for Cheshire, Cumberland, Durham, Lancashire "*- James Pigot and Co, London and Manchester, 1828-9
31	LRO DDX 29/89		
32	BC 28-3-1846		
33	LRODDX 29/72		
34	LRO DDX 29/77	68	Map of Bury - W Benson, 1845
35	LRO DDX 29/80	69	LG 8-3-1842
36	LRO DDX 29/81	70	LG 21-7-1846
37	Probate records	71	*"Early Locomotives of the L&YR"* - E Craven - *Journal of the Stephenson Locomotive Society*, Vol XXXVIII, No 439 February 1962 and No 444 July 1962
38	MJ 20-9-1873		
39	LRO PDR 1033		
40	BC 30-6-1888		
41	*"Archaeology of Radcliffe and the Irwell Valley"* - K Howarth - in *Industrial Archaeology* Spring 1974	72	*The Engineer* 16-7-69
		73	MJ 17-7-69
		74	MG 3-7-69
42	*"Concerning the Bleaching Industry"* - compiled by Sir Alan John Sykes 31-12-1925 - publ Bleachers Association Ltd, 1925	75	*"British Locomotive Catalogue 1825-1923, Vol 3B"* - compiled by late Bertram Baxter - Moorland Publishing Co, Ashbourne, 1982
		76	*"British Locomotive Catalogue 1825-1923, Vol 2A"* - compiled by late Bertram Baxter - Moorland Publishing Co, Ashbourne, 1978
43	BRO item 1586		
44	BRO item 1449		
45	Iron 12-8-1876	77	*Iron* 8-7-1876

78   *"General and Commercial Directory of Bury, etc"* - P Barrett and Co, Preston, 1883

79   *"The Lancashire and Yorkshire Railway"* - John Marshall - David and Charles, Newton Abbot, 1969

80   *"The Lancashire and Yorkshire Railway and its Locomotives 1846-1923"* - R W Rush - Railway World Ltd, London, 1949

81   *"History, Topography and Directory of Mid Lancashire"* - P Mannex and Co, Preston, 1854

82   *"Industrial Locomotives of South Staffordshire"* - R M Shill - Industrial Railway Society, London, 1993

83   *"The British Internal Combustion Locomotive 1894 to 1940"* - Brian Webb - David and Charles, Newton Abbot, 1973

84   Copy in Author' possession

85   *"Town and County Directory for Bury"* - Town and County Directories Ltd, Edinburgh, 1954/5

86   *"Bridge Hall Mills - Three Centuries of Paper and Cellulose Film Manufacture"* - Martin Tillmanns - Compton Press, Tisbury, Wiltshire, 1978

87   L&YR Sdg Diag 203, 30th October 1899

88   *The Engineer* 25-6-1880

89   *"Yellow Pages"*, 1980 and 1981

90   *"Yates Duxbury and Sons, Papermakers"* - Tom Green - Published by Yates Duxbury and Sons Ltd, 1963

91   L&YR Sdg Diag 358, 27th August 1909

92   BLN 240

93   CJ 9-11-1898

94   BT 17-12-1898

95   L&YR Sdg Diag 198, 30th October 1899

96   BT 4-6-1929

97   Information from Industrial Railway Society list

98   Line Plan of Liverpool Bolton and Bury Railway - 2 chains to 1 inch - LMSR, Euston, 1936 to 37 - at BRPB, Manchester

99   *"History, Directory and Gazeteer of the County Palatine of Lancaster"* - Edward Baines, Liverpool, 1824

100 BT 17-5-1902

101 L&YR Sdgs Diag 219, 11th July 1900

102 *"The Holcombe Brook Branch"* - Davis Westall - L&Y Society Journal,1988

103 Information supplied by Mr H D Bowtell

104 Letter Joseph Scholes and Sons Ltd to Frank Smith 16-4-1958

105 Line Plan of Tottington Branch - LMS Euston, 1934 - at GMRO A 19/1/6

106 *Bury Library Correspondence* - May 1972

107 L&YR Sdg Diag 106, 15th Dec 1896

108 Endorsement on another copy of 105 at BRPB, Manchester

109 *"Directory of Bolton, Rochdale, Bury, Oldham, Burnley, Bacup"* - J Williams, Manchester, 1845

110 BT 15-3-1969

111 BT 6-4-1990

112 *"Royal National Commercial Directory of Bury, Heywood, Radcliffe, Ramsbottom and Districts"* - Isaac Slater, Manchester, 1888

113 40&41 Vic cap clvii; 2nd August 1877

114 LRO PDR 1029

115 *"Chronology of the Railways of Lancashire and Cheshire"* - M D Greville - Railway and Canal Historical Society, 1981

116 BC 25-6-1881

117 BC 14-1-1882

118 BC 29-8-1885

119 BC 2-1-1894

120 L&YR Sdgs Diag 184a, 26th June 1903

CHAPTER 6

OUTWOOD, CLIFTON AND KEARSLEY

In Chapter 6 we return to the Radcliffe area, to look at the industrial railway systems on the south side of the town, in the former township of Pilkington. Unlike many of the districts described so far, coal mining here does not seem to have started on any significant scale until well into the nineteenth century. Although most of the pits had closed before 1900, Outwood Colliery remained in production until the 1930s and the coal preparation plant there continued in use until after the second world war.

Two other establishments in the same district also claim our attention. The Outwood Iron Company, which was set up in the latter half of the nineteenth century, erected the only blast furnace in this part of the county. The Lancashire Electric Power Company's first generating station was built later on a nearby site.

We then cross the River Irwell to the township of Clifton, where we explore the history of the Clifton and Kersley Coal Company and its railways. The first pits were sunk in the early part of the eighteenth century and were, for many years, worked by the members of the Fletcher family. The collieries were developed extensively during the nineteenth century and one pit, Newtown, did not cease production until well after the second world war.

Leaving the remaining industrial railway systems in the Clifton area until Chapter 7, we move north westwards to Kearsley where, again, coal mining had been firmly established before the end of the eighteenth century. A few pits were able to take advantage of facilities offered when the Manchester, Bolton and Bury Railway opened for traffic in May 1838, but the majority relied on landsale trade, their products being distributed by horse and cart. Most had closed by the end of the nineteenth century.

We conclude with a brief description of the electrified railway system at Kearsley Power Station, built by the Lancashire Electric Power Company in the 1920s to complement and later replace the firm's earlier power station at Outwood.

OUTWOOD AND RINGLEY

Stand Lane and Whitefield Collieries

Stand Lane Colliery was situated between Edward Street and Henry Street, just off the main road leading from Radcliffe towards Manchester. An old coal pit is marked here on the first edition of the 6" map, surveyed in 1844 to 1846, and the site must have been redeveloped a few years later. The Mines Lists show that Stand Lane Colliery was being worked by Thomas Grundy and his brothers in 1853 and that it was taken over by Stott and Pickstone around 1860.

We believe that it was Stott and Pickstone who opened out the Whitefield Colliery, which first appears in the mines lists for 1866. A take plan of the period [1] shows three pits here, all near the East Lancashire Railway.

In 1868 the Mines Lists show that both collieries had been taken over by the Stand Lane Colliery Company, in which the partners were Joseph Grimshaw and William Pickstone. Pickstone retired on 1st April 1873 [2] and the firm was subsequently converted to a limited liability company. Springwell Colliery first appears in the Mines Lists for 1878 and seems to have replaced the nearby Whitefield Colliery which is not shown after 1879.

The Mines Lists for 1883 show Springwell and Stand Lane in the occupation of W J and H S Grimshaw. Springwell seems to have closed in the same year and Stand Lane in 1884. Neither reopened and the coal was later worked by Thomas Fletcher from his Outwood Colliery.

Stand Lane Colliery was never connected to the railway system and the coal was taken away by horse and cart. On the other hand, as will be seen from the map of Outwood and Ringley of 1890, which appears later in the chapter, the Whitefield and Springwell Collieries were quite close to the East Lancashire line and we think that they may have been provided with a private siding.

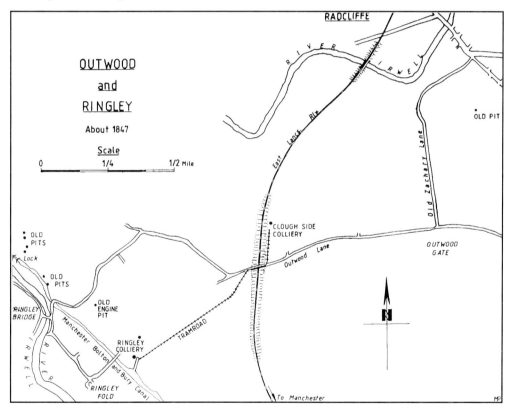

Outwood Colliery from the 1840s to 1909

Outwood Colliery was known in its early days as Clough Side. It lay to the south of the Whitefield and Springwell Collieries, again on the east side of the East Lancashire Railway. It predates the railway and was probably sunk in the late 1830s. It was linked to the Manchester, Bolton and Bury Canal by a tramroad which terminated at a basin to the west of Giants Seat Lock. The tramroad appears on the 2" drawings of about 1840 which were used in the preparation of the first edition of the 1" map and also on the Deposited Plans for the Manchester, Bury and Rossendale Railway [3], drawn up in 1843. The level sections of the line were presumably worked by horses, but there must also have been some form of rope worked incline where the tramroad descended into the Irwell valley.

The schedule to the Act [4] authorising what was to become the East Lancashire Railway shows that the colliery was on land owned by the Earl of Derby and that the lessees were Thomas Brownbill, David Bromilow, Henry Foster, Edward Ellam, John Taylor and John Walker. By 1850, the occupiers were described as Messrs Brownbill and Bromilow [5].

The new railway, opened in September 1846, provided an alternative outlet for coal from Clough Side and it seems likely that a siding was laid in at an early date. The tramroad to the canal was diverted on to the bridge which was built to carry Ringley Road, at that date known as Outwood Lane, over the railway.

In 1857 or 1858, Bromilow and Brownbill disposed of their interests in Clough Side Colliery and the nearby Ringley Bridge Colliery, which we describe later. Clough Side was taken over by Thomas Fletcher and Sons, whom we have met in Chapters 4 and 5 at Stopes and Bradley Fold. It first appears under the new ownership in the Mines Lists for 1858.

There followed a period of redevelopment, with an eventual total of five pits on the site. Perhaps to mark the new era the name was changed to Outwood Colliery, this title being first recorded in the Mines Lists for 1865. The main line sidings appear to have been extended to cater for the increased output of coal, probably in the mid 1870s.

The tramroad to the canal was reconstructed so that pit tubs could be hauled on an endless chain. Motive power was provided by a stationary steam engine which was installed at Higher Heaps [6]. In some places the route was realigned and a new bridge was provided over the East Lancashire line, a hundred yards or so to the north of Ringley Road. A new canal basin was built, with improved loading facilities, and the arm of the canal serving the original tip was abandoned, later to be filled in.

At the north end of the colliery site a second tubway was constructed, terminating near the end of James Street. This conveyed coal to a landsale yard and also to a brickworks which had been established by the firm in the same locality. Apparently tubs loaded with coal ran down by gravity towards Radcliffe. The empty tubs were hauled back to the colliery on a rope attached to a windlass, later replaced by a small stationary steam engine [6]. We do not have a precise date for these developments. However the rebuilding of the line to the canal and the construction of the tubway to James Street must have been completed before the end of the 1880s. Both are shown on the second edition of the 6" map.

In the 1860s and 1870s there were several changes to the partnership, which we have described in Chapter 4. A limited liability company, Thomas Fletcher and Sons Ltd, was formed on 11th May 1898, with a capital of £164,000, to take over the Outwood Colliery, as well those at Bradley Fold and Stopes [7].

Some improvements appear to have been put in hand around the turn of the century, including rebuilding the screening plant and providing an enlarged siding layout. Extra connections with the main line were provided under an agreement with the Lancashire and Yorkshire Railway dated 29th August 1899 [8].

By 1908 the firm was in financial difficulty and, as a result of an action in the Chancery Court, a liquidator was appointed. Outwood Colliery was put up for sale as a going concern on 2nd April 1909 [9,10,11]. Bids at the auction failed to reach the reserve price and the property was withdrawn from the sale [12, 13, 14] . A few weeks later it was sold privately, reputedly for

£100,000 [15,16], to the Clifton and Kersley Coal Company Ltd. A subsidiary company, Outwood Collieries Ltd, was registered on 13th May 1909 to take over the assets [17]. We shall be following its subsequent history a little later.

A report prepared in connection with the sale [18] and the various notices in the newspapers provide a good contemporary description of the colliery and its plant. There were three shafts - No 2 downcast 480 yards deep, No 4 downcast 240 yards deep and No 5 upcast 480 yards deep. The plant included locomotives and railway wagons. The coal was worked under two leases from the Earl of Derby dated 17th November 1896 and 17th November 1906, the latter for a 75 year period, and there was an agreement that the Ladyshore Coal Co Ltd would provide drainage for the mines.

Thirty percent of the output was stated to be sold at the coal yard at James Street and by landsale at the colliery itself. The James Street yard and the associated tubway from the colliery were included in the sale. There was also a coal wharf at Radcliffe on the north side of the canal, held under a 33 year lease from 1st May 1903.

By this date the brickworks at James Street had apparently ceased production. The tubway to the canal at Giants Seat may also have closed, as it is not mentioned in descriptions of the colliery. It still marked on the third edition of the 6" map, surveyed in 1907 and 1908, but it is not shown on later revisions.

The screens at Outwood Colliery, with the three shafts in the background. One of the Peckett locomotives is shunting wagons in the sidings. The photograph is taken from the entrance to the power station sidings, looking across the East Lancashire line.   John Ryan collection

We have already mentioned, when dealing with Thomas Fletcher's Bradley Fold Colliery, the almost complete lack of information about locomotives used by the firm until the end of the nineteenth century. It is possible, as we have pointed out earlier, that the six coupled saddle tank purchased from Hudswell, Clarke and Company in 1882 may have seen service at Outwood Colliery. The same applies to the FARMERS FRIEND which was hired from Thomas Mitchell and Sons Ltd in 1901.

We know that two locomotives were purchased from Peckett and Sons of Bristol - a six coupled saddle tank in 1901 and a four wheeler in 1902. The manufacturer's records which survive are incomplete and it not possible to find out whether these engines were delivered to Bradley Fold or Outwood. On balance, we think it was probably the latter, as both were taken over by the Outwood Colliery Co Ltd.

Ringley Colliery

The first reference to this colliery which we have found is on a royalty plan of 1850 [19], which shows the coal mined by Ellam and Company under a lease from the Earl of Derby up to that date. The workings stretched along the canal from a point near Prestolee village to Giants Seat. The plan marks a series of small pits on both sides of the canal which presumably had been used originally to raise the coal. By the mid 1840s, when the surveys were made for the first edition of the 6" map, it is evident that coal winding had been concentrated at what is described as Ringley Colliery. This was situated on the north side of the canal, alongside the basin which formed the terminus of the tramroad from Clough Side.

According to a note on the royalty plan, it appears that one of the pits caught fire in April 1850. We think that this is when Ellam and Company gave up its lease. The colliery was subsequently taken over by Bromilow, Brownbill and Company, who are shown as occupiers in the Mines Lists for 1853/4.

Bromilow and Brownbill's operations at Ringley and at Clough Side came to an end in 1857 or 1858. Ringley Colliery was put up for auction on 28th July 1858 [20]. The plant included an atmospheric engine with a 41" cylinder, a condensing beam engine with an 18" x 4ft cylinder and a portable condensing beam engine, also with an 18"x 4ft cylinder, together with boilers, pit head gear and sundry other machinery.

On the transport side, there were 12 narrow canal boats to carry 18 tons, 63ft long with a 6ft beam, and 14 coal wagons. The latter were described as 4'2" gauge, to carry 30cwt, and were 6ft long, 4ft wide and 2'6" deep. A large drum and rope for an incline were also mentioned. This makes us think that the sale also included plant at the firm's Clough Side Colliery and that the coal wagons, the incline drum and the rope were associated with the tramroad from Clough Side to the canal at Giants Seat.

As we have described above, Clough Side Colliery, soon to be renamed Outwood, was taken over by Thomas Fletcher and Sons. Ringley Colliery does not appear separately in the Mines Lists again until 1874. This does not necessarily mean that it was closed during the intervening period; it was probably considered, in the official returns, as part of the Outwood workings.

As at Outwood, there were new developments at Ringley in the latter part of the nineteenth century which appear to have included modernisation of the pits and the colliery plant. The new basin on the canal which was built to accommodate coal coming down the tubway from Outwood was made sufficiently large to serve Ringley Colliery as well. The old boat loading facilities and the arm of the canal which gave access to them were abandoned and a short tubway constructed from the colliery to the new basin.

Ringley Colliery continued in production until towards the end of the century, when the workings were taken over by Outwood. It is shown as "discontinued" in the Mines Lists for 1893 and following years.

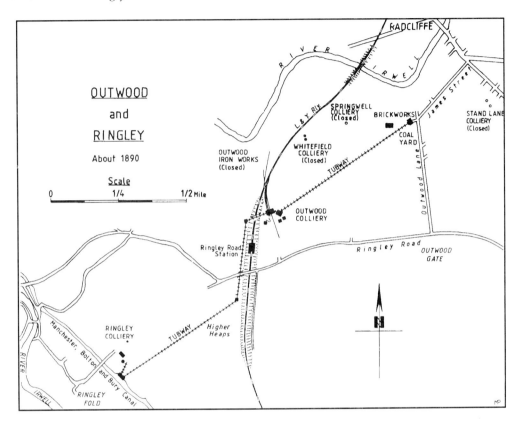

Outwood Colliery 1909 to 1929

Following the transfer to Outwood Collieries Ltd, major changes took place which led to a reorganisation of the railway system. A new washery and coal preparation plant were erected, occupying land adjacent to the site of the earlier Whitefield and Springwell Collieries. The records of the company [21] show that there were repairs to the locomotive shed and extensions to the sidings at the colliery and the washery in 1910. There were further extension to the sidings at the washery in 1911.

In 1913 the work of cutting new connections with the Lancashire and Yorkshire was completed. Additional exchange sidings were provided under agreements with the railway company dated 21st April 1913 and 6th May 1915 [22]. Work on extending the internal railway system continued until 1915. Standard gauge track was laid into the coal yard at James Street, replacing the original tubway from the colliery, probably in 1913 [21].

At the south end of the colliery site, a new brick works was built and came into full production early in 1927 [23]. This was served by a standard gauge track laid in from the pit yard. There was also a short narrow gauge line for the skips of clay which came from an open pit on the south side of Ringley Road.

The first locomotives used by the Outwood Colliery Co Ltd were the two Pecketts taken over from Thomas Fletcher and Sons Ltd. The six wheeler was subsequently known as OUTWOOD No 1 and the four wheeler as OUTWOOD No 2. According to a former employee No 1 was generally used about the colliery yard, while No 2 shunted at the washery.

OUTWOOD No 2 was transferred in 1912 to the books of the Pilkington Colliery Co Ltd [21], another Clifton and Kersley subsidiary. It was sent to Astley Green Colliery and does not seem to have returned. Meanwhile, ROBIN HOOD, a four wheeled saddle tank built by Chapman and Furneaux of Gateshead in 1901, had been sent to Outwood from another of the Clifton and Kersley Coal Company's pits [21].

OUTWOOD No 1 was delivered to Thomas Fletcher and Sons Ltd in 1901. It is seen here as plain OUTWOOD at Wheatsheaf Screens, Pendlebury, in May 1954
Alex Appleton

Outwood Colliery 1929 to 1956

In 1929, the Clifton and Kersley Coal Co Ltd and its subsidiaries merged with other South Lancashire mining companies to form Manchester Collieries Ltd. However, shortly afterwards there was a serious underground fire at Outwood and all coal production ceased. The colliery was formally abandoned, according to the Mines Lists, on 2nd February 1931. One of the pits was retained for pumping purposes and the washery continued in operation, processing coal from other collieries of the new company. From at least 1936 onwards much of this came from Astley Green Colliery and Wheatsheaf Colliery at Pendlebury via Molyneux Junction in main line trains.

The washery and the pumping station were taken over by the National Coal Board on 1st January 1947. The washery was kept in operation until 1956. The private sidings agreement was terminated on 22nd April 1957 [24]. The majority of the buildings were subsequently demolished, except for a single storey block near to Ringley Road. The remainder of the site had not been redeveloped by the end of 1993 although there are plans to landscape the area for recreational purposes.

CLIFTON, built by the Vulcan Foundry in 1895 for the Clifton and Kearsley Coal Co Ltd, is seen here at Outwood in May 1936. It was broken up shortly afterwards.   B D Stoyel

Shortly before the merger it had been intended to send ROBIN HOOD to the Spindle Point Colliery in exchange for CLIFTON [25], a locomotive built by the Vulcan Foundry in 1895 for the Clifton and Kersley Coal Company. CLIFTON was then undergoing under repairs at Spindle Point. These seem to have been completed in July or August 1928 [26] and the engine was subsequently sent to Outwood. If ROBIN HOOD was transferred to Spindle Point, it must have only been as a temporary measure.

In the early 1930s OUTWOOD No 1, ROBIN HOOD and CLIFTON were all at Outwood. CLIFTON was sold for scrap on 8th May 1936 to Harry Stephenson and Co Ltd, of Hindley [27]. It was observed by one of the authors' colleagues in a derelict condition, still at Outwood, on 21st June of that year and was cut up soon afterwards.

OUTWOOD No 1, now known as plain OUTWOOD, and ROBIN HOOD shared the work at the washery until 1946. ROBIN HOOD was then sent to Robin Hood Screens to deputise for KEARSLEY which was undergoing repairs. When KEARSLEY returned to service, ROBIN HOOD was itself sent to Walkden Yard for overhaul.

Following the formation of the National Coal Board, there was a shortage of four coupled and small six coupled engines, which were the only ones suitable for work at Outwood, Robin Hood, Wheatsheaf and other places with restricted siding layouts. As a result, there were frequent movements from location to location to cover for overhauls and breakdowns.

ROBIN HOOD returned from Walkden Yard to Outwood under its own steam on 1st September 1947. It was transferred to Wheatsheaf in the following year. It then saw various spells of duty at Robin Hood Screens and Moston Colliery as well as Wheatsheaf Screens before arriving back at Outwood on 25th January 1951 [28]. It was sent to Walkden Yard two months later, on 10th March. From there it went in turn to Ashton Moss Colliery, Robin Hood and Wheatsheaf before reappearing at Outwood on 27th May 1952 [29]. It left again for Robin Hood in October or November of the same year and later saw service at Ashton Moss and Bradford Collieries. After a final spell at Robin Hood Screens, it was broken up at Walkden Yard in December 1961.

OUTWOOD continued in use at Outwood until mid 1950, when it was sent to Walkden Yard for repairs and for a new boiler. It did not emerge from the workshops until 28th February 1954 [29]. There was a short period of work at Wheatsheaf Screens before it came back to Outwood on 14th June [29]. It was still at Outwood when the coal preparation plant closed and was sent to Walkden Yard under its own steam on 2nd August 1956, travelling via Clifton Junction and Linnyshaw Sidings. It never worked again, lying out of use at Walkden for several years before being broken up in January 1962 [29].

To provide a replacement for OUTWOOD, a small six coupled saddle tank was transferred from Wheatsheaf Screens on 24th January 1950 [29]. Built by Peckett and Sons of Bristol in 1890, it had been supplied to Andrew Knowles and Sons Ltd and had been taken over by Manchester Collieries Ltd in 1929. Most of its working life had been spent at Clifton Hall and Wheatsheaf and although originally carrying the name CLIFTON HALL, this had been dropped latterly. It was given the name PECKETT, painted on the saddle tank, some time early in 1950. It remained at Outwood until 15th January 1955, when it travelled to Walkden Yard under its own steam. It never returned to Outwood and was finally broken up in January 1962.

The Outwood Iron Company

The Outwood Iron Co Ltd was formed in 1872 to build an iron works on land leased from the Earl of Derby [30] across the East Lancashire line from Thomas Fletcher and Sons' colliery.

The works took two years to complete and the first and only blast furnace was blown in during August 1874 [31]. A contemporary article in "*Iron*" [32] stated that the furnace was 70ft high with a 20 ft bosh, with a beam blowing engine and that it was capable of producing 300 tons of pig iron per week. Although plans had been made to erect a second furnace and a forge, the works does not seem to have prospered financially and the extensions were never carried out.

The works was closed down in the mid 1880s and the furnace, along with the blowing engine, boilers and other plant was put up for sale on 14th May 1888 [33]. The site was subsequently cleared and, up to the time of writing, has not been redeveloped. A considerable amount of blast furnace slag still remains to mark the position of the tips.

There was a connection with the adjacent Lancashire and Yorkshire Railway, under an agreement dated 30th January 1874 [34]. There had been an earlier siding at the same point, which gave access to a loading mound for the use of the Earl of Derby's tenants and this had to be repositioned to make way for the lead into the iron works. The Earl's siding seems to have been provided shortly after the opening of the line, as there is reference to it in the East Lancashire Railway Board Minutes for 28th February and 14th March 1853 [34].

The first edition of the 25" map, surveyed in 1891 shows only a very limited railway system within the works. It is doubtful whether a locomotive was ever employed. None is mentioned in the sales notices in 1888, although there is reference to railway wagons and a weighbridge.

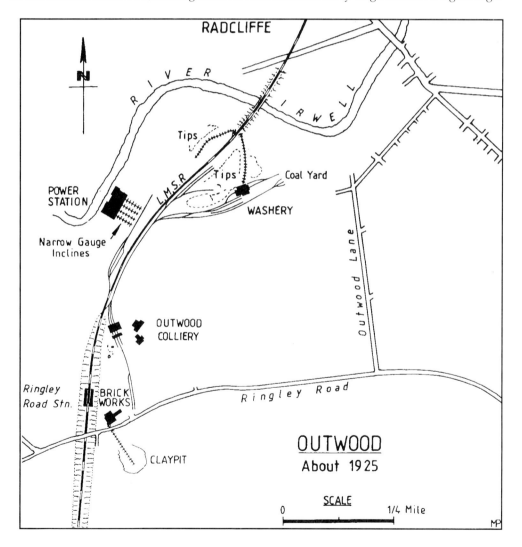

171

Radcliffe Power Station

The Act of Parliament of 1900 [35], under which the Lancashire Electric Power Company was incorporated, specified that power stations should only be built on a site adjoining the Albion Ironworks at Aspull, near Wigan, at Parr near St Helens, at Little Lever and at Trafford Park. This restriction was removed by a further Act, obtained in 1904 [36]. Finally an Act of 1906 [37] gave the company powers to provide a supply of electricity to local authorities and private consumers and to absorb other undertakings.

Instead of the four small stations specified in the 1900 Act, the company decided to centralise operations on a site to the north of the old ironworks, not far from the River Irwell. Radcliffe Power Station started operations in October 1905, equipped with four BTH 1500 Kw vertical turbo-generators. A fifth similar set was added in 1911. There were extensions in February 1913, in April 1914 and September 1917, by which time there was generating capacity of 23,000 Kw. A further 20,000 Kw was added during 1922 [38].

Radcliffe Power Station in the 1920s. A view from the boiler house looking up one of the pairs of narrow gauge inclines. The electric locomotive built by Stothert and Pitt can just be seen at the left of the picture on the overhead gantry.   Courtesy of Radcliffe Library

Coal came in by rail and by 1924 some 7,500 tons was being delivered each month. The connection with the Lancashire and Yorkshire Railway was provided under an agreement of 20th October 1904 [24] and, within the works boundary, a pair of tracks led into a single line on an overhead gantry, some distance above the power station itself. The internal sidings were equipped with overhead wiring and shunting was performed by a small electric locomotive, supplied by Stothert and Pitt of Bath in 1904.

The coal handling arrangements were of an unconventional type, supplied by Babcock and Wilcox Ltd. The standard gauge wagons were tipped by an electrically operated ram to discharge the coal into a pair of steel bunkers. From here the coal dropped into steel cars, each with a capacity of about 1 ton, which ran on narrow gauge inclines. When released, the cars moved by gravity towards the boiler house, where they came into contact with a barrier connected to a heavy pendulum, which slowed them down. The coal was emptied automatically and the car was sent back uphill to the bunker by the return swing of the pendulum [39].

The second edition of the 25" map, published in 1907, shows only one pair of narrow gauge inclines. Later editions of the map, published after the first world war, show that the number had increased to four as the station had been extended. There was also a short narrow gauge system at ground level, presumably to take ash from the boilers to a tip near the river.

The power station became the property of the British Electricity Authority as from 1st April 1948. In consequence of reorganisations within the industry it passed to the Central Electricity Authority on 1st May 1955 and to the Central Electricity Generating Board on 1st January 1958.

With the commissioning of more up to date plant elsewhere in Lancashire, the works was gradually phased out and finally ceased generating around 1960. In June 1962, it was observed that the overhead wiring had been removed and that the locomotive was derelict. By September of that year the staging had been demolished and the locomotive had disappeared, presumably for scrap. The agreement with British Railways in respect of the private sidings was not formally terminated until 2nd June 1965 [24].

THE CLIFTON AND KERSLEY COLLIERIES

The Clifton and Kersley Collieries under the Fletchers

We move now to the south side of the Irwell valley to a district with a long history of coal mining. Several shallow pits had been sunk in the 1730s, not far from the banks of the river, by John Heathcote [40]. His Clifton Colliery, better known by its later name of Wet Earth, passed into the hands of the Fletcher family.

In the 1740s, John Heathcote engaged Matthew Fletcher (1729-1808) to carry out improvements [41]. Matthew was the second son of Jacob Fletcher (1696-1766), a colliery proprietor with mines at Breightmet and Harwood, and he was responsible for sinking the Gal Pit at Clifton to reach the deeper seams [42]. James Brindley, later to become famous as a canal engineer, was brought in to devise a scheme to drain the new pit. Power for the pumps was supplied by a water wheel, fed by an underground culvert from a weir a mile or so upstream [43].

By the end of 1750s Matthew Fletcher had became the owner of the Clifton estate and had taken over the Wet Earth Colliery. He went on to sink the Little Mine, Doe, Woodgate and Botany Bay pits.

With the exception of some coal which may have been sent away from Wet Earth using small tub boats in the River Irwell [43], all the Clifton pits initially had to rely on road transport. Improved access to markets in Manchester and elsewhere was provided by the Manchester, Bolton and Bury Canal, which was opened through Clifton in the middle of 1796 [44]. By extending the leat serving the Brindley Water pump, Matthew Fletcher built a private canal from Wet Earth Colliery to join the Manchester, Bolton and Bury at the south end of Clifton Aqueduct. There was also a short branch serving the Botany Bay Colliery, where the canal continued underground to reach the coal workings.

Matthew Fletcher died in 1808 and the estate and collieries were left to Ellis and John, sons of Matthew's brother, Jacob (1734-1767). John died soon afterwards and Ellis, now in sole charge [41], continued to develop the collieries, sinking new pits on the higher ground away from the river.

In 1820 a coal depot was established at the Turnpike Gate at the top of Clifton House Road and linked to the Little Mine by a short tramroad on the site of what later became Little Mine Lane [41]. Robin Hood Pit, taking its name from a nearby public house on Manchester Road, was sunk in 1821 [41].

Ellis Fletcher died on 26th April 1834 and his son, also named Ellis, was too young to manage the estate [41]. Trustees were appointed, who embarked on a further programme of colliery expansion. They started to sink the Cannel Pit north of the Manchester road in 1838 and this was followed by the Moss Pit, the Manor Pit [45] and presumably the Bus Pit.

While these mining developments were taking place, the canal company had changed its name to the Manchester, Bolton and Bury Canal and Railway and had started to construct a line from Salford to Bolton along the Irwell Valley. The original Act of Parliament [46] had authorised a line built on the bed of the canal, which would have been filled in. This Act also authorised a branch railway to Farnworth which would have left the main line at the south end of Clifton Aqueduct. The branch would have run parallel to Fletcher's canal, past Botany Bay and Wet Earth, and then climbed up the side of Unity Brook by means of a cable worked incline. A further short branch off the Farnworth line, near the top of the incline, was to give access to Fletcher's Bus and Doe Pits and to Andrew Knowles and Sons' Clifton Moss Colliery. Ellis Fletcher was to be allowed to use the branches serving his collieries free of toll by way of compensation, as his private canal would have been made redundant.

A change of plan meant that the railway from Salford to Bolton was built on a separate course. Navigation on the canal was maintained and the clause in the 1831 Act giving Fletcher toll free use of the colliery branches was repealed [47]. Wet Earth and Botany Bay Collieries continued to be served by the private canal and rail access was not provided until some 60 years later.

The route of the railway north-west of Clifton was not finally settled until 1835 [48]. Although the main line was opened for traffic throughout in May 1838 [49], there was considerable delay in completing what now became known as the Clifton Branch. It was finally opened on 30th April 1840 [50], but only in a truncated form as far as the Moss Pits, which we believe may have been another name for James Stott's Unity Brook Colliery. The continuation to Farnworth and the line from the incline top, past the Bus and Doe Pits, to Clifton Moss Colliery were never built.

A short private siding was built to the Manor Pit from a point near the top of the incline. It was probably contemporary with the Clifton Branch and had certainly been completed when the surveys were carried out for the first edition of the 6" map in 1844 to 1846.

Although Ellis Junior came of age in 1854 and took over from the Trustees, he died a few months later [51]. The estate passed to Jacob Ramsden, illegitimate son of Ellis Senr, who then changed his name to Jacob Fletcher [41]. Jacob died two years later and the estate passed to

Jacob's daughter, Charlotte, aged 10. The property was administered on her behalf by trustees, the principal of whom was John Fletcher (1807 - 1876), son of Colonel Ralph Fletcher of Bolton (1707-1832) [41].

During the period that John Fletcher was responsible for the collieries, improvements were made at Robin Hood, where a start was made on widening the shaft in April 1856 [45]. The Manor Pit was also modernised at this period [41] and the new Spindle Point Colliery, often referred to as the Trencherbone Pit, opened out on an adjacent site in the 1860s to replace the Little Mine and the Doe Pit [41].

The private railway from the Bus Pit (at this time usually spelt Buss) to join the Clifton Branch at the top of the Unity Brook incline also appears to date from this period. It is not shown on the Deposited Plans of the Manchester and Southport Railway, dated November 1852 [52]. It had however been completed by November 1860, when the Deposited Plans were prepared by the Lancashire and Yorkshire Railway for its proposed Wigan to Clifton line [53].

The colliery developments appear to have overtaxed the trustees' financial resources and, in 1865, arrangements were made to lease the collieries to Joseph and Josiah Evans of Haydock. An inventory of plant as it existed on 31st December 1865 [54], presumably prepared in connection with the lease, provides some interesting information.

The collieries were listed as Wet Earth, Trencherbone, Manor, Bus, Robin Hood, and Botany Bay. There were 239¾ yds of railway track, including sidings, at the Trencherbone Pit, 600 yards at the Manor Pit and 713 yards at the Bus Pit, together with a further 34 yards at the top of the incline. There was a 10-ton weighing machine at the bottom of the incline. The firm owned 84 railway trucks - 78 square and 10 hopper. Wagon shops had been established near the Trencherbone Pit by this time.

There is no mention of a locomotive, but there is reference to two railway ropes each 240 yards long and two chains 38ft long by ¾" diameter. This suggests that stationary engines at Spindle point and at the Bus pit were used to haul the empty wagons from the Lancashire and Yorkshire sidings at the incline top, but we lack firm evidence of this. The gradient in both cases would have been sufficient for the loaded wagons to descend by gravity.

There was evidently still a considerable waterborne traffic, presumably from Wet Earth and Botany Bay Pits and there is mention of a new tramway from Wet Earth to the canal. The Boat Yard was apparently located at Wet Earth and the firm owned 57 coal boats, 1 ice boat and 1 weir boat. There were wharves in Manchester and Salford at Oldfield, Gaythorn, Stanley Street, Ordsall and Albion Street.

The Clifton and Kersley Coal Company 1865 to 1880

Following the lease by the brothers Joseph and Josiah Evans, their nephews Edward and Alfred Pilkington, sons of Richard Pilkington the glassmaker, were brought in as managers. Together with the Evans, they formed the Clifton and Kersley Coal Company [45]. Twenty years later, on 31st July 1885, the concern was turned into a limited liability company, which still retained the spelling 'Kersley' in its title, rather than the modern Kearsley [55]. The work started by the Fletchers at Manor and Spindle Point was completed and the Billy Lane Brickworks was opened [45]. The Bus Pits closed in the early 1870s, being shown for the last time in the Mines Lists for 1873.

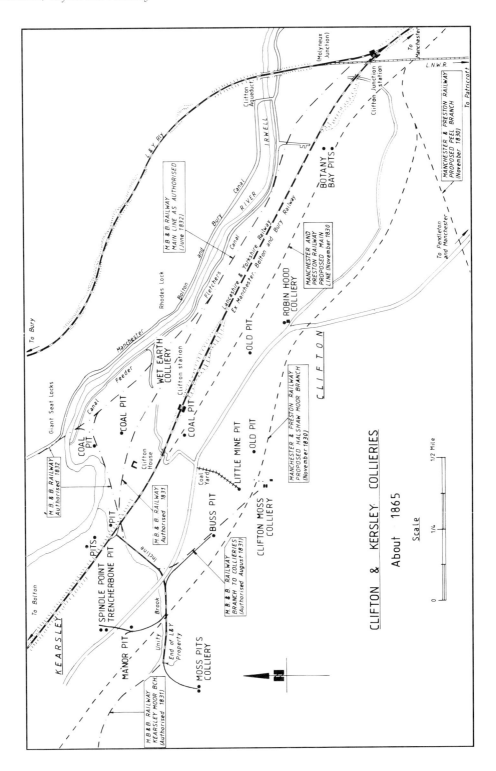

CLIFTON & KERSLEY COLLIERIES

About 1865

The colliery workshops and the timber yard alongside Manchester Road, established by the Fletchers, were enlarged by the new company [45]. A railway connection was provided, probably at this time, by extending the line which previously served the Bus Pits. Later, an engine shed was constructed at the timber yard to house the locomotives which worked at Spindle Point and the Manor Pit.

The rope worked incline on the Lancashire and Yorkshire's Clifton Moor branch was replaced by a steeply graded railway, suitable for locomotives, which included a reversal on the hillside above the Manchester to Bolton line. The date at which this alteration was made has not been recorded, but it appears to have been in the early 1870s. The plans relating to a new siding agreement with the Clifton and Kersley Coal Company in 1875 show the new line in place [56].

The colliery company appears to have financed the deviation line, at least in part, and to have been responsible for working their own trains over it. It is evident from later sidings diagrams [57] that the greater part of the new alignment was on land belonging to the colliery company, which was also responsible for maintaining most of the trackwork.

In the eastern part of its property, the Clifton and Kersley company turned its attention to providing a rail outlet for its Robin Hood and Botany Bay Collieries. Tubways were constructed from the pits to a screening plant which was erected alongside the L&YR Manchester to Bolton line. Work started on 30th March 1870 [45], the siding connections with the main line being provided under an agreement with the Lancashire and Yorkshire Railway dated 14th October 1870 [58].

On 6th August 1875 Alfred Pilkington cut the first sod at the Newtown Colliery, alongside Manchester Road [40]. This too was connected to Robin Hood Sidings by means of double track tubway which ran down the side of the hill. Eventually there were three shafts on the site [42].

In 1871 the Clifton and Kersley Coal Company purchased what was probably its first locomotive, presumably to work over the new line from Spindle Point to the Lancashire and Yorkshire Railway. We have no other information apart from the fact that it was named CLIFTON and that it was sold for £118.15.0 in 1895 [59]. An old employee told us that he remembered seeing it lying out of use near the timber yard at about that time [60].

CLIFTON was followed by KERSLEY, a six coupled saddle tank which came from Black, Hawthorn and Company of Gateshead in 1874 and by BLACK DIAMOND, a four coupled saddle tank from Sharp, Stewart and Company in 1878.

The Clifton and Kersley Coal Company 1880 to 1905

Although Wet Earth Colliery had been modernised in the 1870s, when the two existing pits had been deepened and a third pit sunk [40], it had relied so far on Fletchers Canal for the despatch of its coal. In the 1890s the Clifton and Kersley company constructed a railway, in part on the banks of the canal, to join the LNWR's Patricroft to Molyneux Junction line. There was also a short branch which passed under the L&YR Manchester to Bolton line and connected the Wet Earth line with the sidings serving the screens at Robin Hood. The work seems to have been completed in 1895 or 1896. The agreement in respect of the connection with the LNWR is dated 19th January 1894 [61] and the costs of the new line, together those of a locomotive shed at Wet Earth, were added to the Clifton and Kersley Coal Company's capital account in the year ending 31st December 1896 [62].

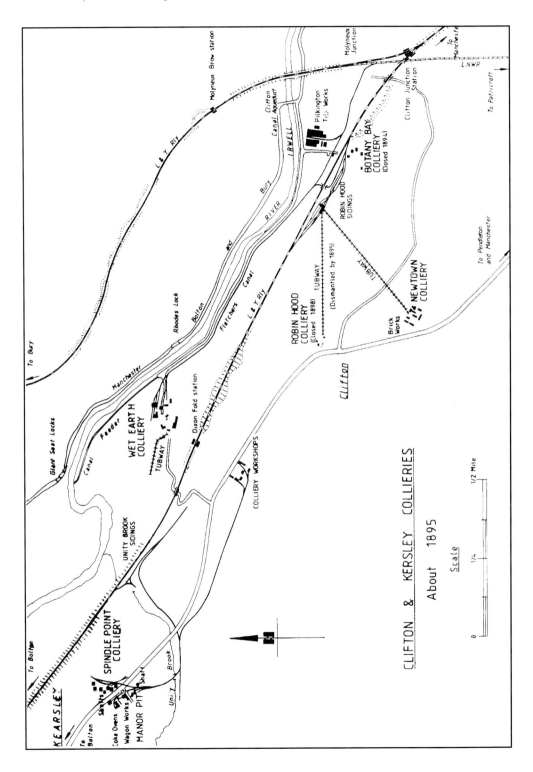

CLIFTON & KERSLEY COLLIERIES

About 1895

Scale

It seems likely that the new railway was also intended to provide access to the Pepper Hill Colliery which the company started to sink in the 1890s on a site near Clifton Junction, north of the Lancashire and Yorkshire Railway. The project encountered considerable difficulty due to flooding and was finally abandoned in 1899.

Marl found during the sinking was suitable for pottery manufacture. This led to the formation of the Pilkington's Tile and Pottery Company's works in 1891, under the auspices of Lawrence Pilkington, brother of Edward and Alfred [45]. The factory had a wharf on the Manchester, Bolton and Bury Canal and it is reputed that china clay was delivered from Manchester Docks by barge. There was also a siding from the Wet Earth to Molyneux Junction line. The colliery company's engines brought in coal, performed any internal shunting which was needed and also worked traffic to and from the LNWR exchange sidings.

Two four coupled saddle tanks were obtained from Black, Hawthorn and Company of Gateshead, VICTORIA in 1887 and ROBIN HOOD in 1893. We presume that these were intended for use at Robin Hood Screens and on the new line to Wet Earth. CLIFTON, also a four coupled saddle tank, arrived from the Vulcan Foundry of Newton-le-Willows in 1895. For reasons which are not known, ROBIN HOOD was returned to Chapman and Furneaux, of Gateshead, successors to Black, Hawthorn in 1901, in exchange for a new engine of the same name.

The Pilkington Tile and Pottery works, looking north from a point near the site of Botany Bay Colliery. The main line from Manchester to Bolton runs across the bottom of the picture, with Pepper Hill Signal Box, at the southern entrance to Robin Hood Sidings, in the foreground. The colliery company's line from Wet Earth Colliery to the ex-LNWR exchange sidings is immediately beyond the main line and wagons can be seen on the spur serving the tile works. Fletcher's Canal is beyond the works, with the branch to Botany Bay Colliery at the left hand boundary of the premises. The Bolton Corporation Rhodes Farm Sewage Works can be seen in the distance. The photograph was probably taken in the mid 1920s.   Arthur Chambers

The last locomotive to be purchased by the company came in 1903. This was NEWTOWN, a four coupled saddle tank, built by Hawthorn, Leslie and Company of Newcastle on Tyne. Some of the earlier engines must have been in need of repair, as in December of the same year the firm was advertising that it wanted to hire a four coupled tank locomotive with 14" or 15" cylinders for three months [63]. We do not know what response it had.

The engine shed at Wet Earth was extended in 1903 to accommodate a second locomotive [64], while a new shed was built at the Timber Yard during 1904 and 1905 for the engines serving Spindle Point and Manor Pit [65,66].

The Clifton and Kersley Collieries 1905 to 1929

Robin Hood Colliery had closed towards the end of 1888 [67], Botany Bay Colliery in November 1894 [45] and Manor Pit in 1905 [40]. With only Spindle Point, Newtown and Wet Earth at work, the company began to look outside the immediate neighbourhood of Clifton to maintain production.

In the late 1870s, the Little Hey Pit at Kearsley had been taken over from Andrew Knowles and Sons Ltd, but that had only been used for pumping. One of the pits formerly worked by Samuel Scowcroft and Sons, probably at Kearsley Moor, was put to similar use in 1888. Then, in 1904, some exploratory work was carried out at Kearsley Moss Colliery, again formerly the property of Samuel Scowcroft and Sons. Production started here a year or two later and continued until 1921.

The first major venture was the construction of a new colliery at Astley Green, to the south of Tyldesley, which we describe in Chapter 9. This was undertaken by the Pilkington Colliery Co Ltd, a subsidiary which the Clifton and Kersley Coal Co Ltd had formed specifically for this purpose on 27th August 1907 [21].

On the north side of the Irwell Valley, Outwood Colliery came up for sale in 1909. As we have described earlier, it was purchased by the Clifton and Kersley Coal Co Ltd on 7th May and transferred to another subsidiary, Outwood Collieries Ltd, registered on 13th May 1909 [68].

A third subsidiary, Collieries (Clifton and Kersley) Ltd, was registered on 11th November 1924 and all the assets not vested in the other two companies were transferred to it on 16th December [69]. Thereafter the Clifton and Kersley Coal Co Ltd became purely a holding company.

Bridgewater Collieries Ltd purchased Newtown Colliery in 1925 to give access to the rich seams of coal north of its existing pits at Sandhole. The contract of sale, dated 1st September 1925, provided for the use of the Robin Hood Sidings together with the screening plant and washery jointly with the Clifton and Kersley company, which retained the option to process coal brought in from its other collieries [70]. The tubway from Newtown Colliery as far as the bridge over Rake Lane passed to Bridgewater Collieries Ltd; the remainder stayed in Clifton and Kersley ownership. The agreement with the London, Midland and Scottish Railway Company relating to the use of the main line connections for Bridgewater Collieries traffic was not signed until 21st October 1926 [71], to formalise what was already the situation.

It appears that Bridgewater Collieries also made some use of the canal arm which had formerly served Botany Bay Colliery, but whether this was to send coal away by boat we do not know. They were told in January 1927 that they had no right to do so, as the site was needed for an extension to the pottery works [72]. The canal arm was duly filled in later that year [73].

The Clifton and Kersley company's operations at Robin Hood seem to have been run down very quickly. Slack coal from Astley Green had previously been processed here [74] but, by June 1925, this had been transferred to the washeries at Spindle Point, Outwood and Wet

Earth [75]. House coal was also sent from Astley Green to Robin Hood sidings, from where it went up the tubway to the landsale yard at Newtown. This traffic seems to have ceased around the end of 1925.

Collieries (Clifton and Kersley) Ltd decided that it no longer required the washery and, in December 1926, it was offered for sale to Bridgewater Collieries Ltd, along with the portion of the tubway north of Rake Lane [76,77]. Negotiations dragged on through 1928 and the early part of 1929, when they were overtaken by the absorption of both firms into Manchester Collieries Ltd.

In 1928 the last two pits owned by Collieries (Clifton and Kersley) Ltd were closed. Wet Earth ceased production on 10th February [40,78] thus ending mining on the site which had started some 187 years previously. The site now forms part of a country park. Much work has been done in recent years to conserve the relics which still remain and to interpret them for the visitor.

At Spindle Point operations were suspended in July 1928 according to the Mines Lists, although the colliery was not formally abandoned until 1931. The washery here was retained for a few more years to deal with coal from Astley Green. In May 1928 it was reported that additional duties there necessitated a second locomotive and, when the washery worked two shifts, one of them would be required to work both shifts [79]. In June of the same year the railway at the timber yard was said to be in a shocking state and could not be used safely much longer [80]. In January 1929 it was agreed that the line from there to Spindle Point should be lifted [81] and we presume that the locomotives were subsequently kept at Spindle Point.

The workshop buildings at the timber yard were later used for other purposes. Some still survive at the time of writing, forming part of a small industrial estate. The site of Spindle Point Colliery is now occupied by a warehouse and distribution depot.

The history of the locomotives used at the Clifton and Kersley collieries during the period from 1905 to 1929 is complicated by the fact that there were several transfers between the subsidiary companies. Although some information is contained in the company archives [21], the documentation, much of it concerned with accountancy, is not always easy to follow. Some information about the engines employed at Robin Hood Sidings is provided in a recent article by Philip Hindley [82].

ROBIN HOOD was transferred to Outwood Collieries Ltd around 1910 and does not seem to have been replaced. In December 1913 the Clifton and Kersley Coal Company advertised for either a four coupled or six coupled locomotive with 14" cylinders [83]. A second hand engine answering to this description arrived at Astley Green Colliery at about his date, so we assume that the advertisement had been placed on behalf of the Pilkington Colliery Co Ltd and that the engine was not intended for use at the Clifton and Kersley collieries.

Thus, leaving aside those on the books of the two subsidiary companies, there were five locomotives in service with the Clifton and Kersley Coal Co Ltd after 1910 - KERSLEY, BLACK DIAMOND, VICTORIA, CLIFTON, and NEWTOWN.

Two were kept in the shed at the timber yard for working between Spindle Point Colliery and the Lancashire and Yorkshire sidings at Unity Brook. According to old employees, KERSLEY and BLACK DIAMOND were allocated to these duties in the period up to the first world war. The former was said to have been normally used for shunting in the exchange sidings, while the latter worked over the steep gradient between the main line and the colliery [69].

The second ROBIN HOOD built by Chapman and Furneaux of Gateshead in 1901, photographed at Robin Hood Sidings in May 1955.   Alex Appleton

A maker's photograph of NEWTOWN, built for the Clifton and Kersley Coal Co Ltd by Hawthorn Leslie and Co Ltd in 1904   Frank Jones collection

By the mid 1920s, CLIFTON, which had been reboilered in 1921 [84], was at Spindle Point [85]. NEWTOWN, which had received a new boiler and firebox in 1922 [86], was also here for a time [85].

One engine was normally kept at Robin Hood Sidings and either one or two at Wet Earth. In the early 1920s it seems that the duties here were shared by NEWTOWN, VICTORIA and perhaps BLACK DIAMOND. However, BLACK DIAMOND was transferred to the Pilkington Colliery Co Ltd for use at Astley Green in 1922 [87] and was not replaced.

Towards the end of 1925 NEWTOWN was working at Robin Hood Sidings, where it presumably carried out the shunting for Bridgewater Collieries Ltd as well the little that was still needed for the Clifton and Kersley company. It suffered on several occasions with boiler tube problems. The management was told that one locomotive was insufficient for the work, but little was done except to institute two-shift working [88,89]. The Pilkington Tile and Pottery Company complained of the irregular and unsatisfactory service provided by the colliery company. It was advised to employ horses or other means to carry out shunting within the factory and to place outgoing wagons in a position to be picked up by the colliery engine [90].

From the end of January or early in February 1926, Bridgewater Collieries Ltd took over responsibility for its own shunting operations at Robin Hood. The firm's fleet of locomotives were all six coupled and unsuitable for the restricted siding accommodation and tight curves. A smaller, four coupled engine, specifically for use at Robin Hood, was purchased second hand, in January 1926, from George Cohen and Sons Ltd for £825 [29] and was given the name KEARSLEY by its new owners. It had been built in 1918 for the war-time Inland Waterways and Docks organisation by Kerr, Stuart and Company of Stoke on Trent and had reputedly been at a government factory at Wednesbury before coming to Robin Hood.

With the arrival of the Bridgewater Colliery Company's locomotive, there appears to have been little, if any, need for the Clifton and Kersley Coal company to keep an engine of its own at Robin Hood. NEWTOWN was transferred to the Pilkington Colliery Co Ltd during the year ending 31st March 1928, perhaps after the spell at Spindle Point mentioned earlier. This left only three locomotives to cover the work at Spindle Point and Wet Earth.

The situation must have been difficult when CLIFTON was stopped for repairs during May, June and July 1928 [79,80,91], particularly as two locomotives were required for the work at Spindle Point washery [79]. A real crisis developed when VICTORIA broke a cylinder and slide bar at the beginning of June 1928 [92] and the company records [93] suggest that NEWTOWN may have been returned temporarily until the repairs had been completed.

Some details have survived in the company archives about the Clifton and Kearsley Coal Company's fleet of wagons and additional information is provided in an article in the Journal of the Lancashire and Yorkshire Railway Society [56].

With numerous coal yards in Manchester and Salford, as well as at Oldham, Bury, Bolton, Blackburn, Darwen and elsewhere, the company maintained a large fleet of wagons suitable for use on the main line. Totals are recorded as 1612 in 1912, 1750 in 1913, 1730 in 1922 and 1678 in 1923 [94]. The wagons were painted red, lettered CLIFTON & KERSLEY COAL CO LIMITED in white [56].

Some 275 new wagons to carry 10 tons had been obtained either on hire or under hire purchase agreements during 1912 and 1913 from the Lancashire and Yorkshire Wagon Co Ltd of Heywood, the Lincoln Wagon and Engine Co Ltd and the Birmingham Railway Carriage and Wagon Co Ltd. These replaced the earlier 8-ton wagons with dumb buffers which had been banned from main line service as from 31st December 1913.

Repairs were carried out in the company's own wagon shops near the site of Manor Pit and some new construction was also undertaken. For example in October 1924 it was decided to build six new 12-ton wagons there [95] and later that year it was decided to build two new 12-ton wagons per month [96].

Although coal was conveyed by canal in 14-cwt boxes from Wet Earth to wharves in Salford, this method does not seem to have been adopted for transport by rail, except for one short lived trial in the 1920s. In February 1924 [97] it was decided to use boxes to bring house coal, destined for the landsale yard at Newtown, from Astley Green to Robin Hood sidings. Seven 12-ton underframes, each to carry four boxes, were purchased from the Central Wagon Co Ltd of Wigan [56]. Two 10-ton underframes and 28 boxes were built in the company's own shops [97]. At the end of 1925 it was recorded that the box wagons were no longer needed. The underframes were to be converted to ordinary wagons and the boxes were to be offered for sale [88].

Wagons no longer fit to run over the main line were used for internal purposes within the collieries. Many of the old dumb buffer wagons taken out of service before the end of 1913 no doubt finished their working lives like this, although at least 75 of them were broken up [98]. In 1924, it was decided to take the remaining 8-ton spring buffer wagons out of main line service. 100 were to be transferred to Outwood, 75 with end doors to be used between the colliery and the washery and 25 to be used for house coal to James Street landsale yard. The other 49 wagons were to be reported on [96].

The scene at Robin Hood Sidings, taken from a train from Manchester travelling towards Bolton in November 1953. The screening plant can be seen in the background, with the tubway from Newtown Colliery descending the incline on the hillside on the left. The locomotive shed, with its mid 1930s extension, is in the centre. At the bottom of the picture, the line to the tile works and the exchange sidings with the ex- LNWR line is just visible, passing under the main line beyond the signal post.   Alex Appleton

Newtown Colliery and Robin Hood Screens 1929 to 1957

The Clifton and Kersley Coal Co Ltd and its subsidiaries were absorbed into Manchester Collieries Ltd in March 1929. The washery at Spindle Point closed shortly after the amalgamation. Newtown Colliery and the associated coal preparation plant at Robin Hood Sidings remained in operation, but these, as we have seen, had passed into the ownership of Bridgewater Collieries Ltd in 1925.

In the early 1930s Manchester Collieries Ltd undertook a considerable programme of improvements. Newtown No 3 Pit was provided with new headgear and the installations at Robin Hood Sidings were up-dated [99]. The washery was sold for demolition in November 1934 [100], and new surface haulage plant was brought into use at the screening plant [99]. Some of the coal processed at the screens was returned up the tubway to the pit yard for landsale and for use in the boilers [101].

During the second world war the closure of Newtown Colliery was considered, but not implemented [40]. The colliery and its associated coal preparation plant at Robin Hood continued in full operation and they were taken over by the National Coal Board on 1st January 1947.

In 1956 a tunnel was driven through to the nearby Wheatsheaf Colliery so that all coal could be wound there [40]. Newtown Colliery ceased production in 1961 [40]. No 2 Pit continued in use as a pumping station for Agecroft Colliery. The greater part of the site was cleared and is now occupied by houses.

The screening plant at Robin Hood was closed towards the end of 1957 and the sidings there had been taken out of use by November of the same year. The line passing under the Manchester and Bolton railway from Robin Hood to the tile works probably remained in use until 1956 or 1957, but traffic on the portion from the tile works to the ex-LNWR exchange sidings had probably ceased somewhat earlier.

Manchester Collieries Ltd and later the National Coal Board had continued to work traffic to and from the Pilkington Tile Works and do the shunting there. Before the second world war, coke for the gas producers came in by main line trains and coal was supplied from Robin Hood screens over the colliery company's lines. In the 1930s, there was a daily van from Patricroft for incoming goods. Those finished products which were sent away by rail were normally dealt with at Clifton Junction Goods Yard [102]. In post war years the traffic gradually faded away, although, for a time, anthracite continued to arrive by rail from South Wales.

The Kerr Stuart locomotive KEARSLEY was taken over by Manchester Collieries Ltd and remained here for many years. The Engineering Department Report for the year ending 31st March 1935 [103] notes that the locomotive shed had been extended so that the spare engine could be kept under cover. The spare engine in the early 1930s was presumably VICTORIA as CLIFTON had been transferred to Outwood Colliery around the time of the merger. It is not clear whether the Black, Hawthorn locomotive KERSLEY passed into the ownership of Manchester Collieries Ltd.

VICTORIA was sold for scrap in May 1936 [27]. THE SIRDAR, a four coupled side tank, acquired by Manchester Collieries Ltd in 1929 from the Bedford Colliery of John Speakman and Sons Ltd, was transferred to Robin Hood. Although the date of the move has not been recorded, it seems to have taken place around 1935.

KEARSLEY and THE SIRDAR continued to perform the shunting duties at Robin Hood until after the second world war. THE SIRDAR was condemned in June 1945 and broken up early in the following year. ROBIN HOOD was then transferred from Outwood Washery to allow KEARSLEY to be overhauled.

An April 1947 photograph of KEARSLEY, the Kerr Stuart locomotive purchased by Bridgewater Collieries Ltd for use at Robin Hood. It has just passed under the Manchester to Bolton line and is working hard up the steep gradient with a train of empty wagons, probably from the tile works.   Alex Appleton

Both engines were taken over by the National Coal Board on 1st January 1947. KEARSLEY had been returned to traffic by the end of February 1947 and remained at Robin Hood until two years or so before the screens were closed. During this period it paid one visit to Walkden Yard, for general overhaul. It left Robin Hood on 16th December 1954 travelling under its own steam via Linnyshaw Moss Sidings. It returned by the same route on 25th March 1955. In the middle of 1956, KEARSLEY was sent from Robin Hood to Ashton Moss Colliery. After a another transfer to Wheatsheaf, it went to Walkden Yard towards the end of 1961. Here it remained out of use until it was scrapped in February 1967.

ROBIN HOOD left for Walkden Yard under its own steam on 22nd March 1947 [29]. After repairs, it joined the group of small locomotives which were transferred from colliery to colliery as the need arose. It came back to Robin Hood Sidings for brief periods during 1949, 1950, 1951 and 1952 when KEARSLEY was out of service. Then, in the middle of 1954, it returned on a more permanent basis. It was sent to Walkden Yard under its own steam on 18th August 1955 via Linnyshaw Moss and, after repairs, travelled back by the same route on 26th November 1956. It was seen shunting at Robin Hood Sidings as late as September 1957, but by November of the same year all work had ceased here. ROBIN HOOD was sent to Walkden, where it was broken up in December 1961.

THE SIRDAR, a powerful side tank locomotive, built in 1897 by the Vulcan Foundry for John Speakman and Sons. It was transferred to Robin Hood Sidings after the formation of Manchester Collieries Ltd and worked there until 1945.   *Alex Appleton*

The Avonside locomotive taken over by Manchester Collieries Ltd from the Bradford Colliery Co Ltd, seen here working at Bradford in 1952 before its transfer to Robin Hood.   *Alex Appleton*

Two other locomotives which were used at Robin Hood Screens in National Coal Board times were CARBON and an engine which did not actually carry any name, but which was usually referred to as BRADFORD.

CARBON was a four coupled saddle tank, built by Andrew Barclay Sons and Company of Kilmarnock in 1920. It had been taken over by Manchester Collieries Ltd from the Atherton Collieries of Fletcher, Burrows and Co Ltd and been working at Astley Green Colliery on vesting day. CARBON subsequently worked at Cleworth Hall Colliery and was transferred to Robin Hood for a short period early in 1955. It arrived under its own steam on 28th February and returned to Cleworth Hall, again under its own steam, on 25th April. CARBON was later sent to Bank Hall Colliery at Burnley and was broken up there in November 1968.

BRADFORD was a four coupled saddle tank, built by the Avonside Engine Company of Bristol in 1928 for Bradford Colliery, on the eastern side of Manchester, which had been purchased by Manchester Collieries Ltd in 1936. The locomotive remained at Bradford Colliery until closure. It was then sent to Robin Hood Sidings under its own steam on 7th February 1956. By September 1957 it had been laid aside and was still lying out of use at Robin Hood in August 1958. It was broken up there shortly afterwards.

KEARSLEY

Unity Brook Colliery

We have been unable to discover the precise location of this colliery. The 6" Geological map of 1929 shows it just to the south of Fletcher's Spindle Point Pits. The map accompanying Gaskell's *"History and Traditions of Clifton"* [45] equates it to the Moss Pits.

The Mines Lists from 1853/4 through to 1879 show Unity Brook as being worked by James Stott. A somewhat puzzling aspect is that the branch serving the Moss Pits had been taken up by November 1860, when the Deposited Plans were drawn up for the Lancashire and Yorkshire Railway's proposed Hindley to Clifton line [53]. Perhaps the Moss Pits formed the original Unity Brook Colliery and new pits were sunk near Spindle Point later.

There was a serious explosion at Unity Brook in March 1878 [104]. This may have hastened its closure but it was seemingly nearing the end of its life. Production ceased in November 1880 when it was stated to be worked out [105].

The plant was auctioned on 25th November [106]. Included in the sale were 31 8-ton wagons, which suggest that a connection with the Clifton Branch had been maintained up to the closure.

Knowles and Stott's Ringley and Kearsley Collieries

We move on now to three groups of pits opened out in the late 1830s and early 1840s by members of the Knowles family in various partnerships with the Stotts. Those collieries which survived until 1873 became the property of Andrew Knowles and Sons Ltd, which was formed in September of that year.

Kearsley Hall

The first edition of the 6" map, surveyed in 1844 to 1846, marks a number of coal pits on the west bank of the River Irwell upstream of Fletcher's Wet Earth Colliery stretching as far as Kearsley Hall.

Most seem to have been quite small undertakings dating from an earlier period. The only group of significance were those forming the Kearsley Hall Colliery, which the firm of Knowles and Stott had opened out about 1836 [107]. The principals in the firm at that time were Andrew Knowles and his sons John and James, together with William Stott [108]. The colliery may have closed before 1853 as it is not specifically mentioned in the first issue of the Mines Lists.

Ringley Fold

Messrs Knowles and Stott's Ringley Fold Colliery, on the opposite side of the river, in Pilkington Township, seems to have started work in August or September 1839 [107]. The lease, from the trustees of William Bromilow and Thomas Brownbill to Andrew Knowles, his sons, John and James, and William Stott, was signed on 1st January 1840 [108]. It covered an area between the Irwell and the Manchester, Bolton and Bury Canal, which we think Bromilow and Brownbill may have been working earlier.

The colliery had a life of more than 30 years. Following the death of Andrew Knowles in 1847, the property was taken over by a new partnership consisting of John Knowles, James Knowles and William Stott. On the death of John Knowles in 1852, James was joined by his brothers Robert and Thomas. The colliery passed to the firm of Andrew Knowles and Sons Ltd in 1873 and must have closed around 1876, the last year that it appears in the Mines Lists.

Unlike Kearsley Hall Colliery, which seems to have been served by road transport throughout its life, Ringley Fold was joined by a short tramroad to the Manchester Bolton and Bury Canal. The first edition of the 6" map, surveyed in 1844 to 1846, shows a line running from two pits on the bank of the Irwell to Giants Seat Locks. It presumably continued in use until the colliery closed.

Little Hey and Singing Clough

There are records of mining leases in Kearsley and Stoneclough granted to Andrew Knowles and his sons John and James in 1835 and 1838 [109,110,111] but we have been unable to locate the pits which they sank to work the coal. We think that one of the collieries, held under a lease from the Starkie family [111], was on the west side of the Manchester to Bolton railway, to the south of Stoneclough Station. The first edition of the 6" map marks the Coppice and Clough pits in this area. The lease authorised the construction of waggonways, tramroads and railways, but there is no evidence that any were built.

The Knowles pits seem to have been closed down before 1855 as they are not marked on the Kearsley Tithe Map of that date [112]. There were new leases in 1857 and 1858 to James Knowles and William Stott [113,114] and the Knowles and Stott's Kearsley pits appear in the Mines Lists for 1856 for the first time. In 1868, when the Mines Lists go into more detail, they are identified as the Little Hey and Singing Clough Collieries.

Little Hey was on the west side of the Bolton and Manchester railway, near the site of the later Kearsley Junction. The Deposited Plans for Lancashire and Yorkshire Railway's Kearsley

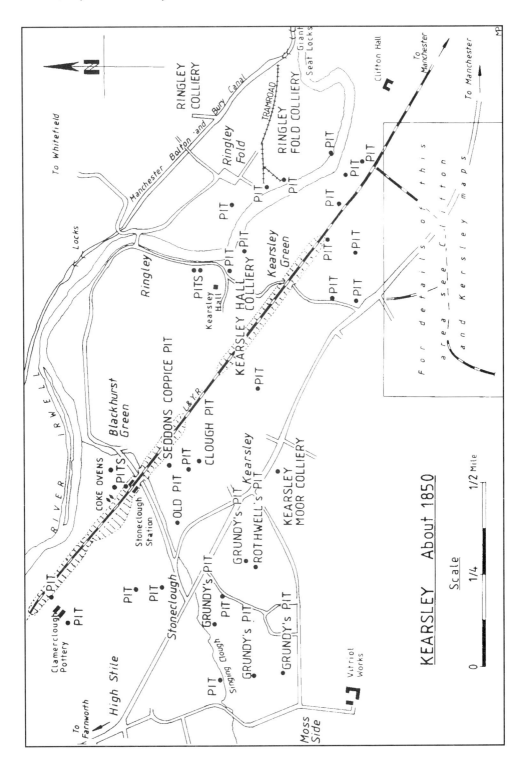

KEARSLEY About 1850

Scale

0   1/4   1/2 Mile

Branches [115], dated November 1872, show that there was a siding connection into the colliery. We think it likely that any internal shunting which was necessary was carried out using horses, as the colliery seems to have been too small to justify a locomotive. Little Hey ceased production in the late 1870s, having been taken over by Andrew Knowles and Sons Ltd in 1873. It was purchased by the Clifton and Kersley Coal Company around 1878 and was used as a pumping station until 1913. No coal was produced after the sale by Andrew Knowles and Sons and we presume that the siding connection was taken out at this time.

The Singing Clough pits are identified on the Deposited Plans at the top end of the valley, to the west of the lane from Halshaw Moor to Moss Side. They were on the point of being closed at this time and are not shown in the Mines Lists after 1872. They were unable to benefit from the new railway, which was opened in 1878, and must always have relied on road transport to take the coal away.

Rhodes Farm and Ringley Sewage Works

All remaining traces of the pits at Ringley and the tramroad associated with them disappeared when a new sewage works for Bolton Corporation was built in the 1950s, covering the area between the canal and the river from Ringley Fold to Giants Seat.

The installations here supplemented an earlier works at Rhodes Farm, to the east of Giants Seat, which had been opened in August 1899 [116]. The Rhodes Farm works provided a certain amount of traffic on the adjacent Manchester, Bolton and Bury Canal and two lay-byes were built in 1902 to accommodate the boats [117].

A 2'0" gauge railway system was used at Rhodes Farm to transport materials around the site and probably represents a development that took place after the second world war. A small diesel locomotive was purchased in 1949 from Ruston and Hornsby of Lincoln for use on the line. It was sold in February 1965 to the Lancashire Moss Litter Company for use at Horwich.

Kearsley Moor and Kearsley Moss Collieries

A directory of 1834 [118] shows Jackson and Scowcroft as proprietors of a colliery at Kearsley. In directories of 1848 and 1851 [119,120] the firm is given as Longworth and Scowcroft. We believe that it was John Scowcroft who was the partner in these firms and that the entries relate to the Kearsley Moor Colliery, marked on the first edition of the 6" map on the west side of the Manchester to Bolton Road, near the centre of the village. The Mines Lists show that by 1854 it was being worked by T and S Scowcroft and the executors of John Scowcroft. By 1856 it had become the property of Samuel Scowcroft.

By 1872, when the Deposited Plans were prepared for the Lancashire and Yorkshire Railway's Kearsley Branches [115], Samuel Scowcroft had sunk a new Kearsley Moss Colliery on a site near the Vitriol Works. An earlier pit, on the opposite side of Moss Lane had been retained, and is shown as sublet to Samuel Scowcroft by Thomas Grundy.

The Kearsley Collieries, along with Scowcroft's Rosehill Colliery at Bolton, were put up for sale as a going concern on 13th June 1883 [121]. The Kearsley Collieries remained unsold, apparently for family reasons. Two of the pits were closed in August of that year [122] and the few remaining men at the third pit ceased work on 15th September [123]. The plant and equipment was auctioned at sales on 9th, 10th and 24th April and on 10th May 1884 [124 to 127].

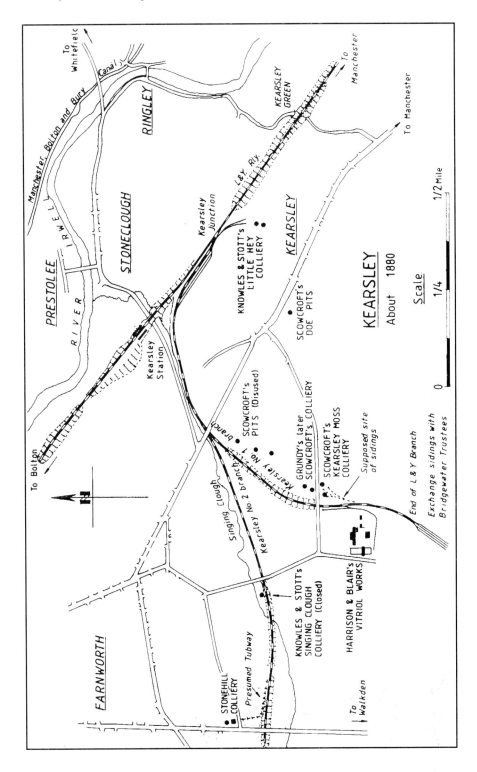

The leases appear to have been transferred to the Clifton and Kersley Coal Company, which took over one of the pits for use as a pumping station. Then, in 1904, the Clifton and Kersley company started work to reopen the Kearsley Moss Colliery. Production seems a to have commenced a year or two later and continued until 1921, The Mines Lists show that the colliery was abandoned in 1923.

There was some discussion in 1926 about reopening Kearsley Moss again, but nothing materialised [128]. Bridgewater Collieries considered taking it over, but waived their option to purchase early in 1927. It was then decided that it should be dismantled [129].

Scowcroft's Kearsley Moor Colliery was never connected to the main line railway system. Following the opening of the L&YR's Kearsley No 1 Branch in 1878, sidings were evidently provided to serve the Kearsley Moss Pits, as they are mentioned in the sales notices in 1883. Railway wagons were included in the sale on 24th March 1884, but it is unlikely that the firm ever employed a locomotive here. The Clifton and Kersley Coal Company's operations here in the present century presumably required the sidings to be relaid, although it is again doubtful that a locomotive was used.

Stonehill Colliery

We have been unable to trace the early history of Stonehill Colliery. It is marked on the first edition of the 6" map, surveyed in 1844 to 1846. In the Mines Lists for 1864 it shown in the occupation of Roscoe and Lord, an old established firm which had been working collieries at Rochdale and Bury in the 1840s [130].

There was no direct rail connection before the opening of the Lancashire and Yorkshire Railway's Kearsley No 2 Branch in 1878. It appears that a short tubway was then constructed from the colliery to a loading dock where the coal was transhipped into standard gauge wagons. Road transport had evidently been used to distribute the coal before this, as a sale of horses was advertised for 18th March 1878 because "a new mineral line to the collieries is open" [131].

Ten years later, the lease expired and the colliery plant was advertised to be sold on 28th February 1888 [132]. The colliery does not appear to have reopened and as it provided the only traffic on the Kearsley No 2 Branch, this too was closed.

Harrison Blair and Company's Vitriol Works

The firm was founded in 1833 [133] by Harrison Blair to build a Chemical Works on Kearsley Moss to make vitriol, hydrochloric acid, bleach liquor and soda by the Leblanc process.

Blair was associated in the project with George Cottingham, who had previously been works manager at Benjamin Rawson's vitriol works at Prestolee. Cottingham died a few years after the works was started and Harrison Blair was joined in the partnership by his brother Stephen. The partners took over a bleach works at Mill Hill, in Little Bolton, but later the property was divided between them.

The Bleach works went to Stephen and Harrison retained the chemical works at Kearsley [134,135]. By 1872 the works had been taken over by a partnership of James Warburton and Thomas Chester Blair [136], who continued to trade as Harrison Blair and Company. The firm was turned into a limited liability company, registered on 11th May 1891, when it was stated that the works made soda ash, soda, sulphuric acid and other chemicals [137,138].

A number of railway projects had been put forward which would have served the works. The Farnworth Branch of the Manchester, Bolton and Bury, authorised in 1831 would have passed close by, but was only built in a truncated form, stopping a mile or so short. A branch from the top of Unity Brook to the Vitriol Works had been proposed in the Lancashire and Yorkshire Railway's Clifton Branch Extension scheme of 1847 [139] , in the Manchester and Southport scheme of 1852 [52], and in the Lancashire and Yorkshire's Wigan to Clifton scheme of 1860 [53]. It was not until the opening of the Kearsley No 1 Branch in 1878 that the works was eventually served by rail. The siding connection was provided under an agreement with the L&YR dated 19th July 1873 [140].

The earliest locomotive we have discovered was a vertical boilered machine of unknown make, which was sold in March 1907 to Thomas Mitchell and Sons Ltd, the Bolton machinery merchants. It was taken in part exchange for a second hand four coupled saddle tank, originally built by the Hunslet Engine Company of Leeds in 1888.

Correspondence with the firm suggested that the Hunslet locomotive was itself replaced around 1918 [133] and, according to a old employee, it was broken up on site by William Whitelegge, a Farnworth scrap dealer. From about 1924, a road tractor was used to move the wagons in the works yard [133], but we have been unable to discover if there was another locomotive in the intervening period.

The sidings remained in use until after the second world war, rail traffic finally ceasing probably in the late 1950s or early 1960s. The agreement in respect of the connection with the Kearsley No 1 Branch was cancelled as from 31st December 1965 [140]. The works subsequently closed and the site is now used by a road haulage firm.

The Stoneclough Colliery Company

In the 1890s mining was restarted by the Stoneclough Colliery Co Ltd at the lower end of Singing Clough, in an area where there had been a number of small pits in the first half of the century. The firm first appears in the Mines Lists for 1892, when the colliery was recorded as "sinking". The 1929 6" geological map shows the Stanley Pit on the east side of the road leading to Ringley Bridge, while the Starkie Pit was on the south side of the L&YR's Kearsley Branch Sidings.

The firm was unsuccessful and the colliery ceased work in 1902 or 1903. The Mines Lists for 1904 describe it as abandoned. The plant was sold by auction on 5th October 1904 and the pits were never reopened [141,142].

The Stanley Pit had no rail connection, but the Starkie Pit was served by a small bank of sidings which joined the L&YR Kearsley Branch. Included in the dismantling sale were 750 yards of track. The relevant L&YR sidings diagram records that the siding was taken up in 1904 to 1905 [143].

Kearsley Power Station

By the 1920s the demand for electricity was beginning to outgrow the limited capacity at the existing plants and the Lancashire Electric Power Company decided on the construction of a new power station at Kearsley, extra capital for the work being authorised by the Company's Act of 1929 [144].

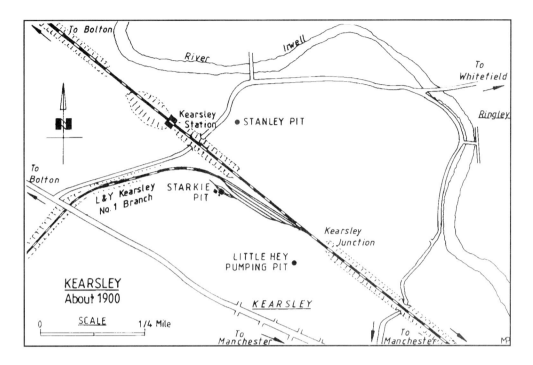

KEARSLEY
About 1900

The site chosen was on the low ground near the River Irwell, occupied in former times by Kearsley Hall Colliery. Electricity production started in 1929. The civil engineering work was undertaken by Jarvis and Sons. According to employees at the power station, four narrow gauge steam locomotives were used on the contract, but we have been unable either to confirm this or to find out further information about the engines.

Rail access was provided by a line which connected with the Kearsley Branch sidings and passed under the Manchester and Bolton railway. Much of the coal came from former Bridgewater pits, by this date owned by Manchester Collieries Ltd. It was handed over to the LMSR at Linnyshaw Sidings and hauled by main line locomotives over the short distance from there to Kearsley Junction.

Between the power station and the exchange sidings, all empty wagons returning to the collieries had to be hauled up steep gradients, mainly 1 in 22, with short stretches of 1 in 27 and 1 in 48 [145]. Electric traction was chosen, with overhead wire current collection. As well as the internal railway system itself, eight of the roads in the exchange sidings at Kearsley Junction were also electrified.

Current was supplied at 550 volts DC from motor generator sets, with mercury arc rectifiers as stand-by. Because of the steepness of the gradients a double bogie design of locomotive was purchased. Each axle was driven through single reduction gearing, by a 45 HP motor. The motors were connected in pairs and each pair could be worked either in series or parallel.

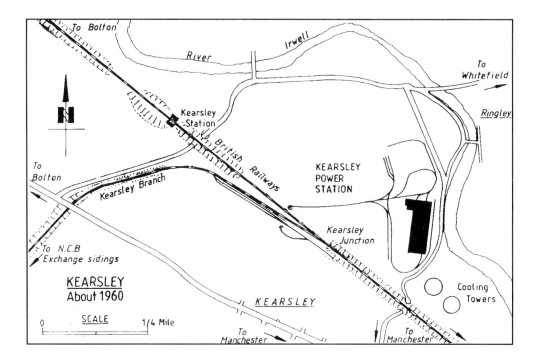

The first locomotive was delivered in 1927 by Hawthorn, Leslie and Company of Newcastle on Tyne, with electrical equipment supplied by BTH. It is said to have been used during the construction of the power station, when an external power supply was provided. For twelve years it worked all the traffic. Then, in 1936, to coincide with extensions to the Power Station, a second identical locomotive was purchased from the same manufacturers.

To cater for further extensions being planned towards the end of the second world war two more locomotives were acquired, one in 1944 and one in 1945. These were built by the Robert Stephenson and Hawthorn, successors to the earlier firm. The design was similar to that of the pre war engines, except that 65 HP motors were fitted.

With the nationalisation of the industry, the British Electricity Authority took over the power station as from 1st April 1948. As a consequence of reorganisations, it passed to the Central Electricity Authority on 1st May 1955 and to the Central Electricity Generating Board on 1st January 1958.

At the peak of electricity production, the railway system handled around 20,000 tons of coal each week, operating on a three shift basis. This involved moving about 180 wagons in and out of the sidings every 24 hours. Only 7 or 8 wagons could be handled on each trip to and from the main line sidings, so the electric locomotives were kept fully occupied. In 1962, they were joined by a 150 HP four coupled diesel, built by John Fowler of Leeds, which was transferred from Ince Power Station. This does not appear to have been employed for traffic purposes, but was used on maintenance duties when repairs were needed to the overhead wires.

By 1969, the power station was being run down and the railway operations had been reduced to two shifts, handling 60 to 80 wagons per day, although some coal was also delivered by road. By 1977 only limited amounts of electricity were being generated and, after the middle of the year, such coal as was required came by road. In October the main line sidings were being removed and most of the overhead wire had been taken down [146].

The four electric locomotives at Kearsley Power Station, lined up for what is assumed to have been an official photograph, taken about 1945. Note that the wagons are still in the livery of the Lancashire Electric Power Co Ltd and had escaped the general pooling of rolling stock which took place during the war years.
Industrial Railway Society - Brian Webb collection

The electric locomotives were still being used on a short section of track, from the lorry tippler to the bunkers, and this continued until the middle of 1981, when the power station ceased work [147]. The track within the power station yard was not taken up immediately and the electric locomotives were moved about from time to time.

The main use of the internal railway system was, however, for research on remote controlled driverless vehicles, apparently under the auspices of the General Electric Company Ltd. Two trams, previously owned by Blackpool Corporation, had appeared by January 1981 and these were run around the site as part of the experiments. By August 1982, two more trams had arrived, this time from Lisbon.

Around 1980, the Central Electricity Generating Board established a central workshops at Kearsley, to serve its North Western Region. A number of diesel locomotives and one fireless steam engine were sent there from other power stations, either for repair or storage, but, by the end of 1985, they had all been moved away. Further information about them can be found in the Locomotive Summary at the end of the chapter.

The five cooling towers were demolished on 28th April 1985 [148]. The power station buildings were cleared away during 1987 and 1988 and a housing estate was built on the site in the early 1990s.

Of the four electric locomotives, two went for preservation, No 1 to the Greater Manchester Museum of Science and Industry, Liverpool Road, in 1981 and No 3 to the West Yorkshire County Council's Spen Valley Railway in July 1983.

No 2 had been sent to Back o' th' Bank Power Station, at Bolton, in the middle of 1978 for conversion to a battery locomotive for use at Llanberis Power Station, Gwynedd. However, the work was not carried out and it was returned to Kearsley in June 1980. It was transferred on 19th July 1983 to Padiham Power Station, near Burnley. This was another former Lancashire Electric Power Company plant where overhead wire electric traction had been adopted in the private sidings. However, the electric locomotive had been replaced by two diesels in 1961 and the overhead wire system taken down. In autumn 1992 No 2 was sent to the Arbour Locomotive Works of Ian V Riley Engineering Ltd at Kirkby, near Liverpool, for a similar conversion.

No 4 was converted into a battery locomotive at the Kearsley Workshops in 1982. Given the name DOUG TOTTMAN, it went to Heysham Power Station in January 1984. It was still there at the end of 1993.

LOCOMOTIVE SUMMARY

Outwood Colliery

> Originally known as Clough Side Colliery
> Name changed to Outwood in 1865
> Brownbill and Bromilow until 1858
> Thomas Fletcher until about 1875
> Thomas Fletcher and Sons until 1868
> Thomas Fletcher and Sons Ltd from 11th May 1868
> Outwood Collieries Ltd from 13th May 1909
> Manchester Collieries Ltd from 4th March 1929
> Colliery abandoned 1931, washery retained
> National Coal Board from 1st January 1947
> Washery closed 1955

Thomas Fletcher and Sons Ltd (until 1909):

	0-6-0STOC	P	923	1901	14"x20"	3'7"

Class B1, new
To Outwood Collieries Ltd in 1909

	0-4-0STOC	P	935	1902	10"x14"	

Class M4, new
To Outwood Collieries Ltd in 1909

Note that Hudswell Clarke 240 and FARMERS FRIEND may also have been used at Outwood - see text

Outwood Collieries Ltd (1909 to 1929):

OUTWOOD No 1	0-6-0STOC	P	923	1901	14"x20"	3'7"

Ex Thomas Fletcher and Sons Ltd in 1909
To Manchester Collieries Ltd in 1929

OUTWOOD No 2	0-4-0STOC	P	935	1902	10"x14"	

Ex Thomas Fletcher and Sons Ltd in 1909
To Pilkington Colliery Co Ltd in 1912 and transferred to Astley Green

ROBIN HOOD	0-4-0STOC	CF	1200	1901	14"x19"	3'2"

Ex Clifton and Kersley Coal Co Ltd about 1909
To Manchester Collieries Ltd in 1929

Manchester Collieries Ltd (1929 to 1947):

OUTWOOD No 1	0-6-0STOC	P	923	1901	14"x20"	3'7"

Ex Outwood Collieries Ltd in 1929
To NCB on 1-1-1947

ROBIN HOOD	0-4-0STOC	CF	1200	1901	14"x19"	3'2"

Ex Outwood Collieries Ltd
To Robin Hood Sidings about 1945

CLIFTON	0-4-0STOC	VF	1450	1895	15"x20"	3'7"

Transferred about 1928 or 1929 from Collieries (Clifton and Kersley) Ltd at Spindle Point
Sold to Harry Stephenson and Sons Ltd, Hindley, 8-5-1936 for scrap

National Coal Board (1947 to 1955):

OUTWOOD   0-6-0STOC P 923 1901 14"x20" 3'7"
  Ex Manchester Collieries Ltd on 1-1-1947
  To Walkden Yard for repairs in early 1950 and then to Wheatsheaf
  From Wheatsheaf to Outwood 6-1954
  To Walkden Yard 8-1956 and scrapped there 1-1962

ROBIN HOOD   0-4-0STOC CF 1200 1901 14"x19" 3'2"
  Temporarily here from 9-1947 to 5-1949, 11-1949 to 1-1950, 1-1951 to 3-1951, 5-1952 to late 1952/mid 1953

PECKETT   0-6-0STIC P 518 1890 13"x18" 3'0"
  Transferred from Wheatsheaf 1-1950
  To Walkden Yard for repairs 1-1955 and did not return to Outwood

Radcliffe Power Station

  Lancashire Electric Power Co Ltd until 31st March 1948
  British Electricity Authority until 30th April 1955
  Central Electricity Authority until 31st December 1957
  Central Electricity Generating Board from 1st January 1958

        4wOHW Stothert   1904
              and Pitt
 New
  Derelict by 6-1962 and scrapped by 9-1962

Clifton and Kersley Collieries

  Various members of Fletcher family and their trustees until about 1865
  Clifton and Kersley Coal Company until 31st July 1885
  Clifton and Kersley Coal Co Ltd until 16th December 1924
  Collieries (Clifton and Kersley) Ltd until 4th March 1929
  Newtown Colliery sold to Bridgewater Collieries Ltd September 1925, with joint use of Robin Hood
    Screening Plant
  Manchester Collieries Ltd from 4th March 1929
  National Coal Board from 1st January 1947

Locomotives used at :
  Spindle Point Colliery and Manor Pit from about 1870 to about 1930
  Robin Hood Screens from about 1870 to about 1926 by Clifton and Kersley Coal Company, Clifton and
    Kersley Coal Ltd and Collieries (Clifton and Kersley) Ltd and from early 1926 to 1957 by Bridgewater
    Collieries Ltd and successors
  Wet Earth Colliery from about 1895 to about 1930

Clifton and Kersley Coal Company, Clifton and Kersley Coal Ltd and Collieries (Clifton and Kersley)
  Ltd (1865 to 1929):

CLIFTON
  Acquired in 1871
  Sold 1896

KERSLEY   0-6-0STOC BH 308 1874 14"x20" 3'7"
 New
  Possibly to Manchester Collieries Ltd in 1929, but may have been scrapped before amalgamation

BLACK DIAMOND	0-4-0STOC	SS	2742	1878	16"x20"	4'0"

New
To Pilkington Colliery Co Ltd in 1922 and transferred to Astley Green Colliery

VICTORIA	0-4-0STOC	BH	896	1887	15"x20"	3'8"

New
To Manchester Collieries Ltd in 1929

ROBIN HOOD	0-4-0STOC	BH	1038	1893	14"x19"	3'2"

New
Returned to Chapman and Furneaux Ltd in 1901 and resold to Steetley Lime and Basic Co Ltd, Coxhoe,
    Co Durham

CLIFTON	0-4-0STOC	VF	1450	1895	15"x20"	3'7"

New
To Outwood Collieries Ltd about 1928 or 1929 and transferred to Outwood Colliery

ROBIN HOOD	0-4-0STOC	CF	1200	1901	14"x19"	3'2"

New
To Outwood Collieries Ltd about 1909 and transferred to Outwood Colliery

NEWTOWN	0-4-0STOC	HL	2580	1904	15"x22"	3'9"

New
To Pilkington Colliery Co Ltd by 3-1928 and transferred to Astley Green Colliery
May have returned temporarily to Spindle Point, see text

Bridgewater Collieries Ltd (at Robin Hood Sidings - 1925 to 1929):

KEARSLEY	0-4-0STOC	KS	3123	1918	15"x20"	3'2"

Originally IWD, Portsmouth
Purchased from George Cohen and Sons Ltd, £825, 25-1-1926
To Manchester Collieries Ltd in 1929

Manchester Collieries Ltd (1929 to 1947):

KERSLEY	0-6-0STOC	BH	308	1874	14"x20"	3'7"

New
Possibly ex Collieries (Clifton and Kersley) Ltd in 1929, but may have been scrapped prior to
    amalgamation

VICTORIA	0-4-0STOC	BH	896	1887	15"x20"	3'8"

Ex Collieries (Clifton and Kersley) Ltd in 1929
Sold to Harry Stephenson and Sons Ltd, Hindley, for scrap 5-1936

KEARSLEY	0-4-0STOC	KS	3123	1918	15"x20"	3'2"

Ex Bridgewater Collieries Ltd in 1929
To NCB 1-1-1947

THE SIRDAR	0-4-0STOC	VF	1541	1897	15"x20"	3'5"

Ex Bedford Colliery about 1933
Boiler condemned 3-1945, scrapped 3-1946

ROBIN HOOD	0-4-0STOC	CF	1200	1901	14"x19"	3'2"

Ex Outwood in 1945 or 1946
To NCB at 1-1-1947

National Coal Board (1947 to 1958):

KEARSLEY   0-4-0STOC   KS   3123   1918   15"x20"   3'2"
    Ex Manchester Collieries Ltd 1-1-947
    To Walkden Yard for repairs 16-12-1954, returned on 25-3-1955
    To Ashton Moss Colliery 6-1957

ROBIN HOOD   0-4-0STOC   CF   1200   1901   14"x19"   3'2"
    Ex Manchester Collieries Ltd 1-1-1947
    To Walkden Yard for repairs 22-3-1947
    Temporarily at Robin Hood 23-8-1950 to 25-1-1951, 8-11-1951 to 5-3-1952, 26-3-1952 to 17-4- 1952, End
        1952 or early 1953, Mid 1954 to 18-8-1955, 26-11-1956 to late 1957
    To Walkden Yard late 1957 and broken up there 12-1961

CARBON   0-4-0STOC   AB   1704   1920   14"x22"   3'5"
    Temporarily at Robin Hood 28-2-1955 to 25-4-1955

BRADFORD   0-4-0STOC   AE   1995   1928   14"x22"   3'6"
    Did not carry name
    Ex Bradford Colliery 7-2-1956
    Scrapped at Robin Hood 9-1958

Rhodes Farm Sewage Works

    Bolton Corporation

2'0" gauge
                            4w DM   RH   273525   1945   20DL Class
    To Lancashire Moss Litter Co Ltd, Horwich 1-1965

Kearsley Chemical Works

    Harrison Blair and Company

                            0-4-0 VB VC
                            or 4wl VB VC
    Sold to Thos Mitchell and Sons Ltd 3-1907, in part exchange for HE 238-1880

                            0-4-0STOC   HE   238   1880   10"x16"   2'8"
    Purchased from Mitchell 3-1907
    Scrapped, reputedly about 1918 by Wm Whitelegge, Farnworth

Road tractors used for shunting after about 1924

Kearsley Power Station

    Lancashire Electric Power Co Ltd until 31st March 1948
    British Electricity Authority until 30th April 1955
    Central Electricity Authority until 31st December 1957
    Central Electricity Generating Board from 1st January 1958

Working locomotives :
1   4w-4wOHWE HL   3682   1927   210HP
    New
    To Greater Manchester Museum of Science and Industry, Liverpool Road, 1981

2		4w-4wOHWE HL	3872	1936	210HP

New
To Back o' th' Bank Power Station, Bolton about 7-1978 for conversion for use at Llanberis Power Station, Gwynedd.
Not converted and returned 6-1980
To Padiham Power station 19-7-1983
From Padiham to Ian V Riley Ltd, Kirkby, late 1992, for conversion to 4w-4w Bat elec for Heysham Power Station

3		4w-4wOHWE RSH	7078	1944	230HP

New
To West Yorkshire County Council, Spen Valley Railway, 19-7-1983

4		4w-4wOHWE RSH	7284	1945	230HP

New
Rebuilt 1982 to 4w-4w Bat elec at Kearsley, named DOUG TOTTMAN, and sent Heysham Power Station 1-1984.

No 1	0-4-0DM	JF	4210078	1952	150HP

Number removed by 9-1964
Ex Ince Power Station, Cheshire 5-1962
To Chadderton Power Station circa 4-1973, retd about 1977 or 1978
To Marple and Gillot Ltd, Sheffield, for scrap 2-5-1984

Locomotives sent to Kearsley for repair or storage :

1	0-6-0DM	HE	7179	1969

Rebuild of HE 5642-1959, ex BR No D2593
Ex Chadderton Power Station 24-9-1981
To East Lancashire Light Railway, Bury, 3-1983

2	0-6-0DM	HE	7180	1969

Rebuild of HE 5636-1959, ex BR No D2587
Ex Chadderton Power Station 11-1981
To East Lancashire Light Railway, Bury, about 3-1983

FW7 LORD ASHFIELD	0-6-0FOC	AB	1989	1930	15"x18"	3'0"

Ex Fleetwood Power Station 17-3-1982
To Greater Manchester Museum of Science and Industry, Liverpool Road, by 8-2-1985

	0-4-0DM	JF	4210068	1952	150HP

Ex Fleetwood Power Station 6-1982
To Shipbreakers (Queenborough) Ltd, Kent, 1985

	0-4-0DM	JF	4210059	1951	150HP

Ex Carrington Power Station 17-9-82
To Marple and Gillot Ltd, Sheffield, for scrap, 2-5-1984

10 D ARTIS	0-4-0DM	JF	4210001	1949	150HP

Ex Connah's Quay Power Station, Clwyd, 18-10-1984
To Padiham Power Station late 1985

References to Chapter 6

1   BMB ZLA 16/68

2   LG 27-2-1874

3   LRO PDR 363

4   7&8 Vic cap lx; 4th July 1844

5   BC 27-7-1850

6   *"Industrial Archaeology of Radcliffe and the Irwell Valley"* - K Howarth - in *"Industrial Archaeology"*, Spring 1974

7   FJ 28-5-1898

8   L&YR Sdgs Diags 5, 10th April 1895 and 5A, 16th June 1908

9   WEx 12-12-1908

10 WO 12-12-1908

11 BJ 19-3-1909

12 BJ 8-4-1909

13 WO 10-4-1909

14 FJ 8-4-1909

15 BJ 14-5-1909

16 WO 22-5-1909

17 Clifton and Kersley Coal Co Ltd Minutes 25-5-1909 in SMM U64

18 *Report on the Outwood Collieries of Thos Fletcher Ltd* by C E Rhodes and Son, Rotherham, 6th Feb 1909 - at Bury and Radcliffe Libraries

19 BMB ZLA 16/27/3

20 BC 17-7-1858

21 SMM U64

22 L&YR Sdgs Diag 5B, 6th July 1916

23 Clifton and Kersley Coal Co Ltd Minutes 1-3-1927 in SMM U64

24 Note on Line Plan of East Lancashire Railway, Clifton Junction to Radcliffe Branch - BR, Euston 1950 - 2 chains to 1 inch - at BRPB, Manchester

25 Collieries (Clifton and Kersley) Ltd Minutes 21-5-1928 in SMM U64

26 Idem 29-6-1928

27 Records formerly kept at Walkden Yard

28 Observed in transit by Mr C A Appleton

29 *"From Walkden Yard Records"* - CA Appleton - in *"Industrial Locomotive"*, Nos 62 and 63, 1991

30 MJ 18-5-1872

31 BC 15-8-1874

32 Iron 19-9-1874

33 MG 5-5-1888

34 L&YR Sdgs Diag 365, 6th July 1916

35 63 & 64 Vic cap ccxxv; 6th August 1900

36 4 Edw VII cap liv; 24th June 1904

37 6 Edw VII cap cxcix; 4th August 1906

38 *"The Undertaking of the Lancashire Electric Power Company"* - Brochure published by the company in January 1923 - Reprint of article in Engineering 22nd and 29th December 1922

39 *"The Radcliffe Generating Station of the Lancashire Electric Power Co Ltd"* - British and Colonial Review - April 1924

40 *"Collieries in the Manchester Coalfield"* - Geoffrey Hayes - De Archaeologische Pers, Eindhoven, nd about 1980

41 Article by Alfred Gaskell in Swinton and Pendlebury Journal, 19-7-1961

42 *"Coal Mining in Salford"* - Geoff Preece - City of Salford Cultural Services, 1985

43 *"Brindley at Wet Earth"* - Banks and Schofield - David and Charles, Newton Abbot, 1968

44 *"The Canals of North West England"* - Hadfield and Biddle - David and Charles, Newton Abbot, 1970

45 *"The History and Traditions of Clifton"* - Alfred Gaskell - Swinton and Pendlebury Public Libraries, 1964

46 1&2 Wm 4 cap lx; 23rd August 1831

47 2 Wm 4 cap lxix; 1st June 1839

48 5&6 Wm 4 cap xxx; 17th June 1835

49 *"Chronology of the Railways of Lancashire and Cheshire"* - M D Greville - Railway and Canal Historical Society, 1981

50 *"The Lancashire and Yorkshire Railway"* - John Marshall - David and Charles, Newton Abbot, 1969

51 BC 28-10-1854

52 LRO PDR 592

53 LRO PDR 707

54 LRO DDX 326/7

55 CG 14-8-1885

56 *"The Clifton and Kersley Coal Co and the LYR"* - D Richardson - in *"Platform 33"*, L&YR Soc Jnl, Autumn 1990

57 L&YR Sdgs Diags 31, 10th July 1895 and 31a, 26th June 1903

58 L&YR Sdgs Diag 237 10th May 1901

59 Clifton and Kersley Coal Co Ltd stock returns for 1895 - in SMM U64

60 *"The Clifton and Kersley Coal Co Ltd"* - C A Appleton - *Industrial Locomotive Society Journal* Vol XIX No 4 Sept to Dec 1965

61 Line Plan of Clifton Branch - LNWR, Euston, 1919 - 2 chains to 1 inch - BRPB, Manchester

62 Clifton and Kersley Coal Co Ltd Financial Records - SMM U64

63 MM 17-12-1903

64 Clifton and Kersley Coal Co Ltd - Additions to stock year ending 31-12-1903 - SMM U64

65 Idem 31-12-1904

66 Idem 31-12-1905

67 BC 3-11-1888

68   Clifton and Kersley Coal Co Ltd Minutes 25-5-1909 - SMM U64

69   Idem 16-12-1924

70   Idem Sept 1925

71   Endorsement on L&YR Sdgs Diag 237a, 27th Aug 1909

72   Collieries (Clifton and Kersley) Ltd Minutes 14-1-1927 - SMM U64

73   Idem 21-9-1927

74   Idem 13-8-1924

75   Idem 18-6-1925

76   Idem 16-12-1926

77   Idem 9-2-1927

78   WO 25-2-1928

79   Collieries (Clifton and Kersley) Ltd Minutes 21-5-1928 - SMM U64

80   Idem 6-6-1928

81   23-1-1929

82   *"Kearsley"* - Philip Hindley - *"Industrial Locomotive"* Vol 6, No 65 1992

83   CG12-12-1913

84   Clifton and Kersley Coal Co Ltd Additions to stock year ending 31-12-1921 - SMM U64

85   Collieries (Clifton and Kearsley) Ltd Stock returns 1924-28 - SMM U64

86   Clifton and Kersley Coal Co Ltd Addition to stock year ending 31-12-1922 - SMM U64

87   Pilkington Colliery Co Ltd Additions to stock year ending- 31-3-1928 - SMM U64

88   Collieries (Clifton and Kersley) Ltd Minutes 19-11-1925 - SMM U64

89   Idem 2-12-1925

90   Idem 17-12-1925

91   Idem 29-6-1928

92   Idem 6-6-1928

93   Collieries (Clifton and Kersley) Ltd Additions to stock half year ending 30-9-1928 - SMM U64

94   Collieries (Clifton and Kersley) Ltd Minutes 30-1-1924- SMM U64

95   Idem 8-10-1924

96   Idem 24-10-1924

97   Idem 29-2-1924

98   Idem 13-9-1912

99   Cbn Jan 1932

100   LRO NCMc 33/17

101   Cbn Dec 1932

102   Article by Arthur Chambers - in *"Mancunian"*, Journal of the Manchester Locomotive.Society, 1984

103   LRO NCMc 33/17

104   BC 16-3-1878

105   FJ 6-11-1880

106   FJ 27-11-1880

107   BC 28-1-1840

108   LRO DDX 29/70

109   LRO DDX 29/11

110   LRO DDX 29/12

111   LRO DDX 29/23

112   LRO DRM 1/61

113   LRO DDX 29/24

114   LRO DDX 29/13

115   LRO PDR 954

116   BC 26-8-1899

117   *"Towpath Guide to the Manchester, Bolton and Bury Canal"* - Steven Parker and Richard Chester-Browne - Manchester, Bolton and Bury Canal Society, 1989

118   *"National Commercial Directory for the Counties of Chester, Cumberland, Durham and Lancaster "*- James Pigot and Co, Manchester, 1834

119   *"Royal National Commercial Directory and Topography of the County of Lancaster"* - Isaac Slater, Manchester, 1848

120   *"Royal National Commercial Directory and Topography of the County of Lancaster"* - Isaac Slater, Manchester, 1851

121   BC 19-5-1883

122   FJ 25-8-1883

123   FJ 15-9-1883

124   BC 19-1-1884

125   FJ 26-1-1884

126   FJ 30-1-1884

127   FJ 29-3-1884

128   Collieries (Clifton and Kersley) Ltd Minutes 10-2-1926- SMM U64

139   Ibid 23-2-1927

130   LG 22-11-1844

131   BC 9-3-1878

132   BC 4-2-1888

133   Letter Harrison Blair and Co Ltd to Frank Smith dated 19th October 1959

134   LG 30-12-1854

135   Notes on Harrison Blair - Bolton Industrial History Society - BMB B660.2B BLI

136   Book of Reference with LRO PDR 954

137   Iron 22-5-1891

138   BEN 18-5-1891

139   LRO PDR 510

140   L&YR Sdg Diag 171, 5th August 1898

141   BC 17-9-1904

142   FJ 23-9-1904

143   L&YR Sdg Diag No 152, 29th Nov 1897

144   19 Geo V cap xi; 27th March 1929)

145   Article by P J Ashforth in *"Railway Observer"* Vol 39 No 484 June 1969

146   BLN 331

147   BLN 407

148   Information supplied by Cyril Golding

To be Published as a separate volume:

Part II

Contents:

.

At ⟨...⟩ re able to see ⟨...⟩ the voices were coming from. Norton and Marigold Bicker were standing near the trash can, and they were eight inches tall. Marigold was an eight-inch woman in a checkered dress and tiny fluffy bedroom slippers. Norton was an eight-inch man with a bald head and tiny glasses.

'Uh-oh,' said Marie. 'We've got trouble now.'

THE
TINY
PARENTS

Ellen Weiss and Mel Friedman

RED FOX

A Red Fox Book
Published by Random Century Children's Books
20 Vauxhall Bridge Road, London SW1V 2SA

A division of the Random Century Group
London Melbourne Sydney Auckland
Johannesburg and agencies throughout the world

First published by Alfred A. Knopf, Inc. 1989

Red Fox edition 1991
Reprinted 1991

Set in Melior
by JH Graphics Ltd, Reading

Printed and bound in Great Britain by
Cox & Wyman Ltd, Reading

ISBN 0 09 978350 9

To Nora and Nadja

Contents

CHAPTER ONE

The Weirdest Parents in New York

The Bickers were at it again.

'Norton Bicker, I just don't know what you use for brains sometimes! The epsilon confabulator goes on the other end!'

'You don't know what you're talking about, Marigold — as usual! Do you want to blow us up? The epsilon confabulator goes on *this* end. And *you* pointed the vector field in the wrong direction!'

'I did not!'

'Did too!'

'Did not!'

'Did too!'

'Did not did not did not!'

Upstairs, on the second floor of the tall, narrow brownstone house in Brooklyn, Eddie and Marie Bicker were trying to do their homework.

'I've had it,' said Marie, throwing down her pencil. 'How can I think about the Mexican Revolution when they're screaming downstairs in the basement? You know what I'm going to do! I'm going to walk down the block and look in windows, and when I find a really normal-looking family, eating Pop-Tarts and feeding their goldfish, I'm going to knock on their door and ask if I can live with them.'

The night outside was dark and bitter cold. Marie looked at her reflection in the frost-covered window, and a perfectly normal-looking twelve-year-old girl looked back at her. Well, of course her nose *was* just a little too large. She rolled her eyes.

'All I want is to have normal parents, like other kids. Is that too much to ask?'

'Umm,' said Eddie, chewing his pencil absently. Basil, their aging basset hound, lay at his feet chewing on Eddie's slipper.

Marie knew there was no point in continuing the discussion. Being normal was not something that particularly interested Eddie. He wasn't stupid — in fact, he was probably the smartest kid in the fourth grade at P.S. 217 — but he just didn't care about the finer things in life. He could wear the same mismatched pair of socks for two weeks and not notice. And it didn't much bother him that he probably had the weirdest parents in New York City.

A crash sounded from downstairs.

'You potato-head!'

'You slug!'

'You — you wing nut!'

Eddie twirled one of his curls around his finger and didn't look up from his reading. 'You know they don't really mean it,' he said. 'Besides, they'd never get anything invented if they didn't scream at each other.' He breathed on his glasses and rubbed them with his shirttail, which just made them smearier.

'Would that be so terrible?' demanded Marie. 'I don't know about you, but *I* think the world could survive without an electronic toothpaste-tube roller or a mechanical pillow fluffer.'

'This one's really important to them, though,' said Eddie. 'This one would change the world. They'd be famous.'

'You want to know what I think? I think it's scary, that's what I think.'

'It does have a bit of risk attached to it, I guess.'

'A bit of risk,' snorted Marie. 'A bit of risk. Remember what happened when they tested the first model? On the cheeseburger? It took us three days to clean it up. And remember trying to get rid of all those six-pound sesame seeds without attracting the neighbours' attention?'

'Well, they did say it needed a little adjustment.'

'I hope the Proton Enlarger never gets built. Some scientific advances should never be unleashed on the world. Especially a machine with a ray that makes things bigger.'

There was a loud bang from the basement and then an earsplitting electronic hum. 'Not that switch, the other one!' yelled Marigold.

'What? I can't hear you!' shouted Norton.

'Pull it, you dim-bulb! Pull it now!'

'What? What?'

'Quick, before it's too late! The ray! Oh, nooo!'

Eddie sat up in his seat, finally paying attention. 'Does something sound funny about their voices?' he asked Marie.

'Wait a second, let me listen,' she whispered.

There was silence for a moment.

'Now look what you've done!' shrieked Marigold.

Eddie blinked. 'Don't their voices sound sort of . . . high?'

'Yeah. Kind of . . . tiny,' agreed Marie. They looked at each other.

Then they sprang out of their chairs and barrelled downstairs, tripping all over Basil in their rush to get to the basement.

When they got to the heavily padded door at the bottom of the stairs, they burst into the laboratory. The lab was even messier than usual: there were test tubes, beakers, flywheels, gears, bent spoons, and plungers everywhere.

But Norton and Marigold weren't there.

'Good lord,' whispered Marie. 'They've vapourized themselves.'

They stood there silently, in awe and terror.

'We haven't vapourized ourselves,' said a small, squeaky voice from somewhere near the trash can. 'Your *father* attached the "on" switch upside down.'

'That's because your *mother* bought the wrong kind of switch at the hardware store,' said another voice in tiny fury.

'That's because your *father* wrote down the wrong thing on the shopping list,' said the first little voice.

'That's because your *mother* was rushing me, as usual,' said the second voice.

At last, Eddie and Marie were able to see where the voices were coming from.

Norton and Marigold Bicker were standing near the trash can, and they were eight inches tall. Marigold was an eight-inch woman in a checkered dress and tiny fluffy bedroom slippers. Norton was an eight-inch man with a bald head and tiny glasses.

'Uh-oh,' said Marie. 'We've got trouble now.'

'It's not my fault,' squeaked Marigold.

'Well, then, whose fault is it, Mrs Brilliant Inventor?' squeaked Norton.

They went on like this for a minute, screaming and jumping up and down, until Eddie broke in.

'HOLD IT!' he yelled. 'JUST SHUT UP FOR A SECOND, WILL YOU?'

They shut up, surprised.

'Look at yourselves,' he said. 'You're still shrinking! You were as tall as that pile of newspapers a minute ago, and now you only come halfway up it! You're getting shorter every second. We'll have to do something fast, or you really will disappear.'

'Oh God,' said Norton. 'Oh God, oh God.'

'Quick,' ordered Marigold. 'Run over and reverse the field alternator, Eddie! The red button.'

Eddie leaped to the machine and punched the large red button. There was a small popping noise, but nothing happened.

'Try the polar multiplexer,' suggested Norton. 'The big black switch with the bobby pin sticking out.'

Eddie pushed the switch up. There were a lot of sparks, and then all the lights went off on the machine.

'We're still shrinking,' squeaked Marigold, an edge of hysteria creeping into her voice. 'We're only three newspapers high now!'

'Time for desperate measures,' said Marie. 'Try kicking it.'

Eddie shrugged. 'Nothing to lose,' he said, and gave the machine a tremendous kick that made him dance with pain. This time the machine hiccupped. 'Ow, ow, ow,' moaned Eddie.

'You've done it,' said Norton. 'We've stopped shrinking!'

And a good thing, too. Norton and Marigold Bicker were now two and half inches tall.

CHAPTER TWO

Hungry, Hungry, Hungry

There didn't seem to be much to say for a while. There was, however, a lot to think.

Eddie was thinking, Well, I'm nine years old, and Marie's twelve. I guess we can take care of ourselves. But how are we going to get the money to buy groceries? And what are we going to feed Norton and Marigold anyway?

Marie was thinking, This would be a really good time to go find that nice, normal family. Yes, maybe this is really the day to do it.

It's impossible to say what Norton and Marigold were thinking.

'I have an idea,' volunteered Eddie at last. 'Maybe we could reverse the effects of the machine — make it do what it was supposed to do before it zapped you.'

'You could try it,' said Marigold. 'Try flipping that red switch a couple of times.'

Eddie flipped the switch. The machine didn't even blink.

'It's no good,' said Norton mournfully. 'The circuits are all fused now. The machine is gone. Dead. Defunct.'

Marie sat down on a lab stool and stared into space. She tried to make sense of this new situation. My parents are two and a half inches tall, she imagined herself explaining to the people from the newspapers. Then she imagined making her little speech in a more casual tone of voice: Hi, I'm Marie Curie Bicker. My brother's name is Edison Newton Bicker. We're named for famous scientists, isn't that cute? Our parents are two and a half inches tall. She kept on staring into space but her chin was trembling a little. The world was swimming in front of her eyes. 'Yikes,' she sighed. 'This is bad.'

'There, there, dear,' said Marigold, in a rare moment of motherly tenderness. 'It'll be all right. We'll figure something out. Here, pick me up.' Marie picked her up. 'It's very high up here,' squeaked Marigold, looking down.

Marie brought her mother very close to her face and Marigold leaned over and kissed her on the cheek. 'There, there, dear,' she repeated.

'Ahem,' said Norton. 'Sorry to bring this up, but I'm awfully hungry.'

'How can you think of food at a time like this?' asked Marigold.

'Well, I'm sorry, but I am. I really am,' repeated Norton.

Marie stared into space, sniffing quietly. There was a long silence.

'You know something?' said Marigold. 'I'm hungry too. I'm very, very hungry.'

'It makes sense,' reasoned Eddie, who had been thinking about it. 'The tinier you are, the faster you burn up food. Little birds and mice and shrews and things, they have to eat practically all the time, just to keep their little hearts beating. All they do all day is look for bugs and stuff.'

'Bugs? Yucch!' cried Marie, suddenly coming to life. 'Eddie, we're not going to have to feed them *bugs*, are we?'

'I don't think so,' said Eddie.

'We're still *people*, for heaven's sake,' said Norton. 'We'll need to eat people food. I wouldn't mind a nice bacon, lettuce, and tomato sandwich right now, to tell the truth.'

'I think a BLT might be a little hard for you to manage, Dad,' said Marie. 'Eddie and I better go upstairs and figure out something you *can* eat.'

They started with the refrigerator. There were a lot of furry things in there. Norton and Marigold were not into housework.

'Old roast beef,' said Eddie. 'No good — we won't be able to cut it up small enough.'

'What if they waste away in a couple of days?' said Marie.

'How about this cottage cheese?'

'What if they stay tiny forever?' said Marie.

'Don't think about it,' said Eddie.

'Maybe the cottage cheese will work for Marigold,' said Marie. 'Norton hates cottage cheese. Why don't you give him some of that creamed spinach?'

'Each one of those little flakes of spinach is almost as big as his head,' observed Eddie.

'Here, let's put all this stuff in the blender. That will smooth it out, and it'll be sort of balanced. Throw in this leftover oatmeal too. And those sardines, way in the back.'

'This is going to get to be a big pain in the neck very fast,' said Eddie, dropping a teaspoonful of each thing into the blender. As a final touch, he shook in a few globs of ketchup. 'There,' he said, turning on the blender. 'Now it has another vegetable.'

Marie tasted it. 'It's disgusting,' she said. 'Maybe some salt would help.'

'We're out of salt,' said Eddie. 'I'll put in some pepper instead. It's the best we can do. They'll just have to eat whatever we can figure out.'

'I have an idea,' said Marie. 'I'll run out to the store and buy a few jars of baby food. It's got to be better than this.'

Marie put on her jacket, rummaged in the old glass beaker they used for spare money, and ran out the door. Eddie sat at the table for a while, scratching Basil behind his big, floppy ears and thinking about life. Idly, he stuck a finger into the foul-smelling glop. Could be worse, he thought. He rolled it around in his mouth and made a face. 'Nope, couldn't be worse.'

What would Julia Child do to give this dish a little extra something? he wondered. He opened the cupboard and took out a jar of strawberry jam. Perhaps just a suspicion of strawberry, he thought, stirring in a spoonful. And a dash of coconut for garnish. He sprinkled on a huge amount of the white flaky stuff.

Then he looked around the kitchen for something his parents could use for silverware and plates. His eye fell on a root-beer bottle cap that had been left lying on the counter. Okay, he thought, here's their plate. They can share it. Now what are they going to eat with?

After another few minutes of looking around, he had just about decided they'd have to eat with their fingers when he noticed a box of flat toothpicks on the shelf above the stove. He climbed up on a stool to get them. The box had sticky brown kitchen dirt all over it. He took out two toothpicks and broke off about a quarter of an inch from the end of each one. He filled the bottle cap with the greenish mush and stood the two toothpick pieces up in it, as attractively as he could. 'Bon appetit,' he muttered, and headed for the basement.

Downstairs, Norton and Marigold were waiting impatiently for their dinner. They sat down on the floor, and Eddie placed the bottle cap between them.

'Boy oh boy, I can't believe how hungry I am,' said Norton, shovelling the food into his mouth at an incredible rate.

'Me, too,' agreed Marigold, eating just as quickly. 'This stuff is horrible, Edison. Is there any more?'

'There's more in the blender,' said Eddie. He was amazed at how much they'd eaten in thirty seconds. 'I'll go get it.'

He trudged upstairs, already feeling like a prisoner in a forced-labour camp. He could imagine himself spending his days and nights going up and down, up and down, the little voices chirping like little birds for more and more and more. . . .

Marie came in and slammed the kitchen door, bringing in a cloud of cold air with her. Her hands were red when she pulled off her woollen gloves.

'I got Peas and Carrots, Squash, and look at this — Veal Dinner. Pretty good huh?'

'Looks delicious,' chuckled Eddie. 'Especially those Peas and Carrots. Mmm-mmmm.' If there was one good thing about this situation, it was the delightful feeling of revenge he was experiencing. He thought of all the times Norton had cooked liver and onions with wheat germ on top, and Marigold had made him eat it. Biologically correct food, they called it.

Marie sat down at the table. Eddie saw that she had an armful of bottles and jars, gathered from the forbidden top shelf of the cupboard. These were all the strange and mysterious foods Norton and Marigold kept for 'special occasions' — red syrup to put into liquor, tiny onions, maraschino cherries, little silver balls for decorating cakes, and chocolate-covered after-dinner mints. She lined them all up in front of her on the table and stared hard at them for a few moments. Then she shrugged. 'What the heck,' she said, opening them up one by one. 'Here goes nothing.'

'Can I try one of those cherries?' asked Eddie.

'Sure,' said Marie, digging into the mints.

'I wonder if those silver things are really edible,' said Eddie, reaching for one. It was an incredible feeling, knowing that there was absolutely nobody to yell at them.

'You'll never guess what Mildred Grackle is doing now,' Marie said conversationally, chewing noisily on a silver ball. Mildred Grackle lived in the house next door.

'I can hardly wait to find out. Is she raising catfish in her bathtub again?'

'No, this is even better. She's starting a lemming farm in her backyard.'

'A lemming farm? What for?'

'She read someplace that lemmings have good fur for coats and they taste just like chicken. So she got five hundred of them from a mail-order catalogue. The new guy that works in the store told me.' She took a long swig of red syrup.

'Hold on. You mean lemmings, those little brown furry animals that jump into the ocean every few years? Those lemmings?'

'Those lemmings.'

'Sheesh.'

'Then again, who are we to call anyone else weird? Our parents are two and a half inches tall.'

'Oh, nuts!' cried Eddie, jumping up from his chair. 'I forgot about their next capful of food. They must be starving down there.'

'I hope they like the Veal Dinner,' said Marie.

'If they don't like it, we can play airplane with them,' said Eddie. 'That's what they did to us with the liver and wheat germ.'

They went downstairs to feed Norton and Marigold, who were so hungry they would have eaten absolutely anything.

'I'm awfully thirsty,' said Norton, shovelling more Veal Dinner into his mouth. 'Could you please give me a little water to drink?'

'Sure, Dad,' said Eddie with a sigh.

'I've been thinking,' said Marigold in her funny little squeak. 'Until we figure out how to get out of this mess your father got us into, we'll need to set things up down here so we can take care of ourselves.'

'I had an idea about that,' said Marie. 'Remember that old dollhouse of mine, up in the attic? Maybe you could live in there for the time being.'

'What a good idea,' said Norton. 'Kind of a little home within a home.'

'I think we could make that work,' said Marigold. 'Why don't you go and get it, Marie?'

Eddie, who was starting to go up the cellar stairs, suddenly gasped. 'Look! The window!' He pointed to a small window high up on the basement wall that was at ground level outside the house. There, seeming to float behind the dirty glass, was a ghostly face.

'Mildred Grackle!' cried Marigold. 'Quick! Hide! She's spying on us again! She can't see us like this!'

The tiny parents scooted behind the trash basket.

CHAPTER THREE

OOPS!

The four of them stood frozen in the basement for a minute. 'Shoo! Shoo!' Marigold whispered, trying to make Mildred disappear.

'Be quiet, Marigold!' hissed Norton.

Eddie and Marie, getting their breath back, sprang into motion and bounded up the stairs, tripping over Basil again.

'That nosy witch!' said Eddie under his breath. 'Every window in this house has her nose print on it!'

'Well, we really have to keep her away from here now,' said Marie in alarm. 'She can't see Mom and Dad!'

Mildred Grackle was not a witch, but she looked like one. She had a big pointy nose, snaggle teeth, eyes like hot coals, and hair like barbed wire. All she needed was a big black hat. She lived with an extremely ugly and bad-tempered cat called Belladonna, and was always beating out rugs in front of her house, raising clouds of dirt that made people cough for blocks around. Her favourite activity was trying to snoop into other people's business.

Eddie and Marie flung open the front door. They could see Mildred at the side of the house, bent down in a very undignified position to peer into the basement window. She was wearing a pink quilted housecoat, and she had little curlers all over her head, rolled very tight.

'Um — can we help you?' said Marie loudly. Mildred stood up fast and patted her curlers, trying to collect herself.

'I need to see your parents, young lady,' she said in a voice like a chain saw.

'They're not at home just now,' said

Marie, trying to be as polite as she could. 'Can I tell them what it's about?'

'You can tell them what it's about, all right. It's about that stupid mutt of yours digging up my begonias and scaring my cat! That's what it's about.' Basil growled at Mildred. She scowled at him, turned on her heel, and then marched across the cracked concrete driveway toward her house.

'Whew!' said Eddie. 'That's over.' Basil put his big cold nose into Eddie's hand. 'I think you're going to have to stop digging up her garden, Basil,' said Eddie. 'She might turn you into an onion.'

They went inside and closed the door.

Downstairs, Norton and Marigold were still hiding behind the trash can. 'All clear,' said Eddie. 'You can come out now.'

'Thank goodness,' said Marigold. 'I'm hungry.'

'Oh, brother,' said Eddie.

'Mom and Dad,' said Marie, squatting on the floor beside them, 'we're going to have to think about this thing. Eddie and I don't have the scientific knowledge to get you big again, and you're too little to do much for yourselves. I think we have to get some outside help. Let's call the police, okay?'

'No police! No police!' squeaked Norton.

For once, Marigold agreed with him. 'We can't have the police come snooping around here,' she said firmly. 'Why, once this invention is perfected, it'll make us millions! We'll get the Nobel Prize! I've got my speech prepared already. We can't have people with little minds stealing this invention away from us.'

'Now hold on a second,' interrupted Norton. 'I'm the one who's giving the acceptance speech. It was my idea to begin with.'

'It was not. It was mine,' said Marigold.

'Mine! It was mine!'

'Would you two stop it? They're not going to give a Nobel Prize to a pair of two-inch people,' said Marie in exasperation. 'We have to get help from *someplace*.'

'I know,' said Eddie. 'Why don't we call somebody from OOPS?'

'Hmmm,' said Norton. 'You might have an idea there.'

OOPS, which stood for the Organization of Practical Scientists, was an association of peculiar people who were busy inventing toenail-cleaning machines, lettuce shredders, and other wonderful inventions in messy basements all over the country. There were probably about fifty members of OOPS. This year Norton was serving his term as president.

'Hmmm,' repeated Norton, rubbing his tiny chin.

'I don't know,' said Marigold. 'There are lots of people in OOPS who would sooner steal your idea than look at you.'

'We'd have to find someone we trust absolutely,' said Norton.

'Someone who doesn't need to steal ideas, because he has plenty of his own,' Marigold added.

'Someone who's honest and pure.'

'Someone who can keep a secret.'

'Someone who can figure out how to get us out of this mess.'

'Ozzie,' they both concluded together.

Oswald Regenbogen, otherwise know as Ozzie, was head of the OOPS Crisis Task Force. He had gotten Norton and Marigold out of quite a few messes before. For instance, there was the time they had crossed a Venus's-flytrap with a dogwood tree to make a watchdogwood, a tree that would keep your front yard free of intruders. Unfortunately the trees got nasty, and Ozzie had to figure out how to get them under control. And then there was the time Norton and Marigold had invented instant-water powder, but couldn't figure out what to add to the powder to make the water. They had worked in the basement for six solid weeks until Ozzie had just told them to forget it. And, of course, there was the talking toaster that wouldn't shut up. But there had never, never been anything quite *this* bad.

Within the membership of OOPS, Ozzie was rumoured to be the smartest human being in the world. It was whispered that he had invented Detroit. It was also said that he had invented the buttonhole, and that nobody in the world had known what to do with all those billions of buttons until Ozzie Regenbogen came along.

The only reason he had never gotten famous was that he didn't care about being famous. He only cared about thinking. He thought all day and all night. He thought in the bathtub and while playing the saxophone. He drew little doodles and diagrams and mathematical formulas on napkins. Hardly anybody understood what Ozzie was thinking, even after he explained it.

Actually, there was one other reason why Ozzie had never gotten famous, and that was his shyness. He wasn't just a little shy, like people who sit in the corner at parties or who find themselves answering 'Fine, thank you,' just out of pure nervousness when somebody says 'Good morning.' Ozzie Regenbogen was so shy he hardly ever left his house. He had most of his groceries delivered. He did not ever announce his incredible discoveries to the newspapers. And when there was a meeting of OOPS, he used a special one-way television-and-telephone hookup he had invented, so that he could see everybody and talk to them without actually going there. Nobody in OOPS knew what Ozzie looked like.

'Do you think he can figure this thing out over the phone?' asked Marigold.

'I've heard of him solving worse things than this on the phone,' Norton pointed out.

'Great,' said Eddie. 'Let's get going. Where's his phone number? I'll call him up. That is, unless you think you can dial the phone, ha-ha-ha.' He laughed a mirthless laugh.

'Young man, that kind of humour is not going to be appreciated, so you may as well just stop it right now,' squeaked Marigold.

'I'm sorry, Mom,' said Eddie. He struggled to be serious. 'But it is a little funny, you have to admit. Okay, where's Ozzie's number?'

'You don't call Ozzie Regenbogen. He calls you,' said Norton.

'What do you mean, he calls you?' said Marie. 'How does he know he's supposed to call here?'

'He has his ways,' said Norton. 'Nobody knows what they are. But Ozzie calls you, that's all I know.'

'Great,' said Marie. 'Ozzie calls us. Just great.'

CHAPTER FOUR

Little House
in the Basement

The next morning, Saturday, Eddie and
Marie met at the kitchen table. Marie had
orange soda and chocolate chips for
breakfast. Eddie poured himself a three-
day-old cup of coffee. He was wearing a T-
shirt that had four large holes in the front.

'I thought Mom made you throw that
shirt out,' said Marie.

'I was sort of saving it. I couldn't stand to
throw it out,' said Eddie. He took a sip of
the coffee. 'Yucch, this stuff tastes awful,'
he said. He poured it into the sink and got
himself some cold cereal and milk.

'I had some really weird dreams last

night,' said Marie, munching her chocolate chips. 'I was being chased by a teensy army with darning needles for swords.'

'I had weird dreams too,' said Eddie, rubbing his eyes. 'It would probably be weird if we *didn't* have weird dreams, considering what's going on in our house.'

'You want to go up in the attic with me and look for my old dollhouse?' asked Marie with a yawn.

'Sure,' answered Eddie. 'We probably have about five minutes before they start yelling for food.'

The Bicker attic wasn't like any other attic in Brooklyn, or even in the world. Norton and Marigold didn't save things like dusty photo albums or old baby quilts. They saved old welding equipment, pieces of heavy machinery, and parts from cars and motorcycles, because they might come in handy for an invention someday.

But when she was eight, Marie had put her foot down and insisted that her dollhouse had to stay.

And there it was, in the corner. Even in the dim light, covered with dust, it shone with perfection. The dollhouse had been given to Marie by her aunt Beth, and it had been Beth's when she was a girl. It had two stories, shingles on the outside, and flowered carpeting on the stairs. There were lace curtains on the windows, and real electric lights. The windows went up and down, and the doors opened and shut with painted china doorknobs. The house was full of old-fashioned, overstuffed furniture, including a four-poster bed in the upstairs bedroom.

'This should make a nice little home for them,' said Marie with satisfaction, as she blew the dust off the top. 'The ceilings look just about the right height.'

They wrestled it down from the attic without losing any of the furniture and carried it down to the basement.

'We were wondering where you were,' said Marigold. 'We're starving.'

'I had a terrible night's sleep on the floor,' complained Norton.

'Stop complaining, Norton,' said Marigold.

'We brought you the dollhouse,' said Eddie. 'It should make things easier.'

They all inspected it together. Norton and Marigold stepped inside it, and it seemed as though it had been made for them. They found tiny, tiny metal dishes and silverware in the kitchen cabinets, and the little kitchen table and chairs were just the right size.

'Whoever decorated this place,' Marigold said, squinting at the purple leaves on the linoleum, 'I hate their taste.'

Norton climbed up the stairs, which were a bit steep, to the second floor. 'Look,' he called down, 'the beds are actually soft, and there are blankets and everything.'

'You can't cook here, but if we bring you a jar of baby food in the morning, you can eat it all day,' suggested Marie. 'We can even put an ice cube in the icebox, to keep food from spoiling.'

'Good idea,' said Marigold, tearing her eyes away from the kitchen floor.

'And now for the crowning touch,' said Marie. She found the old, frayed cord that hung from the back of the dollhouse. After some searching amid the tangle of wires and extension cords that covered the floor, she found a place to plug it in.

Instantly the house was filled with light. Fancy chandeliers blazed in the hallways, lamps lit up in the bedrooms, and the overhead light in the kitchen glowed pleasantly.

'I told you we'd be glad someday if we saved this dollhouse,' said Marie.

'It's nicer than our house,' said Eddie.

'I guess when it's bedtime, one of us will have to come downstairs and unplug the lights,' said Marie.

'And we can cover up the whole thing with a cloth, just like a birdcage,' added Eddie.

'Don't be funny,' warned Marigold.

'No, I think that's a good idea,' said Norton. 'Give us some privacy.'

'What I want to know,' said Marigold, 'is where we're going to set up our lab. If we can get some work done, we may be able to figure out how to fix the machine.'

'It's too tiny in there!' said Marie.

'You can do incredible things with transistors,' said Marigold firmly. 'I'll give you a shopping list on Monday.'

'Speaking of shopping,' Eddie said, sitting on the floor, 'we're going to need a way to get money. I was thinking maybe we could get money out of the bank machine with your card.'

'It's in my wallet,' said Marigold. 'Just don't spend it all on science fiction books and bubble gum.'

'What's your secret number, so we can use the machine?'

'It's 3—14—1879. Einstein's birthday.'

'We should have known,' said Marie.

'Ahem,' said Norton. 'I think it's breakfast time.'

'Okay, I'll bring you a jar of Liver Dinner,' said Eddie, getting up. 'Sorry it doesn't have any wheat germ in it.'

Just as he reached the top of the stairs, the doorbell began ringing. Not ringing, exactly; screaming was more like it. Eddie had never heard their doorbell being rung so insanely.

Had somebody come to tell them the whole neighbourhood was on fire, and that they'd all better get out right away? He flung open the door, his heart pounding.

There stood Mildred Grackle, wearing her housecoat and hair curlers. This time, though, her face was covered with stuff that looked like mud, her mouth was working without making any sound, and her eyes were bulging almost out of her head.

'What happened? What's wrong?' asked Eddie. She looked as though she had been in armed combat.

'What's wrong? What happened?' she spluttered, wiping some of the beauty-treatment goo off her face with the back of her hand. 'I'll tell you what happened. I'll tell you what's wrong. That criminal dog of yours sneaked into my backyard this morning and let out all my lemmings, that's what happened. And you know what's *going* to happen? I'M GOING TO KILL HIM, THAT'S WHAT'S GOING TO HAPPEN! Where is he? I'm going to flush him down my toilet! I'm going to take him to the Grand Canyon and drop him off!'

Eddie was so relieved that the neighbourhood wasn't burning down that he hardly heard Mildred as she kept on raving about what she was going to do to Basil. He knew she wasn't really going to do anything to Basil, anyhow.

But he gradually did become aware of another sound, the sound of the telephone ringing again and again. Suddenly it stopped

'EDDIE!' yelled Marie. 'IT'S OSWALD REGENBOGEN ON THE PHONE!'

Eddie shut the door in Mildred Grackle's face.

CHAPTER FIVE

Nine Weeks to Live

It was very hard not to laugh at Ozzie Regenbogen's voice. He sounded like a person who was holding his nose. But as soon as Marie felt a giggle rising up in her, she squashed it immediately. Laughing at Ozzie Regenbogen's voice would have been like laughing at Albert Einstein's ears.

'Oh,' he said after she had told him what the problem was. 'Sounds like a twitch in the neutron field. That happens sometimes. Never seen it happen to a person, though. Interesting problem.'

There was a long silence on the line.

'Er — can you help us?' asked Marie finally.

'Ah. Help you,' he said as if that thought hadn't crossed his mind. 'Hmmm. Help you. Well, it's possible. Can't guarantee anything, though. Interesting problem.'

Marie got the chilling feeling that the problem was much more interesting to him than Norton and Marigold were.

'I'll tell you what,' he said to Marie finally. In her mind's eye, she could see a funny man holding his nose on the other end of the phone. 'I'll give this a think. Maybe talk to some other members of the Crisis Task Force about it. Meantime, I'll need to speak to one of your parents. Want to know how they built their machine. Could you put one of them on the phone?'

'Sure,' said Marie. 'Hold on a minute, okay?'

She ran down the stairs. 'Mom! Dad!' she yelled. 'One of you has to come upstairs with me and talk to Ozzie Regenbogen!'

'I'll come!' squeaked Marigold. 'Your father will get all the facts wrong.'

'I'd better do it,' said Norton. 'Who knows what *she'll* tell him!'

Marie snatched one of them up in each hand, trying not to squeeze them too hard around the middle. Then she sprinted up the stairs again.

When they reached the kitchen, Norton and Marigold looked around as if they were in a foreign country.

'This place is a mess,' said Marigold.

'I know, Mom. We've been busy,' said Marie with a sigh. Then she set her parents down on the counter near the phone receiver.

'Let me talk to him first,' demanded Marigold. Marie moved her so she could stand next to the mouthpiece.

'Ozzie,' said Marigold. 'Thanks for calling. Now, here's the thing. Norton attached the epsilon confabulator on to the wrong end.'

Ozzie's voice came buzzing out of the earpiece like a bee in a bottle.

'What?' yelled Marigold. 'I can't hear you.' She left the mouthpiece, ran over to the earpiece, and put her head against it.

Ozzie's voice buzzed a question and Marigold ran back to the mouthpiece to answer it. 'Positive,' she called.

Now Norton walked over to the phone and stood near the earpiece. 'I'll listen. You talk,' he told his wife.

The phone buzzed again as Ozzie spoke.

'HE WANTS TO KNOW WHICH WAY THE VECTOR FIELD WAS POINTING,' Norton yelled to Marigold.

'North,' said Marigold smugly. 'The right way.'

Norton listened to yet another question from Ozzie, and his face fell.

'HE SAYS WE'RE BOTH WRONG!' he called to Marigold. 'SAYS HE'LL HAVE TO THINK ABOUT IT. WE MAY HAVE SET UP A DOOLEY-BENZ WAVE PATTERN. HE'LL CALL US BACK TOMORROW, HE SAYS.'

'Good-bye, Ozzie,' squeaked Marigold

into the mouthpiece. 'We'll talk to you soon.'

'He wants to talk to you again, Marie,' Norton said. 'Can we go downstairs and have a little snack now?'

Marie picked up the receiver, and Eddie picked up their parents. He headed downstairs with them.

'Hello?' said Marie nervously. She wasn't sure why, but Ozzie Regenbogen made her uncomfortable. She wasn't sure he was quite human.

'What day did your parents get small?' he asked her.

'Yesterday,' she answered. 'Why?'

'Well, I've made some calculations. I figure they have about nine weeks to live. Give or take.'

'WHAT?'

Eddie had come back upstairs, and was watching Marie closely.

'You know, of course,' said Ozzie, 'that very small animals have short life spans. They have such fast metabolisms, burning food up very quickly and whatnot, that they burn themselves out at quite a clip. Well, it's the same with your parents now.'

'Could you be wrong about this?' said Marie, whose heart was suddenly beating as fast as any mouse's.

Ozzie seemed taken aback by the question. 'Of course not,' he said, sounding injured. 'So we'll have to work this out fast. I'd say we have a two-in-seven chance of reversing the effects before it's too late. Good-bye.'

He hung up abruptly, leaving Marie staring openmouthed at the phone.

'What was *that* about?' Eddie asked.

Marie hung the phone up slowly.

'They're going to die in nine weeks if we can't get them big again,' she said. 'Their lives have been speeded up, he says. Because they're so small.'

'I thought they looked a tiny bit older just now,' said Eddie.

'I don't want them to die,' said Marie. A big tear rolled down her cheek. 'I love them. Even if they're not normal parents.'

'It's *better* that they're not normal

parents,' said Eddie. 'And they're not going to die. We're not going to let them.'

A tiny, squeaky voice wafted up from the basement. 'Are there any more mashed bananas?' it called.

CHAPTER SIX

The Wrath of Mildred

A grey, sleet-filled week began, with no more word from Ozzie Regenbogen. Eddie and Marie trudged off to school and trudged home again. They had a hard time keeping their minds on their schoolwork.

Later that afternoon they stopped off at the radio hobby store and bought a collection of things that Norton and Marigold had requested for their lab: transistors, printed computer circuits, very fine wire, and several items Eddie and Marie could hardly see, let alone identify. Their parents immediately began setting up a lab in the family room of the dollhouse.

On Tuesday, Eddie's best friend Lewis called to see if Eddie wanted to work on Lewis's model battleship with him, but Eddie's heart wasn't in it.

That night Marie was sitting in the living room munching on a dinner of Cheeze Dandies and watching the eleven o'clock news, when Eddie wandered in. He was eating a dish of rum raisin ice cream.

'. . . And that's the bad news about the weather, everybody,' the weatherman was saying. 'Back to you, Bob.'

'Well, folks,' said Bob with a grin, 'here's a really weird one from Long Island. It seems that a pack of lemmings has been seen heading up the Brooklyn-Queens Expressway. That's right, a pack of lemmings. And yesterday several people walking their dogs on Jones Beach saw this same pack of little brown rodents disappear into the Atlantic Ocean. Nobody knows how they got to New York, because their normal habitat is the Arctic circle! Quite a little puzzle for the scientists, isn't it? And now, here's Trixie with the sports.'

Eddie turned the television off. 'Oh, cripes, those have to be Mildred's lemmings,' he said. 'I forgot all about them. We're in big trouble now.'

'Basil's in trouble, anyway,' said Marie. 'He's the one that let them out.'

'Liberated them,' Eddie corrected her. 'At least they died with honour, their own way.'

'Mildred's going to be wild when she hears about it,' said Marie. 'This is not what we need right now.'

In fact, they hadn't seen Mildred Grackle in days, which was unusual and a little surprising, considering what had happened. She didn't even seem to be looking in the windows.

On Thursday afternoon the doorbell rang and Eddie answered it. A small man in a striped suit stood on the stoop. He had a skinny little moustache, like someone from an old movie.

'Hello there, young fellow,' said the man.

Hello there, young fellow? Eddie stared at him.

'Are your parents about?' asked the man. He stood on tiptoe and peered around Eddie into the house.

Eddie moved a little to block his view. 'They're busy right now. Can I give them a message?'

'Norton and Marigold Bicker, isn't that right?' said the man, still trying to look over Eddie's shoulder.

'That's right,' said Eddie. He was beginning to feel very edgy.

The man smoothed his moustache with his thumb and forefinger. 'I have something for them,' he said, with an unpleasant smile.

'You can give it to me,' said Eddie.

'I'm supposed to give it to them.'

'They're both really sick right now,' said Eddie. 'Incredibly sick.' He felt as though a big 'L' for Liar must be burning on his forehead.

'All right,' said the man. 'I've got to go. But you will promise to give it to them, won't you?' Eddie nodded, and the man pulled a grimy white envelope out of his jacket.

'Nice working with you, young fellow,' he said with a wink. He turned and ran down the stairs. Eddie shut the door, mystified.

'What was that?' asked Marie, coming up from the basement with an empty jar of Peas and Carrots in her hand.

Eddie ripped open the envelope and studied the paper inside, trying to make sense of it.

'Looks official,' he said.

Marie took the paper from him and moved toward the light so she could read the small print better. 'Oh, great,' she said. 'Wonderful. It's a summons.'

'A summons?'

'Yeah, Mildred Grackle is suing us. 'Loss of Lemmings,' it says here. Mom and Dad are supposed to appear in court next Wednesday.'

Basil, sitting in the corner, scratched himself energetically behind the ear.

CHAPTER SEVEN

Shadow Dancing

Wednesday came and Wednesday went but Norton and Marigold did not appear in court. They were completely preoccupied with setting up their tiny new lab. Besides, you can't appear in court if you're two and a half inches tall.

'Lots of people don't show up in court,' said Marigold. 'And we have a better excuse than most. We'll deal with it when we're big again.'

If you're big again, thought Marie, studying her mother's tiny face. Were there a few more lines on it, or was it just her imagination? 'Oh, where is that Ozzie Regenbogen, anyway?' she said. 'And who says he's right about everything? I think he's weird.'

'He'll call, he'll call,' said Marigold. 'Things have to kind of ferment in his mind. And he *is* right about everything. No one has ever heard of his being wrong.'

Marie's heart sank a little further. Why didn't he call? Time was running out!

'Mildred shouldn't have been raising lemmings for fur coats anyway,' said Eddie, coming down the basement stairs with an ice cube for the little plastic refrigerator. 'It's cruel and unusual.'

'Just like Mildred,' said Marie.

'Especially the unusual part,' snickered Eddie.

'Sssh!' warned Norton, darting behind the workbench. 'The window!' Everybody froze.

Sure enough, a large shadow was darkening the basement window. Two shadows, in fact. Mildred had brought someone with her.

'Down there,' she whispered, in a voice that could have been heard in Ohio. 'I'm sure they're down there!'

'Why are you so sure?' asked a man's voice.

'They didn't appear in court, their car hasn't moved in a week, nobody has seen them — I'm absolutely positive those children murdered their parents. They're horrible little creatures. They always have been. If you search the basement, I know you'll find the bodies. I'm never wrong about things like this!'

'All right, pumpkin, I'll make sure it's looked into. Now can we go home and eat some goulash, please? I'm freezing.'

The blood of the entire Bicker family ran as cold as ice when they recognized the deep, slow voice of Mildred's boyfriend, Lenny. Lenny was a sergeant with the New York City police force. He was not too bright, however.

The shadows moved away.

'Good grief,' said Norton in disbelief. 'She thinks you killed us.'

'He calls her pumpkin,' snorted Eddie. 'Pumpkin.'

'It would be funny, if I could remember how to laugh,' said Marie. Then she laughed anyway.

'The thing is,' said Eddie, 'if the cops come, we won't be able to prove we *didn't* kill you. We can't very well bring you to the door in our hands.'

'You know, it might not be so bad if we just came right out with this thing,' said Marie. 'We need help, lots of help. And soon.'

'We have all the time in the world,' said Marigold testily. 'And once we start asking people for help, the whole world is going to know about the Proton Enlarger. Revolutionary inventions get stolen from little people like us just like *that*.' She snapped her microscopic fingers.

'No joke intended,' said Marie under her breath.

'I'm not giving up my Nobel Prize so some fancy college scientist can grab it away from me,' Marigold concluded.

'No, indeed. We're waiting for Ozzie to call.'

'What are we going to do in the meantime?' inquired Norton. 'The police will be ringing the doorbell any minute.'

'We have to convince Mildred that you're alive and well,' said Eddie. 'And I've got an idea.'

'Such a bright boy,' said Marigold, beaming. 'He must get it from me.'

By the time it was dark, Eddie had the whole thing set up. The window shades were all pulled down tight. Eddie had gone over to his friend Lewis's house and borrowed his high-intensity photographer's lamp, and it was set up next to the sofa. A Fred Astaire record was on the record player, ready to start. Marie had her jacket on. And Norton and Marigold were standing on the coffee table.

'Okay, are you ready?' whispered Eddie.

'Ready,' squeaked Norton and Marigold.

'I guess so,' said Marie.

'All right, here we go,' said Eddie tensely.

'Hold it, hold it,' whispered Marie. 'I forgot my cup.' She ran into the kitchen and returned in a second with a china cup. 'Okay, now we can start,' she said.

Eddie switched on the lamp and turned the record player on very loud. Norton and Marigold started dancing the fox trot. Marie slipped out the door.

In five minutes she was back again, giggling uncontrollably.

'What happened? Tell us everything!' demanded Marigold.

'Keep dancing! Keep dancing!' whispered Eddie urgently.

Norton and Marigold resumed dancing, while Marie caught her breath. 'Well, I rang her bell,' she began, wiping tears of suppressed laughter from her eyes, 'and she came to the door. She was shocked to see me. And I said very sweetly, "Can I please borrow a cup of sugar, Ms Grackle? My parents are so busy working these days, we're running out of everything!"' She started giggling again.

'And? And?' prompted Eddie.

'And when she came back with the sugar, I started talking very casually about the weather. Then I said, "Oh, look at that, isn't it wonderful, my parents are finally taking a break, they're even dancing," and I pointed over at our living room window. And there you were! The plan really, really worked! These big shadows were projected right on to the window shades, so it looked like you were your regular size, just dancing away!'

'What did Mildred do?' asked Eddie.

'She just about jumped out of her slippers,' said Marie.

'Eddie, you're a genius,' said Norton, trying to do a fancy twirl with Marigold. 'Where did you get that idea, anyway?'

'It was on the Late Late Movie the other night,' Eddie said modestly. 'I thought it might work.'

Marigold broke free of Norton. 'You two should not be staying up so late,' she said. 'And when was the last time you had any vegetables? This place is a mess, too.'

'I wouldn't have had this good idea if I

hadn't watched the Late Late Movie,' said Eddie. 'And we just had some vegetables for breakfast, didn't we, Marie!'

'What kind of vegetables?' asked Marigold. Her eyes narrowed with suspicion.

'Potato chips. Potatoes are a vegetable.'

'When we're big again, things won't be so whoopee,' said Marigold. 'You just wait and see, Mr Big Shot.'

'Um, I guess I better go put this cup of sugar away,' said Marie, edging toward the kitchen.

CHAPTER EIGHT

Ozzie Has a Brainstorm

In the middle of the night the phone rang.

Eddie and Marie both snapped awake instantly, their hearts pounding. They spilled out of their rooms together and were in the kitchen by the third ring.

'Hello!' said Marie.

'Good evening.' Marie recognized the nasal voice instantly. 'Regenbogen here. I've figured it out. Just came to me, right in the middle of a dream. I was eating an ice-cream cone in King Tut's tomb, and there was the solution, written right on the wall of the pyramid.'

'You know how to get them big again?' asked Marie.

'I know how they got themselves small. It's the Random Occipitor.'

'What's the Random Ox-whatever?'

'Random Occipitor. It's a little gadget they must have used in their machine. Produces startling changes in molecule size, sometimes. Also makes the function of the machine a bit — well, unpredictable.'

'What do you mean?' asked Marie.

'You can't build a machine that enlarges or reduces without a Random Occipitor,' said Ozzie. 'And that means you'll never be able to predict what your machine will do. Might make things smaller, might make things larger. You just don't know.'

There goes the Nobel Prize, thought Marie.

'So, can we get them big again?' she asked. 'Before it's too late?'

'It's possible,' replied Ozzie. 'We can try using the machine on them again. See what happens. There's a fifty percent chance they'll be restored to their former size. If you do it quickly, they won't be much the worse for wear.'

Eddie was rubbing his eyes sleepily, trying to read the conversation in Marie's face.

'And what happens if the machine doesn't work? What's the other fifty percent chance?' asked Marie.

'They'll be reduced so much that they'll be atomized.'

Marie gulped. 'Is trying this our only hope?' she asked at last.

'That's it,' he said. 'And I've figured out something else, too. Bit of a problem.'

Marie could hardly bear to find out what it was.

'Your parents made an error when they calculated their polar alignment. For the machine to work properly, it has to be set up exactly twenty-three feet to the north of where it is now. Goodbye.'

And he hung up.

'That man is unbearably weird,' said Marie. 'I just hope he's right.' She repeated for Eddie everything Ozzie had said.

'Twenty-three feet to the north,' said Eddie, frowning as he figured out the geography. 'Let's see . . . that would be toward East Eighth Street, about the centre of the next house . . .' His eyes opened very wide. 'Holy cow! Do you know where that is?'

'No, where?'

'Right in the middle of Mildred Grackle's living room, that's where. How are we ever going to do that?'

'We'll figure it out,' said Marie. 'We have to. Besides that's not the biggest worry we have. What if it doesn't work, and it atomizes them?'

'I guess we have to let them decide whether they want to take the risk.'

'This is horrible,' said Marie. 'I don't want to be an orphan. I wish they had never built the stupid thing.'

'So do I,' agreed Eddie. 'So do I.'

CHAPTER NINE

Life or Death

At six o'clock the next morning it was so bitterly cold and windy that the frost-covered windows rattled in their frames. Eddie and Marie were downstairs in the basement, dressed in several layers of clothing. Their parents were sitting together in an old mitten of Marie's, which was pulled all the way up to their chins. They were eating applesauce from a thimble.

Basil, who had been allowed into the basement for the first time, sniffed curiously at Norton and Marigold. Eddie and Marie kept a close eye on him, making sure he didn't try anything funny.

Marie's teeth were chattering, and she wasn't sure it was just from the cold. The moment of decision had arrived. There had been very little sleep for her or Eddie that night, and they had finally decided that they might as well just go downstairs at sunrise and get it over with.

Eddie was explaining the situation to Norton and Marigold for the second time.

'If there's a fifty-fifty chance that we could be atomized,' Marigold mused, 'maybe we shouldn't do it. Maybe we should just live the rest of our lives tiny. We could get used to it in a couple of years, I guess.'

'You can't do that,' said Eddie grimly.

'Why not, for heaven's sake?' asked Marigold. 'People get used to all sorts of things. I got used to being married to your father.'

Norton harrumphed. '*Some* people have had even *worse* people to get used to,' he said.

Eddie and Marie were exchanging looks with each other, trying to decide whether to tell their parents the awful truth. Finally Eddie shrugged and Marie nodded.

'It's not as simple as that,' said Marie. 'You can't *have* a couple of years to get used to it.'

'Why not?' said Norton.

Marie swallowed hard. 'Because Ozzie Regenbogen says you have only about eight weeks to live. Your lives are speeded up, like little tiny animals'.'

'Maybe Ozzie's wrong,' said Marigold. She looked panic-stricken. 'Maybe he didn't figure it out right.'

'Ozzie's never wrong. We both know that Ozzie's never wrong,' said Norton.

'Eight weeks! Why that's no time at all! Norton, we're going to die in eight weeks!' Marigold threw her tiny arms around his tiny shoulders, weeping little tiny tears.

'Good-bye, my darling!' cried Norton. 'Farewell, my love!' He blew his nose on a little corner of the mitten.

'Norton, you know I never meant all those awful things I said to you, don't you?'

'I know, sugarplum. I never meant all those terrible things I said to you, either.'

'I don't know where I'd be without you!' Marigold dissolved into tears again.

'Be brave, my darling!' said Norton. 'We'll die together, hand in hand.'

They finished the applesauce together.

Eddie looked at the floor and cleared his throat. 'Mom? Dad?' he said. 'What if we tried the machine again?'

'The machine! Yes! Of course!' cried Norton and Marigold together. It was clear that they had forgotten about it.

'Okay,' said Marie decisively. 'We'll get everything ready. You just wait here.' She turned on her heel and marched up the stairs. Eddie followed her.

'Whew!' she said, leaning against the upstairs door. 'That was really heavy.'

'Yeah, I think I like it better when they scream at each other.'

'Okay,' said Marie. 'We're ready for Phase One. This better work. This just better work. I don't know what I'll do if they end up—'

'Don't think about it. It'll work, that's all.'

'Okay,' said Marie. 'I'll start looking for that key. I know we have it someplace.'

Eddie hitched up his shoulders, stood up very straight, and marched across the kitchen towards the phone. On his way he grabbed a blue dish towel.

He picked up the phone and dialled Mildred Grackle's number. Then he quickly crumpled up the dish towel and held it to the mouthpiece.

'Grackle?' he said in his deepest, gruffest voice when she answered the phone. 'Mildred Grackle?'

Oh, please, he thought, don't let me sound like Eddie Bicker talking through a dish towel.

'You think the Bicker kids knocked off their parents, right?' he snarled. 'Well, I have some information that just might interest you. Meet me at the skating rink in Rockefeller Center at two o'clock this afternoon.'

'Who is this? Who is this?' she shrilled.

'Never mind who this is,' said Eddie. 'Just be there.'

'How will I find you?'

Suddenly the light of pure devilry shone in Eddie's eyes. 'You won't find me, I'll find you. Carry a chicken in your left hand. Not the right one, the left.'

He hung up the phone.

'There,' he said, amazed that he'd gotten away with it. 'That should buy us a good couple of hours. She'll have to go all the way into the city, wait around, give up, and come all the way back. And there aren't a lot of trains running at that time of day.'

'Okay,' said Marie. 'But we still have to hurry.'

While she spoke, she was rummaging frantically through the old corks, plastic bags, apple corers, and birthday candles that filled the junk drawer. 'Aha! Here it is!' she yelled, holding up an old key on a frayed piece of string. 'I knew it was in there someplace!'

'Are you sure it's the key to Mildred's house?'

'Yes, it's the one she lent us the day her lemming cages were delivered. She never came and got it back. Perfect!'

'Okay, now I have to call Lewis,' said Eddie, dialling the phone again.

'Hold on, Eddie,' said Marie. 'Are you sure we ought to bring Lewis into this?'

'He's my best friend, Marie.'

'I know, but can we trust him absolutely? And what if there's danger? Do you want to risk exposing him to it?'

'He was here for the watchdogwood experiment. Remember, one of them almost got him? He never even told his parents.'

'All right,' said Marie reluctantly. 'I don't think we can do this without him, anyhow. I just hope he's not totally weirded out.'

Eddie finished dialling the phone.

'Lewis, it's Eddie. I need your help on an important project. . . . What? . . . I know it's six thirty. Just listen to me for a second, will you? Can you come over this afternoon? About a quarter to two. It's life or death. But you can't ask any questions, okay? . . . . No, this isn't another one of my stupid jokes. This is REAL LIFE! Okay, thanks. Don't be late.' He hung up.

'I sure hope he's still good at keeping his mouth shut,' said Eddie. 'Because he's going to have a lot to talk about.'

They spent the rest of the morning making preparations and getting instructions from Norton and Marigold. They dragged some spare boards from the workshop and used them to build a ramp up the basement stairs. Eddie noticed that his hands were clammy from nervousness. At lunchtime Marie dropped two glasses and a bowl of Frosty Crunch. Even Basil was nervous, walking around the house in endless little circles and not lying down at all.

At about one, Eddie and Marie stationed themselves behind the curtains in the living room, watching Mildred Grackle's house. In Mildred's bedroom window they could see the end of the powerful telescope she had just installed. It was pointed straight at their house.

There was no sound but the ticking of the clock. If Mildred didn't leave her house, their plan would fall apart.

'There she goes!' whispered Eddie at a quarter to one. 'Wait, there's something yellow hanging out of her pocketbook. It's chicken feet!' He couldn't restrain a whoop of glee.

'Okay, call Lewis and tell him to come over *now*,' said Marie. She was in no mood for fooling around.

Eddie sprinted for the phone. 'I know it's early,' Marie heard him say. 'Will you just *come*?'

In three minutes the doorbell rang. There stood Lewis, tall and red-haired, looking very perplexed.

'Downstairs,' said Marie. She started to lead him to the basement door. She was glad Lewis was a big kid.

'Just a second.' Eddie threw out an arm to stop Lewis. 'Before you go down there, I want you to swear something.'

'What are you talking about?' said Lewis.

'You must swear on everything that is holy to you that you will never ever divulge what you see in this house today, even if it is stranger than anything you have ever seen in your life,' said Eddie.

'Give me a break,' snorted Lewis. 'What is this, *The Exorcist*?'

'This is serious, Lewis, I want you to swear.'

'Okay, I swear.'

'Pinky swear,' added Eddie.

'Okay, pinky swear.'

They walked down to the basement. Norton and Marigold were just scampering behind the wastebasket, but it was too late. Lewis had already caught sight of them. He stopped dead in his tracks halfway down the ramp.

'Eddie, was that—?' he said in confusion.

'Lewis, say hello to my parents,' said Eddie. Norton and Marigold came back out into the open.

'Um, hello, Mrs Bicker. Um, hello, Mr Bicker.' Lewis was the colour of newly fallen snow.

'Hello, dear,' said Marigold. 'Nice to see you.'

'Over here,' said Marie, pointing to the contraption in the corner. 'We have to move this machine up the stairs.'

'You have got to be kidding,' said Lewis, recovering himself a little. 'That thing must weigh a zillion pounds.'

'Lewis, this is life or death,' said Eddie.

Very slowly and carefully, they managed to manoeuvre the machine on to a wooden dolly, and then wheel the dolly over to the stairway. Then, inch by inch, they began pushing it up the stairs.

Halfway up, Marie suddenly gasped. 'I'm losing it! I can't hold it anymore!' The machine slid back to the bottom before they were able to stop it.

Marie had tears in her eyes. 'I'm sorry,' she said.

'It's okay,' said Eddie. 'We'll just start again.'

They started again, going faster this time. With a last tremendous heave, they got it to the top of the stairs and into the kitchen.

'That was the hard part,' panted Eddie. Their chests were all heaving. 'Now we're home free.'

In another fifteen minutes they had the thing wheeled right up to Mildred's front door. By now, Eddie was praying out loud. 'Oh, please, oh, please let her not come home. Oh, please make her stay out until we're all done. I'll be good forever. I'll never eat another candy bar, and I'll never stay up for the Late Late Movie again.'

Marie was fumbling with the lock. 'It's not working,' she said. 'It's the wrong — Oh, here it goes.' The door swung open.

Mildred Grackle's living room was filled with little china figurines of shepherd boys and pussycats and clowns. Some of them got broken as they wheeled the machine into place. 'We'll have to replace those,' said Marie.

Eddie looked at his watch. A quarter to three.

He grabbed Marie's hand, and they ran out the door. 'Be back in a minute,' he called to Lewis. 'Hold the fort.' Lewis looked terrified.

Eddie and Marie flew down the basement stairs. Norton and Marigold were standing together, looking inconceivably tiny. They were very calm.

On the workbench was a small package wrapped in brown paper. It had arrived as if by magic at the front door, very early that morning. Inside the package was what looked like an ordinary remote-control unit for a television, and a set of instructions written in a small, neat hand. The instructions were signed, 'O. Regenbogen.'

'I sure hope this thing works,' said Eddie.

'It will work, dear,' said Marigold. 'Ozzie has just done a little rewiring on it, that's all.'

'Okay,' said Marie. 'Let's go.'

She bent down and picked Marigold up.

Eddie picked Norton up, and they carried the two of them upstairs and over to Mildred's house. They put their parents down gently on the floor in front of the machine.

At last, everything was set to go. The machine was plugged in and humming.

'Epsilon confabulator,' said Marie.

'Check,' said Eddie.

'On switch,' said Marie.

'Right-side up,' said Eddie.

'Vector field,' said Marie.

'Check,' said Eddie.

'Polar multiplexer,' said Marie.

'Ready to activate,' said Eddie. 'Everything's set just the way Ozzie told us to do it.' He checked all the knobs and dials one last time.

Marie squatted down in front of her parents. 'This will be over in a second,' she whispered.

'I know, dear, I know,' said Marigold. 'Now, go ahead on home.'

'Don't worry,' said Norton to Eddie and Marie. 'You'll do just fine.'

'Don't eat so much junk food,' said Marigold. 'And remember to brush your teeth.'

Marie was starting to cry. 'We'll see you in a couple of minutes,' she said, and then she turned and walked out the door.

' 'Bye, Mom, 'Bye, Dad,' said Eddie in a trembling voice. 'C'mon, Lewis, let's go.' Then he followed Marie.

On the front stoop of their own house, Eddie turned to Lewis. 'Lewis,' he said, 'you've been a good friend. I think you should go home now. If anything awful happens, you shouldn't be here. I don't want you to have it on your conscience.'

'Are you sure you don't need me?' said Lewis.

Eddie nodded, and Lewis shook his hand gravely. Then he walked away, looking relieved. 'Good luck,' he called back.

In the basement, Marie already had the remote-control device in her hand. She was reading the instructions one more time.

'Ready?' said Eddie.

'Ready as I'll ever be,' she replied.

'Okay, push Channel 2 and Channel 8 at the same time.

Marie pointed the end of the device at Mildred's house, shut her eyes tight, and pressed the buttons.

Incredibly, the black plastic began glowing a bright cherry red. 'Ow!' said Marie, dropping the unit. 'That's hot!'

There was a loud bang from the house next door, followed by a blinding flash of light. It was so bright that Eddie and Marie could see it through the small, dirty basement window. They gasped.

Then there was silence.

'It didn't work,' said Marie.

'We never should have tried it,' said Eddie.

Suddenly, Marie put her hand up, signaling Eddie to be quiet. 'Shh,' she said. 'Listen.' A familiar, and very loud, voice was wafting over to them on the breeze from Mildred's house.

'It was your fault to begin with!' yelled

the voice. 'We never should have used the Random Occipitor!'

'Oh, yeah, Mrs Brilliant Inventor? What about that little problem with the vector field?' came the equally loud reply.

'Mom!' said Eddie.

'Dad!' said Marie. 'They have big voices!'

'They're okay!' they whooped.

They dashed out of the house and burst into Mildred's living room. There, with her hands on her hips, was their mother. And beside her, with his fingers in his ears, was their father. And behind *them* was a very bizarre-looking stranger.

'Wh-who's that?' stammered Marie.

They all spun around to look. Staring emptily but pleasantly at Marigold was a six-foot-tall china milkmaid.

'Oops,' said Marigold.

'I guess the Proton Enlarger ray was pointing at her too,' said Norton.

'I think we'd better get her out of here before Mildred gets home,' said Eddie. 'And the machine, too.'

* * *

About half an hour later, Eddie looked out the window and saw Mildred Grackle coming home, carrying a bedraggled chicken by the feet.

Epilogue

Two weeks later, life had returned to normal in the Bicker household — as normal as things got in the Bicker household, anyway.

Mildred Grackle had been disappointed at first to see that Norton and Marigold were well and truly alive. But then she was cheered up by the fact that she could resume her lawsuit about the lemmings. A new court date was set. Several letters from Mildred about the matter were arriving in the mail every day.

And she didn't let up on the snooping, either. There seemed to be fresh Mildred-size nose prints on each window. She even sent Lenny on occasional walks past the Bicker's house to see what he could see.

Basil was under strict orders from Eddie and Marie to stay away from Mildred's backyard, her begonias, and her cat.

Norton and Marigold were not concerned about all this, however. They were working on a new invention, something about gravity.

Eddie and Marie were having regular bedtimes again.

'I have to admit it,' said Marie to her brother in the hallway between their rooms one night. 'I feel a lot better getting enough sleep. And eating some protein.'

'I feel a lot better having regular-size parents,' said Eddie, yawning and stretching. 'Right here in their bedroom.'

All of a sudden there was a huge crash from the basement.

'I thought they were up here,' said Eddie angrily, as they ran to the staircase.

'I'll never forgive them if they're fooling

around with that machine again. This time they can just stay small,' said Marie. 'And I'll go find some normal parents.'

At the top of the stairs, they bumped into Norton and Marigold.

'We thought you were—' said Eddie.

'Then who's downstairs?' said Marie.

They all charged down to see.

Standing in the middle of the basement was Mildred Grackle. She looked very sheepish. She was eight inches tall.

'Help,' she peeped.

'Mildred, explain yourself!' demanded Norton.

'I just had to find out what you were always doing down here,' she said. 'So I came in the window.' Sure enough, the basement window was wide open. She must have had quite a time climbing through it. 'And then I saw that machine,' continued Mildred, 'and I thought I'd just press a few buttons to see what it did, and here I am. And . . . I'm so *hungry*.' She broke down in tears, and her little curlers shook.

'Oh, Mildred, what are we going to do with you?' said Marigold.

Mildred stopped crying. 'Well, can't you make me big again?' She stared at them. 'You *have* to make me big again! If you don't make me big, I'll sue you for everything you've got! It was your machine that did this to me!'

A big smile spread across Eddie's face. 'Speaking of suing,' he said, 'are you still going to sue us because our dog let out your lemmings? I was thinking that you might want to drop that lawsuit.'

'I certainly will not!' she said. 'I mean — er — um . . .' She fell silent as she began to grasp the difficulty of her situation.

'Perhaps you'd like to think about that a little more,' said Eddie. 'Especially since I've been doing some research. You're not allowed to have wild animals in your backyard in Brooklyn, New York, you know. Those were illegal lemmings.'

'Oh. Oh, dear. Well, all right. . . . But, I mean . . . what about me? Look what's happened to me. Aren't you going to get me out of this mess?'

'We'll think about it,' said Marigold slowly.

And they all thought about it for a very long time.

Other great reads ⌇ from **Red Fox**

Further Red Fox titles that you might enjoy reading are listed on the following pages. They are available in bookshops or they can be ordered directly from us.

    If you would like to order books, please send this form and the money due to:

ARROW BOOKS, BOOKSERVICE BY POST, PO BOX 29, DOUGLAS, ISLE OF MAN, BRITISH ISLES. Please enclose a cheque or postal order made out to Arrow Books Ltd for the amount due, plus 22p per book for postage and packing, both for orders within the UK and for overseas orders.

NAME _____

ADDRESS _____

_____

Please print clearly.

Whilst every effort is made to keep prices low, it is sometimes necessary to increase cover prices at short notice. If you are ordering books by post, to save delay it is advisable to phone to confirm the correct price. The number to ring is THE SALES DEPARTMENT 071 (if outside London) 973 9700.

Other great reads ✦ *from* **Red Fox**

THE SNIFF STORIES   Ian Whybrow

Things just keep happening to Ben Moore. It's dead hard avoiding disaster when you've got to keep your street cred with your mates *and* cope with a family of oddballs at the same time. There's his appalling 2½ year old sister, his scatty parents who are into healthy eating and animal rights and, worse than all of these, there's Sniff! If only Ben could just get on with his scientific experiments and his attempt at a world beating *Swampbeast* score . . . but there's no chance of that while chaos is just around the corner.

ISBN 0 09 9750406   £2.50

J.B. SUPERSLEUTH   Joan Davenport

James Bond is a small thirteen-year-old with spots and spectacles. But with a name like that, how can he help being a supersleuth?

It all started when James and 'Polly' (Paul) Perkins spotted a teacher's stolen car. After that, more and more mysteries needed solving. With the case of the Arabian prince, the Murdered Model, the Bonfire Night Murder and the Lost Umbrella, JB's reputation at Moorside Comprehensive soars.

But some of the cases aren't quite what they seem . . .

ISBN 0 09 9717808   £1.99

Other great reads **from Red Fox**

Discover the exciting and hilarious books of Hazel Townson!

THE MOVING STATUE

One windy day in the middle of his paper round, Jason Riddle is blown against the town's war memorial statue.

But the statue moves its foot! Can this be true?

ISBN 0 09 973370 6   £1.99

ONE GREEN BOTTLE

Tim Evans has invented a fantasic new board game called REDUNDO. But after he leaves it at his local toy shop it disappears! Could Mr Snyder, the wily toy shop owner have stolen the game to develop it for himself? Tim and his friend Doggo decide to take drastic action and with the help of a mysterious green bottle, plan a Reign of Terror.

ISBN 0 09 956810 1   £1.50

THE SPECKLED PANIC

When Kip buys Venger's Speckled Truthpaste instead of toothpaste, funny things start happening. But they get out of control when the headmaster eats some by mistake. What terrible truths will he tell the parents on speech day?

ISBN 0 09 935490 X   £1.75

THE CHOKING PERIL

In this sequel to *The Speckled Panic*, Herbie, Kip and Arthur Venger the inventor attempt to reform Grumpton's litterbugs.

ISBN 0 09 950530 4   £1.25